HOUSES

A MEMOIR

Doris Agnes Murphy I.HM.

Dedicated to Carol Simpson
whose hard work made
this memoir possible

ACKNOWLEDGMENT

To the Immaculate Heart Community
for
granting so many story opportunities
that became part of my memories

Houses
A Memoir of Days Gone By

Prologue

I am finally starting to put down the story of my journey from Portland, Oregon to Kenmore Ave, Los Angeles, California where I now live. I am ninety years of age. I have decided to keep track of my life by telling of as many things as I can remember about each of the houses in which I lived for the past ninety years.

Hence, the title is Houses.

I was born in Portland, Oregon on April 27, 1924 in a little house on Alma Street. My mother told me that some of my father's Irish cousins and aunts helped with the birth. She mentioned Aunt Sadie many times. I don't remember her. My mother said that three of us were born there: Barr in 1922, I in 1924, and Beverly in 1926. Our older brother, Bernard or Bernie was born in Red Deer, Alberta, Canada in 1920.

Before I talk about all my houses I want to tell about my parents. In some ways they were a good match, but in other ways a disaster waiting to happen. They were both in their early twenties when they married.

First, I will tell as much as I can about my father. His name was George Morris Murphy. He was born to James Murphy and Agnes Madden Murphy around 1893 in Lynn, Massachusetts. His whole family was

Irish-Catholic through and through. I think his father, James, was born in New England, and His mother, Agnes, was born in Maine. The timing is such that their parents may have been among the millions of Irish who immigrated to America because of the potato famine in Ireland in the middle 1800s. I have very little information about the Irish relatives, except that I do know we have cousins in the Boston area. I have met at least one whose name is Madden.

My father told us the story that when he was born he had two older sisters, Josephine and Frances. They were all close in age, but I'm not sure when or where they were born. In later life they became Josephine Doherty and Frances Byrne. I know nothing else about them because they never visited us. There are no letters that I know of that came from them. If any letters did arrive, my father must have disposed of them for some reason.

The three little children were left motherless when Agnes died a few months after my father was born. He may have become a different person if his mother could have had some influence in his life. We will never know. So now we have a young Irish father with three small children in Massachusetts.

I learned all that I know about my grandfather from the stories my father would tell us when we ate supper together. It seemed that James was basically a gardener and groundskeeper. He must have been very good because he worked on some of the estates on Long Island, and possibly in Rhode Island. My father said he was employed by some of the wealthy families who summered in that area. I actually have some letters that have been miraculously saved written to James by his employers, the Coffins of Park Avenue, New York. The letters are very friendly. It sounds as if they held James in high regard. The only strange thing is that they are describing their European trips to someone who will never be able to enjoy such luxuries. At any rate, he seems to have been a dependable gentleman who was appreciated by his employers. So, I am baffled by what he did next.

At some time while the children were still quite small, James took all three of them up to New Brunswick, Nova Scotia, to live and be brought up by his wife's family, the Maddens. It seems that Agnes was one of about eleven or more children whose parents ran a farm in New Brunswick. I don't have any documentation about the exact location of the farm, but my father used to talk about it many times as being in New Brunswick. So he essentially grew up in Canada. I know that there were many Irish people living in that part of Canada. They had landed there after the potato famine in Ireland.

It seems that he spent all those years in a family of many uncles and aunts who were all older than he. Some were probably still not adults yet, but George was the baby of the lot. The Maddens who were his grandparents took care of the three extra little ones until they grew up. They all either spoiled my father, being the youngest of that large brood, or he may have not been noticed too much in a family that had so many to look after. I have a charming posed photo of my father at the age of about three or four with his two sisters who look to be about five and six. They are dressed in very nice outfits, and look healthy. I do know that my father was close to his Uncle George. My father was referred to as Little George while my great-uncle was called Big George by all who knew them both. My mother would mention it at times.

Another impeccable source is the daughter of Big George, Frances Madden. I have become friends with her since the 1960s because we both entered religious life. I'll talk about that later.

During the sixties I had occasion to visit Boston for one or two days. We had two sisters of the Immaculate Heart of Mary (IHM) studying there at Boston College. While there I spent a lovely afternoon with my Madden relatives. I met a cousin, Don, and his family, but the highlight was visiting with Aunt Olive. She was one of that pile of children on the farm, so she remembered my father very well. Even though she was in her eighties at the time she told me about those days. However, she harbored some resentment either against my father or against James, his father. It was still a bone of contention with her that James never ever gave the Madden family any money to pay for the care of his three children even though he was working steadily all those years. I am not sure that I ever heard from my father that his father ever came to see them. He may have, but it could be that he ignored them all their young lives. That would explain the fact that my father did not want to have very much to do with his father, James.

Now, I am not sure whether or not James wanted to send his three little ones to the Maddens. I do know that in those days it was common for children to be relegated to an orphanage where they would most likely be split up and probably never see one another again. They would even have new names. Remember that this was in the 1890s. Anyway, the three lived with the Maddens, and became such an integral part of the family that they were not called by their family name of Murphy during that time. My father was known as George Madden until after he was married. That explains the use of Big George and Little George – They both were known by the name Madden. This became a matter of concern for my mother and for my older brother, Bernard. I will talk about it later.

I do not have very many anecdotes about my father's childhood. He seems to have grown up healthy and cheerful. He was always a fairly happy-go-lucky type of person. One of his biggest pluses was that he was not violent in any way. I never ever heard him yelling. Sometimes he would mildly curse about something, but it consisted of the word damn or hell. Also, he didn't exhibit any kind of physical abuse ever. In a word, he was mild-tempered, optimistic, a dreamer, and in the end, not able to face the realities of life. I never heard my parents having loud words, but I'm sure there were times when they had to make decisions together and probably had more serious words when the hard times really hit the family.

The only stories I do remember him telling us while we sat at the supper table had to do with some boyhood pranks at the farm which he enjoyed with a cousin who was his own age. They did things like eating all the strawberries picked for the dinner that evening, letting the cows out of one pasture into another without checking with Grandpa Madden. He never talked much about school, so I really don't know how long he attended school or if he graduated from high school. He did sometimes lead us to believe he attended college in Nova Scotia, but I have no letters, transcripts, or diplomas to show this accomplishment. Be that as it may, my father was a good and capable reader, and I have letters showing that he had the most beautiful handwriting of all of us in the whole family.

The most fortunate result of his upbringing, especially for our family, was that he was a faithful and staunch Catholic. Practicing our faith was an ordinary part of our life. He seems to have taken great pride in his religious heritage, and successfully convinced my mother to convert to the faith when they married.

I know that even though the three little Murphys were brought up by the Maddens, their father, James, never let them go entirely. In fact, he may have visited them on occasion. I have no record of it, but it could have happened. I do know that James ended his days in the care of his daughter Josephine. Believe it or not, he died in Portland, Oregon in 1929. I do wonder how he ended up in Portland with Aunt Josephine, his daughter. Neither one had ever lived on the West Coast.

It seems that in young adulthood my father was taken under the wing of Big George and went with him to work in the hotel Uncle George either owned or managed in Didsbury, Alberta, Canada. What his tasks were I do not know, but I do remember my mother saying that my father did not have a realistic idea of work because she saw that when he needed any money he would just go to Uncle George's till and take out what he wanted. However, she wasn't aware of this at first. So, as fate would have it, Big George ran the Rosebud Hotel in Didsbury, Alberta, Canada.

Little George was also part of the scene. That is why he had eyes for Martha Gertz who was a beautiful young woman who grew up in Didsbury. George was in his early twenties, and Martha was two years younger than he was.

On the Irish side we do have some relatives out there. Some are in Boston or thereabout. I have lost contact with the cousin, Don Madden, who I met in the early sixties. The only Madden relative I know, and happily so, is my first cousin, once removed who lives in Portland, Oregon. She is the daughter of Big George so that makes my father her first cousin. She is just a little older than I am so it shows that Big George was maybe a father figure for my father. My cousin's name is Frances Madden. We have had many visits and talks. She is a member of the Holy Names Sisters in the Northwest. She is absolutely the only relative I have, or know of, on the Irish side of my heritage. What a dear person she was. She passed away in 2012.

Now for my mother's story. What a contrast. Martha comes from a one-hundred percent German family. Both of her parents, Andrew and Emily, came to this country around 1890 from Berlin, Germany. My Aunt Hilda, Momma's sister, told me that Gertz might not have been their original name. It may have been Goertz, or some other very Germanic sounding name, they may have changed it or shortened it when they came to this country.

Andrew came from some area in Germany, which belonged to Poland years ago. That is not surprising since that poor country has been divided up between its more powerful neighbors for centuries. So maybe we are a bit Polish. She said we might also be a bit Jewish. Wow.

My mother had always told me the story that my grandfather had left Germany in the late 1800s because he did not wish to serve in the army. In our day and age we would call him a draft dodger. He was learning the tailoring trade, and did not have any inclination to go to war with anyone. I do not know any of the details about his emigration from Berlin, Germany, but I do know that there are a few photographs of his siblings and his own father who all seemed to have ended up in Canada. I wish I knew more about the reasons for their emigration, and for their choice of Canada. I do know that Grandpa first landed here in the United States because it seems he lived in and around New York for a time. He attended business school classes to learn how to run a tailoring shop, and probably to learn English. My Aunt Hilda and Aunt Hannah, another sister of Momma, would talk things over with mother when they would come down to visit her. They would reminisce about family, and talk about their parent's efforts to make it in the new country.

It seems that my grandfather came over from Germany first. A year later, he asked Emily to come over from Berlin. She was able to do it, but I have no details about it. Where did she get on the ship? What was the ship's name? Where did she land? Was it Ellis Island? What family did she leave behind? Did any of her siblings ever come to the U.S., or Canada? There are so many blank holes in that part of their history. My mother told me that her parents never returned to Germany. It seems that Emily and my grandfather, Andrew, met in Berlin, probably in the 1880s. They must have been energetic young people, very serious about life. Emily was especially serious while Andrew had a twinkle in his eye. It shows in the photos. My mother told me that her mother came from the area in Germany known as Alsace Lorraine. That is entirely different from the area where Andrew came from. Alsace Lorraine went back and forth between France and Germany for several wars, the winner always made it part of their territory. In the mid 1800s it must have belonged to Germany because my grandmother was a German, not French.

When Emily finally got to the U.S., she and Andrew were married in Danbury, Connecticut. I have a copy of their marriage certificate given to me by Aunt Hilda. It seems that my grandfather was not letting any grass grow under his feet when he arrived in New York. Besides going to business school, getting his bride to come over from Germany, and getting married, he must have started the ball rolling on gaining citizenship as a U.S. citizen. Also, he applied for, and received a homestead plot of his own, which was located in North Dakota. Parceling out these homesteads was a gift from the U.S., government to anyone who would improve the land for five years. The plan was that at the end of that time, if they had fulfilled the requirements of farming, or grazing, or building a home they could consider the land theirs. I believe it was 160 acres, or a quarter- square mile, which was a pretty sizable piece of land for a young couple to handle, especially when you consider that they were tailors. My grandmother was a very fine dressmaker, so she and my grandfather fit together quite well indeed.

Their homestead was located near Bismarck, North Dakota in a little place called Fessenden. You can imagine that it was quite a change for these two European city-folk to find themselves planted in the desolate plains of North Dakota in 1890. I just cannot imagine how they got along. There may have been many other German folk in that area, so they may have had neighbors they knew. My mother always said that the first four children in her family were born in Fessenden in a little house, partly sod that my grandfather provided for them. Andrew and Emily produced four healthy children while living in North Dakota. Hannah was the first. She was born around 1893. The second child was Martha, my mother, who was born in 1896 on December 31. Then came two boys, Gustave and Walter.

I sometimes wonder how on earth the city-dwelling German immigrants got along in the extreme bleakness that must have been North Dakota at that time. What help did Grandma have when it was time for the births? How did she feel? Were there any complications? Was there anyone to summon to help? I really don't know the answers to these questions. I can just imagine how primitive it must have been compared to their lives in the cosmopolitan city of Berlin when they were planning to come to America.

And then, what comforts did they have in the sod house. There probably wasn't easy access to water. Lights must have been by lamps or candles. What about wash day? I just get tired thinking of all the backbreaking work those pioneers had to do in order to just get through an ordinary day. What hardy and undaunted folk we have for our forbearers. They probably had wells somewhere on the property because it would be needed not only for themselves but also for any animals they had. Remember, those were the horse and buggy days.

They certainly had their hands full during those five years. With four small children to feed and care for, and with a hard working wife, Grandpa must have worked diligently each and every day to provide for them. One thing I do know is that the four little ones seemed to be healthy and happy from the stories my mother told me. I think that my grandparents did not expect to stay on the homestead longer than the five years required for gaining ownership of the property. I think the plan was that they would sell it, and move to a city where they could really become owners of a tailoring business. And therein lays a tale.

One time when my Aunt Hannah came down to visit her sister, my mother, I overheard them chatting about the old days. They started laughing about the days in North Dakota. One of the things they said was that their parents probably didn't get any money for their homestead. It seems that the local minister, what denomination I do not know, talked to a lot of the immigrants who were ready to move on. Somehow he managed to convince them to sign over their land to him, which they did. The story was that the Gertzs ended up with nothing. Probably all the other families had the same experience. I would have to research the ownership of the land grant to see who was the owner right after my grandparents. The year would be early 1900. It would be interesting to see if this person ended up with a very large parcel of land in and around Fessenden. It would be equally as interesting to see what kinds of deeds were passed on to him.

I have not mentioned that both of my grandparents were probably Lutherans or German Baptists. I know that Grandma was especially religious while at the same time very anti-catholic. My mother would often say that her mother was interested in Protestant groups that were nearby, but never interested in associating with Catholics. I suppose there were probably not many Catholics in their neighborhood because in those days immigrants tended to band together by nationality and religion. The Gertz side of the family was German and Protestant while the Murphy side was Irish and Catholic. It has turned out to be an interesting combination.

I sometimes think about how hardy these people were. They had to provide for themselves and their families with primitive amenities, such as a sod house, no running water, or electricity. No place to shop for everyday things, and they had no farming skills. How did they do it? They had to have a drive that finally carried them on to success in later life when they had even more children, and lived in another country, Canada.

I am sure there were adventures after my grandparents left the farm in North Dakota. I have heard names of places like Kitchener, Ontario and Detroit, Michigan mentioned by relatives, but I do not know any details about the why or when regarding these places. As far as I know there might be even more places. What I do know is that the Gertz family ended up in Didsbury, Alberta when my mother was a young child. This is where she grew up, where she went to school, where she eventually met George, my father.

Didsbury is a small town about 20 miles north of Calgary. It is located in the flat plains east of the Rockies which can be seen in the West on a clear day. It has the ever-present grain elevators, which are so common in all of the wheat growing areas of both the US and Canada. Of course, the railroad passed through the town, North to South. My grandparents settled in there.

Andrew opened a tailor shop in which Emily also worked. She was a superb dressmaker. He must have been an expert also because their business seemed to thrive. Grandpa did a lot of his work for the local townspeople and farmers in return for their goods and services. The cut-glass pitcher and glasses we have were payment from a salesman for a new suit handmade by Albert. My mother told me of several other trades made in return for suits and dresses. To me, the most impressive trade was for music lessons for all the children. From what I could gather from Aunt Hilda it seems that my grandfather was an accomplished musician. He could actually play many instruments in the orchestra. I would suspect that the musical talents that his children had were inherited from him. That means that we also could have inherited some of those genes because there are several of his children and grandchildren who have proved to be quite musically talented, myself included.

It wasn't long before four more little ones came along. Their fifth child was Edith, then Oscar, and finally Hilda and Freda. This gave the Gertzs quite a large family. The best part was that all the children were healthy, except for Oscar. Oscar had rheumatic fever, or at least that is what they thought. Everyone considered him a bit sickly. However he lived to be over sixty years old.

Now, back to the music lessons. Since my grandparents both came from a rather cosmopolitan city in Germany, it stands to reason that they had aspirations for themselves and for their children. It seems that one of their dreams was for all their children to have some kind of musical training. My grandfather made some kind of deal with local musicians. In return for suits and dresses they would give the children lessons on various instruments. The result of that was very positive. All the children could play some instrument by the time adulthood came around.

In my mother's case it was a true gift. She became a pianist, which led to her later becoming an expert organist. Aunt Edith was a xylophone and marimba player. I heard her play the marimba when she was in her late seventies during one of our visits to Portland. She was wonderful. Uncle Walter became such a fine violinist that he was a member of the Reno Symphony Orchestra for many years during his stay in Nevada. Aunt Hilda played the piano. I am not sure what instruments the others played, but my mother often talked about the enjoyable evenings they had as they were growing up entertaining themselves, and the town, with melodies made by the Gertz Orchestra. I think Grandma and Grandpa also played some instrument in the orchestra.

Martha's childhood was spent in a carefree manner. All of the children attended school in Didsbury. They were literate, but I don't think any of them attended college. My mother said she liked school a lot. It is true that she never stopped educating herself during the rest of her life. She confided in me one time that she really didn't finish high school. I asked, "Why not?" She said that when she was finished with the tenth grade her parents said she had to stay home and care for Oscar, who was the sickly one, because there was no one to do it. It seems that Hannah had just married so she was not around, so guess who got the honors? Martha said she didn't mind in a way because Oscar, who was later called Ray, was no trouble. He was good-natured. My mother could then do a lot of reading.

When I would hear my aunts and uncles reminiscing about those Didsbury days I would always hear their laughter.

It seems that they all enjoyed their life there very much even though Grandpa was a taskmaster, and Grandma an even stricter one. One thing is certain. My grandparents were hard workers. In fact, the children spent most of their childhood in a large house that my Grandfather built for them. How he knew how to build a house, since he was a tailor, I will never know. Nevertheless, my mother talked about helping with painting, trimming, and generally doing her part. She said all the kids helped. The end product was a beautiful two-story home with four bedrooms upstairs, and living room, dining room, and kitchen downstairs.

One of the most interesting stories my mother told me was about the basement. Grandpa wanted a quiet place to do his thing which in those days was inventing a perpetual motion machine. This was the early 1900s. There was a lot of interest in this project in the US and Canada because I heard that someone offered a very large sum of money to the person who would invent a true perpetual motion machine. My mother said there were people all over who were working on this. So, Grandpa got the bug. She said he would spend hours down in the basement, and would get mad if anyone interrupted him. In the end, though, he couldn't perfect whatever his idea was. It included bicycle wheels and other kinds of wheels that he set in motion somehow. It was hoped that these wheels would overcome whatever friction there was in the homemade machine and keep on spinning forever. The search for perpetual motion kept him busy in the basement during his free time. The kids knew better than to bother him.

My mother's young life was spent in the horse and buggy age. She would tell the great story about when they actually saw their first automobile. She said they were all playing out on the road in front of their house. They had heard about the horseless carriage but they had never seen or heard one. She said that they began to hear a loud unknown noise down the road. There, coming right down their street was the local doctor in an automobile. The kids all stood there dumbfounded and nervous about the noise. They just stood there with their mouths open. Then they all, as if by a signal, knelt down and smelled the tire tracks. It didn't smell at all like a horse. Then they all rushed wherever to tell their parents that they had actually seen a car. When I think of the long life my mother lived I think of the wonders she witnessed: electric lights, airplanes, radio, TV, space travel and landing on the moon, to name just a few.

As time passed in Didsbury the children were growing up. I am sure my grandparents were hoping that some of their brood would follow their footsteps in the tailoring business. Only Gustave, fondly called Gus, became a tailor. He made a good living wherever he lived because there were always men who wanted a handmade suit. The other children went in different directions. I heard my Aunt Hannah and mama talking one time about the close call they both had, as they became young women. They both said they felt pressure from their parents to come into the tailor shop and work in the trade. They said to one another that that was the one thing they did not want to do. Hannah married at age eighteen. Martha became the local telephone operator.

I have some charming photos of Martha posing in front of the telephone office, probably around 1917. She was the head operator. She described how they would sit in front of the exchange that was one mass of wires and plugs, to answer the calls. Her job was to have the caller tell her the number of the person she or he wanted. Then her job was to connect the wire from the caller's telephone to the number asked for. This meant plugging in the wires correctly and swiftly. I am sure that she became expert at this, or she would not have been named head operator. She was always pretty proud of that distinction.

Sometime around 1914 Hannah married David Dickson who worked on the Canadian Railroad. They settled down in Canada for the remainder of their lives. They had five children, my cousins. Jean was the first, then Douglas, Russell, Ronald, and Joyce. Joyce passed away a few years ago. However, Jean was stricken with illness at an early age. After a few years of suffering she passed away in her teens. Aunt Hannah never got over mourning for her. The other four are still living in Canada. I have met all of them on separate occasions. We had nice visits. They were fond of my mother, their Aunt Martha. I believe they live in or around Calgary.

We have a photograph of Aunt Hannah's wedding to Dave. She is in a lovely bridal veil and gown. He is dressed handsomely. The whole wedding party is posing in front of the Gertz house that Grandpa built. It is quite a crowd. I can identify all of the immediate Gertz family including my mother who is seated in the very front row. She is beautiful, and seems to be about 15 or 16 years of age. Grandma Gertz was so furious that Momma married a Catholic, that no one came to their wedding.

It was during this time that World War I was going on in Europe. The only Gertz boy who actually went to war was Walter. He served in England where he met and married an English girl, Nellie, and brought her back to the US to live. They had five children. For a long time this part of my mother's family lived up in Oakland, California. I don't remember meeting any of my cousins except the eldest, Alberta. She came down to Long Beach to visit us for a little while during the thirties. She has since passed away. I have never met the other four. I don't even know their names.

I do not think that my father, George, signed up for service in WW1. He would sometimes intimate that he did, but when Bernie wrote to the authorities in Canada later he was told that there was no record of George's enlistment. It might have been because George was an American in Canada he just did not enlist.

Right after WW1 the whole world was attacked by a terrible flu epidemic. No one was immune. The flu virus was so virulent that a person could die within one or two days of contracting it. It was highly contagious. The history of those years is full of the tragic march of this plague all over Europe, North America and other parts of the world. Didsbury was to finally feel the terrible brunt of the flu. My mother said that there were whole families in that little town that would be stricken, and carried out of their homes as corpses. She said she could remember hearing the loud wailing of the neighbor women when their children would get sick. Her most poignant stories were about the hours she spent at the telephone exchange trying to connect desperate calls for the local doctor. He was so busy and frightened himself that it was sometimes impossible for Mama to find help for the callers. She must have been 21 or 22 at the time. I can imagine the terrible stress it must have been on her to think that she was responsible for life and death situations. Also, on top of that she said she and her whole family were mortally afraid of contracting the disease. For some miraculous reason not one of the Gertzes came down with it. I asked her once what did she think saved them. She said that her mother kept them all covered with a pungent mustard plaster on the chest, and muffling their faces when they went out in public. When the epidemic finally ran its course all of the Gertzes were survivors of a very cataclysmic event in the world.

Aunt Hilda tells about her early childhood that deeply involved my mother. It seems that when Hilda was born in 1909 Martha was recruited to care for her. My mother was twelve years older than Hilda was, so Martha had some important responsibilities at an early age. Hilda said that Martha was so wonderful to her that she thought Martha was her mother. Of course, her mother was busy every day working hard in the tailor shop helping to make a living for the eight children. Grandpa was doing the same. So when little Hilda came along she was like a doll to my mother, only a living one. I don't know who took care of the last child born to the Gertzes. Freda was a couple of years younger than Hilda. Maybe Martha had to do double duty.

One of my mother's strongest features was her sense of responsibility. She never wavered in tackling whatever job needed to be done. I can imagine her as a little teenager doing all the motherly things for Hilda, and later for Oscar. My mother had so many wonderful qualities that would endear her to little ones. She always was very loving and accepting of their mistakes and antics. She had a sense of humor that wouldn't stop.

There were so many times when she would entertain us with remembrances of her life that would turn out to be the funniest we had ever heard in our young lives. Even into old age Martha carried a beautiful smile on her face.

I have a charming photograph of the Gertz family out for a walk or a picnic on the outskirts of town. Hilda is an infant in the baby carriage. Everyone is posing. There are two very interesting things to observe. First, my mother looks to be about 12 or 13. She is sitting right next to the baby carriage and has her hand on it as if she owns it. Grandpa is seated at one end of the family group while Grandma sits at the other end. Secondly, there is a woman in the group that is unidentified. She is also dressed up like the other two adults. Interestingly, she is holding an opened box of chocolates, and is sitting right next to Grandpa. The question is, "Why is this woman next to Andrew, not Emily?" Hilda said she was the assistant in the tailor shop, but now they wonder if she was the other woman. There never seemed to be anything going on, but it is fun to surmise.

Pretty soon Martha became grownup, so to speak. Besides caring for Hilda and Oscar she took the job of telephone operator. She must have been about twenty. That would be 1915 or 1916. I have already talked about her adventures in this job. But, as if she wasn't busy enough, she began using her talent as a piano player. She told us many stories about her few years serving as the accompanist in the local Movie Theater during all the movies. The motion picture fad had truly grown to become a must for any little town worth its salt. Since all the movies were silent it was customary to have some appropriate music played during the show to give expression to the antics going on up on the screen.

Some big theaters had wonderful pipe organs for this job, but the smaller places hired the local talent to do the accompaniment during the show. My mother really enjoyed this job because she got to enter the realm of fantasy, the world of adventure, the beautiful romantic adventures portrayed up there on the screen.

While we were growing up we almost always had a piano in our home. I don't know how this could be in those days, but there it was in the front room. There were countless times when Martha would sit there and play many tunes, all the while she would pretend she was watching a movie unfold before our eyes. As the scenes changed she very deftly played a different tune to express the action. Sometimes the villain was coming to the house to collect the rent. This meant some sinister-sounding music. When the hero would approach to save everyone she would play rousing martial music. At the time of romance Martha had some beautiful lyrical melodies ready. She would go on like this for an hour, all the while giving us a wonderful and exciting narration of the action. We never ceased to be entranced by her stories, her energy, and her ability to charm us. We usually ended up laughing our heads off because she would mimic all the characters. She told us that she did most of the music by heart, but if she needed a light someone would hold a lantern that could be partially covered. This took place in the early part of the 20th century when flashlights and other useful items were not yet in general use.

When Hilda was reminiscing one day she told me that Martha was more fun than anyone else in her whole life. She remembers how Mama would take her down to the movie show at night because she wanted company coming home. Hilda was about six or seven. Martha was around twenty. Hilda would last as long as she could but inevitably she would fall asleep listening to the wonderful music played by her big sister who seemed like her mother.

So, here is Martha doing all kinds of interesting things, showing a lot of gumption because she was escaping a life in the tailor shop, and ready to try her wings in life. All the photos we have of the Gertzes at that time show healthy, happy children, always well dressed, and seemingly well started on their roads to adulthood.

It must have been during those telephone operator days that Martha and George Madden met in Didsbury, They probably ran into each other many times because the town wasn't that large. Mama and Hannah both said that they spent some lunch times in the Rosebud Hotel which was managed by Uncle George, remember Big George? So Little George must have been there all the time. They said he was a rather carefree young man who liked to play practical jokes on others. He would get a good laugh when he got the better of someone. I am sure that sometimes the jokes were not that funny.

So, now Martha and George were young adults in the same little town. It is around 1918 or 1919. Mama spoke about the beaus who were beginning to show up at the Gertz house. I am sure there were dates and times of fun together for the young people. Even though Aunt Hannah was married to Dave she was part of the young people in Didsbury. Dave, who was a bit older than Hannah, went along with whatever his beloved Hannah wanted. So there were outings and other kinds of fun for them all.

I suppose George and Martha struck up an acquaintance when she would sometimes go to the Rosebud Hotel for lunch. I do not know any of the details about their romance, but there was one big problem, George was a Catholic. Whatever happened in their conversations, he was persuasive enough to ask for her hand, and also ask her to convert to Catholicism, which she did.

They were married in St. Agnes Church in the town south of Didsbury.

I am sure she caused a tremendous ruckus in the Gertz household when she showed she was serious about George. I don't know any of the details, such as whether George went to Andrew to ask for Martha's hand, or whether or not the Gertzes were asked to the wedding. All I know is that the photograph I have of the wedding party taken just outside of the church shows only five people. The priest stands in the middle in the classic pose of the hand partly in the waistline of the cassock. On one side of him are two men, the groom, George, and the best man, Uncle George. On the other side of the priest are two women, the bride, Martha, and another women who I believe is Uncle George's wife. When I compare my parent's wedding picture with Hannah's it is striking in that there must have been no one in their families present, and that my mother was wearing a suit instead of a wedding dress. Because I know that my grandmother was very anti-Catholic I suspect that there were a lot of fireworks in that family over the prospect of Martha marrying a dreaded Catholic and on top of that, she became a Catholic herself.

My mother always said that her mother never forgave her for that. In fact I don't think my grandmother ever did anything nice for us ever. I don't have any recollection of any kindness or affection. So even though I had grandparents I feel that I really didn't have them because I don't remember any interaction with them. Of course, I didn't know my Murphy grandparents at all.

My mother embraced her new religion whole-heartedly. She was baptized, received her First Communion and the Sacraments of Penance and Matrimony all on the same day. I can say today that my mother never looked back.

One interesting feature to this saga is that my mother did not know George as a Murphy. He had used the name Madden for many years, and was known as George Madden. I am not sure whether he straightened it out with her before they were married. I learned a lot later in life that when their first child, Bernard Jerome, was born his birth certificate had his name as Bernard Madden. Or maybe it was a case of my mother knowing it wasn't Madden by the time Bernie was born, so she insisted that it was now time to go to the real family name-Murphy. I have not seen any of the papers to verify this, but I do remember coming across letters about it, and wondering what on earth it was all about. Maybe he and his sisters were arbitrarily given the name Madden when they came to live permanently on the farm in New Brunswick. All I know is that George and Martha were married, and started life together in that area near Didsbury. A child soon appeared on the scene. Bernard was born February 3, 1920 in Red Deer, Alberta. That is a town farther north of Didsbury on the road towards Edmonton. I believe he was baptized there also.

My mother told me that when they were married just a while my father took her with him back to the farm to meet the relatives. I am sure he wanted to show off his beautiful bride. My mother said she did not enjoy that visit because she found herself an outsider looking in. I asked her why. She said that it was soon after WWI, she was of German descent, and a convert. She had two strikes against her in meeting the Irish- catholic family. She said the aunts, Sadie, Olive, etc. would grill her on how she was keeping the rules and regulations of the church now that she was a catholic. She said she felt at a real disadvantage because she wasn't well-versed in her new religion. They would take her to church to go to confession. Mama said she wasn't sure what to say to the priest.

I suppose the Madden family thought George made a poor choice. Even though Martha became a catholic to marry George there was still a rather strict view from life-long Catholics of the time that she was not up-to-snuff. Mama said she felt this all her life in regard to her in-laws. The one thing those in-laws didn't know was that George had married a woman who was good, hardworking, faithful, and determined to make a success of her life. She embraced her new religion whole heartedly. Even though she was not receiving approval from any direction she just kept right on doing what she had promised. I think that is an example of the very great strength she had as life went on, and she had to deal with some pretty difficult times. One of her greatest assets was her ability to find humor in almost any situation. This quality carried her, and us, through some of those times.

My mother said that one of the things she tried to do was learn as much as she could about her new religion. I am not sure that the Gertz family attended church services frequently. No one ever talked about it much. The main thing I would hear about is how anti-Catholic Grandma was. Martha realized that she could find a home in the Catholic Church which she cherished for the rest of her life. So it turned out that for her one of the greatest gifts my father gave to her was sharing his Catholic faith with her.

One story Mama did tell about that visit to New Brunswick was that she did want to do the right thing. So, when she wanted to go to church to confession she got away from the Aunts by walking down to the church on the railroad tracks by herself. In this way she didn't have any of them prying into her spiritual business, as it were. I don't know how my father handled any of this. Later years would show that he was not real supportive, but I don't know if he was protective of his beautiful new wife in the face of all those very Catholic aunts and uncles. My mother never returned to that part of the country again. However, some of those aunts and uncles became part of our family story in Canada and Portland.

I mentioned earlier that my oldest brother, Bernard, was born in Red Deer, Alberta. I do not know what took my parents farther north from Didsbury. I suppose George had a job of some kind there. My mother gave up her position as head telephone operator when she married, so I think that George was able to support her and the new baby. We have a photo of the three of them sitting outside at a picnic. They look happy and proud of their little child. I am sure they were like so many newly married - feeling their way, and trying to settle into life together.

My father was a rather happy-go-lucky person. He had a good sense of humor, and was very personable to talk to. In fact, he could carry on a conversation with anyone for hours. I think he inherited that Irish gift of gab. All the photos taken at that time show both my parents looking handsome
and beautiful, and both are well-dressed. By then my mother was an accomplished seamstress herself.

My parents were both in their early twenties when they made another move. Grandpa and Grandma Gertz decided to move back to the US Why, I do not know, but they did move south to Portland, Oregon. This must have been around 1919. My parents also moved down to Portland. Maybe there was a job waiting for Dad. Anyway, they moved to a little house on Alma Street. It was in Assumption Parish.

This is where my story begins.

Top: The Gertz family portrait: Martha back left.
Ctr: George & Martha's wedding, standing next to priest.
Btm: George and Martha with Bernie.

House No 1- 1924
Alma Street - Portland, Oregon

Well, I have finally arrived at the house on Alma
Street where I was born. But first, I must say that my
parents had a second child born at Alma Street. This
child was a little boy named George Barr. I don't
know where my parents got the names for the rest of
us, but it was apparent that the new baby was named
after my father, George. His second name was taken
after Grandma Gertz whose maiden name was Baar.
Yes, that is Baar. That was the way it was always
spelled in our family. She didn't explain why it was
spelled differently. Anyway, for the rest of his life
Barr was Barr to us, his family. We never called him
George because that was my father's name. So, in this
story his name will always be Barr. He was born in
1922. Mama said that the rest of us were all born on
Alma Street.

I asked my mother once who helped her at this time.
She said Aunt Sadie was a midwife, so she assisted in
the births. It turned out that mama didn't have any
complications to speak of. She was hale and hearty.
Aunt Sadie was one of the Irish aunts my father grew
up with on the farm. I know that Mama was grateful
for her help. I am not sure if Momma's sisters or her
mother helped her. At any rate, she survived the birth
of three children on Alma Street. After that there were
no more children added.

During this time my father worked at a huge
warehouse for Montgomery Ward in Portland. He was
some kind of checker or laborer there. When I was

born on April 27, 1924 my birth certificate says that my father was a checker, and my mother was a housewife. One time my mother mentioned that my father also had a job as a trolley operator. It is interesting that my father didn't talk too much about the jobs he had. I think that by this time he was showing the signs of an inability to hold a job for very long before he would do something to be fired. This was in the 20s when there was quite a bit of prosperity in the land. So within about four years the Murphys had three little ones, Bernard, Barr, and Doris. And two years later, Beverly Frances was born November 30, 1926.

Martha had her hands full with four little ones all under the age of six. I sometimes try to imagine her busy with all the care of her babies. She was loving, but I'm sure she felt a lot of worry because Dad was not turning out to be a truly responsible husband. He was beginning to let some bills lapse, and saying he was not going to pay them. He couldn't seem to hold a job for long. All the while he was very personable and cheerful about it all. I sometimes try to imagine how my mother coped with wash day. Portland was always so rainy and gloomy. How did she manage with diapers and clothes for a family of six? Did she have to wash everything by hand on a washboard? How could all the items dry properly? What about the other cares and worries of bringing up the family? She proved to be a woman of resourcefulness and courage.

During one of my visits to Portland to visit Aunt Hilda I spent a fine afternoon with Cousin Frances Madden. I believe my dear mother was with us also. Frances drove us over to the old neighborhood to see the house. I took a few shots. It is small. But, it is situated on a lot separated from neighbors. There is a lawn in front. It looked to be ample for the needs of the little Murphy family.

I have an old photo of Francis and myself when she is about six or seven and I am in the cradle. It seems that Big George's wife, Frances' mother, passed away. Frances was a shy, quiet little girl. My mother's heart went out to her. So she had Frances live with us for a few months until her father could get over his wife's untimely death, and make arrangements for Frances to join him. Frances always commented on how very kind Martha was to her how careful she was to see that Frances was not too lonely. This is one example of the generous love my mother had for someone who needed help. In this case it was a sweet little girl with no mother.

Well, now here we are. Our family is complete. Of course I don't remember too much about my beginnings in Portland. I know I was baptized in Assumption Church on May 11, 1924. I was two weeks old. My name was Doris Agnes. My mother also had a middle name of Agnes. I am not sure if that was her given name or whether she took Agnes at her own reception of the sacraments when she married Dad. Anyway, I always was pleased that she and I had the same middle name. Remember Dad's mother was named Agnes.

The little house on Alma Street was our home long enough for three babies to be born there. It was in the same general location of the house my grandparents moved into on New York Street. In a neighborhood of

Portland called St. John's. Hilda says it was a German neighborhood.

Even though my mother grew up in a household with German parents she herself seemed to be unaffected by dialect or customs. I do know, however, that she actually could speak German because when her sisters would come to visit her in Long Beach I would hear them talking and laughing around the kitchen table speaking German. My mother would often say that she didn't really like the German language because it was guttural. She did retain some knowledge of it into her old age. Of course, she didn't teach us to speak German. World War I had made anything or anyone German a butt of ridicule or worse. She probably had some unpleasant experiences in Didsbury during that war. Whatever it was she did I can say that she spoke beautiful English with not one whit of an accent.

I think that during our stay on Alma Street that my father had various jobs in Portland. It seems that he didn't really have any skills for a particular sort of work. He often said that he was meant for a desk job, not manual labor. He had worked in the Rosebud Hotel in Didsbury, but I'm not sure what he actually did to learn how to manage. His later life with us showed that he really couldn't look at a situation in a realistic manner and do something about any remedies needed. This would prove in the end to bring on a catastrophe for him.

Everything was moving along for the young Murphy family. My father was having the usual trouble holding down a job for very long. His Aunt Sadie was a character in my early memory because she spanked me for going next door when she was taking care of us. I wanted to enjoy the little swing they had on their front porch, so I just went over for a minute thinking she wouldn't know where I was. Well, over she came. She paddled me. Of course, I don't remember anything else about her. In fact, I don't know if I ever saw her again after we left Portland.

We probably interacted quite a bit with my mother's family. Her parents and three of her sisters were living in the next neighborhood. I do have photos of us posing with them in front of their house on New York Street. I believe her brothers, Gus and Oscar, were also part of the scene at the time. I have absolutely no memory of my grandparents ever paying any attention to me. They never gave us special hugs or any little gifts. They just didn't figure in any way in my life experience. I sometimes feel cheated by fate because even though the Gertz grandparents were still alive, we didn't really experience having grandparents. And, of course, Grandpa Murphy came to Portland when I was so small that I have no memory of him. I do know that my mother did not like him at all because she said he was ill tempered with her and with us kids. She never expressed any interest in his memory. It must have been around this time, 1927 that we moved to the next house in my life. I was probably three.

House No 2 - 1927
Buchanan Street – Portland

This chapter will not be very long because my memories of it are so limited. I must have been three and four years old during our stay there. It seemed to be an ample home for a family of six. In fact, all of our homes had at least two bedrooms, one bath with living room, which we called "the front room", and sometimes a dining room. Of course we always had a handy kitchen, but not always a gas stove. Also, I lived at a time when there was always an indoor bathroom. I don't remember ever living where there was an outhouse. So in my view the ordinary home for us was pretty comfortable and safe. My father was providing this in a more or less successful way.

I was now waking up to life around me. I was aware of having two brothers and a little sister. My parents were always there. I am most grateful for the gift they both gave to us children – it was the security of having them with us each day. Another gift they gave to us was providing a peaceful and quiet home life. My parents never ever yelled at one another or said any loud words. In fact, they never argued in front of us. So we enjoyed a rather serene life with excitement every so often. I am sure my mother was having some apprehension about how my father was going to really support us because of the pattern that was developing – start a job, lose a job, etc. However, she never ever let on to us kids her worries about it. And my father kept right on with his happy-go-lucky manner.

Aunt Josephine brought their father James out west to

Portland. I guess James had finally retired from his grounds keeping jobs on the estates in the East. His three children were now all adults, and going on their way. Even though he turned his children over to in-laws to raise he must have remained in contact with them over the years. I don't know how else to explain how Josephine, his eldest child, was now taking care of him in his old age. Anyway it was around this time that they both showed up in Portland. All I can surmise is that Josephine might have been making efforts to have her brother, George, help her with the care of their aging father.

I do know from hearing my father speak of his Dad that he was not especially close to him. My father often would refer to his father as "the old man". Whenever he said this I would feel a bit of wonder about why he didn't call his father "Dad" or "Pop" or some such title of affection. George, my father, never spoke of him or ever related even one time an instance when he and his father had time together. This might explain why he didn't really know how to relate to his own children in a truly caring way. He never had a model, I guess.

I do have a memory of my father carrying me on his shoulders through the big department store in Portland. I think this is actually the very first memory I have. I must have been about three. How much fun it was to be up so high. And the lights were so bright and beautiful. I even remember passing by the beauty parlor of the store where young ladies were having their hair marcelled. They were all being given the latest hairdo for the year 1927 - permanent waves.

This was also the time in my life when I realized that my two older brothers were teasing me. In a way I knew they were a fine protection when I was out in the yard playing with them, but they also could be real scamps. I remember that when we were walking down the road we had to pass by some cows that were grazing. Of course, to me these were giant animals. I wasn't sure just what they were for. My brothers decided to tell me that if one of the cows looked at me I should run because the cow would chase me. Since I was only four years old that was quite a scary announcement. I can still remember the feeling of fright when we would get close to the pasture. In the end it was my mother who steered me straight. She told me that the cows would not chase me, and that they were the source of the milk that we had at breakfast. Well, that was a revelation to me. I stopped running when we went past the cows, but I kept staring at them and wondering where in heck the milk came from.

My parents had now been married about nine years. They had four lively healthy children. Bernie was the only one who seemed to show symptoms of asthma. He sometimes would wheeze and cough. My mother said that she worried about him from the time he was an infant because of his occasional breathing problems.

Otherwise, we were all growing. My mother told me that it was during these days in Portland that she got fed up with the weather. It was gloomy more days than not. It was impossible to dry clothes on the line. This was around 1928 so there were no dryers in existence. Even if there were she probably wouldn't have one because Dad was still going in and out of jobs. That seems hard to believe because this was a time of prosperity in the land. It would be just a year or two before the Great Depression hit the country. It was hard enough for Mama to take care of four children and a husband, but to have very gray and gloomy days on top of it was too much for her. She was probably exhausted. Then something happened that turned her world a lot brighter.

It seems that my parents had a friend who had a relative who worked in the lumber mill in northern California. This friend put in a good word for my father, and a job offer came which couldn't be turned down. I am sure both my parents were elated at the prospect of steady work in a company town, and the chance to move away from Portland. By now the in-laws on both sides were probably giving both of my parents fits. So the decision was made for us to move south to McCloud, California. My mother's joy in this event was ruined by the fact that they still owed quite a few bills. The milkman, the grocer, and others were not yet paid. My mother was in favor of taking what funds they had and paying what was owed, then scrounging enough to make the trip south, even borrowing from her family. My father would have none of that. He said that we were all leaving town in the middle of the night, and forget about paying the bills. And that is exactly what happened. It was so shocking to my mother that she never ever got over it, and was still telling me about it in her later years. The fact that my father had this attitude about paying his bills was a trait that he never faced as far as I can remember. His reaction to this kind of situation was to laugh about it as if it didn't matter. Of course we kids did not know any of this was happening because my parents never let on to us that they were having differences.

So off we all went to beautiful California. I am not sure whether we drove or what because I don't know if we had a car. I don't think we did. We probably took the train south for an overnight trip. Say "goodbye" to the gloom and dampness of Oregon. Say "hello" to sunny California.

House No 3 - 1928

Mt. Shasta City - McCloud, California

Here begins a time that in my memory is very sweet, peaceful, and fun. We arrived first at the small town on Mt. Shasta City. It was located just a few miles north of McCloud where we were headed. My parents found a little house for us, and we waited until the word came from the McCloud Lumber Company that one of their company-owned houses was available. I have only a few memories of our stay in Mt. Shasta City. I always remember that my mother was so persuasive with us kids about anything. I guess she was trying to get us to eat a nourishing breakfast.

You know how kids can be finicky. I can still hear her say to me, "You know that your favorite breakfast is oatmeal, don't you, Honey?" I, of course, agreed with her, and spooned up that big dish of oatmeal like it was ice cream. She had a wonderful way of putting on the best side of anything that came up. She was like that all of her life – very positive in outlook. It saved us a lot of times in our difficult times, which came later.

I have some small photos of us kids sitting on the front steps of that little house in Mt. Shasta City. Beverly is still a baby so she is not in the photo. But, it shows three healthy, happy children looking ready for whatever comes up. Bernie is already the big brother, and Barr is turning out to be the scamp. I was four, so the other two were six and eight years old. The year is 1928 or 1929.

I am sure my parents were looking forward to this new adventure with happy hearts. It was a time to get a new start. Their little family was healthy and happy. They were away from interfering relatives. My father had a job. So the future looked bright. And best of all they could plan the future for their little family in a peaceful way.

My mother took great pride in her brood. She said that Saturday was 'bath day'. She would get us all bathed and gussied up in our Sunday clothes. She then sent us all on a walk around the block with Bernie as our leader. Later, I can remember this special time. We all were smiling and so happy. Mama had a way with doing little things that would bring us a lot of joy and laughter. All the while my father was in the picture too, but he was more benign and quite pleasant, but in the background. He let Mama 'do her thing' with us kids. Of course, we blossomed under such loving care.

Mama would take us on walks to the park and to the steps of a large building, probably the school. I have a photo of us sitting around her on those steps. We are all very little still.

I don't know how long we lived in the house in Mt. Shasta City, but before long we were settled in a nice little home in McCloud. I believe it was on Minnesota Street. 118 is a number that comes to mind. Because my father was now an employee of the McCloud Lumber Company he was assigned this house for his family residence. I believe the plan was that no rent would be paid directly to the company. They would simply take out the rent from my father's monthly paycheck. That made it certain that the rent would always be paid. Also, another plan the company had was that their employees could have a running bill at the grocery store down on Main Street. The lumber company owned the whole town, so they controlled everything. It was quite a different arrangement from what my parents had been used to. I am sure my mother was greatly relieved because now there was a steady paycheck coming in.

I will spend some time now to describe McCloud. By now I am five so my memories are beginning to grow. I can see so many things in my mind's eye. This was a small town nestled in the foothills right at the base of the majestic Mt. Shasta. We could look right up to the mountain from our front yard. It was always beautiful at any time of the year. The company homes were lined up in the town together with rows and rows of cut lumber. We would walk to the store or to school through acres of fresh-cut boards that were neatly stacked in very high, straight piles. In order for everyone to walk along the streets safely the company had constructed sidewalks along all the housing streets. The sidewalks were all made of wood, and were usually several inches off the ground. There were these wooden walks also constructed through the stacks and stacks of cut lumber. So wherever we went we could keep out of puddles and snow.

The one thing I remember my mother worrying about was the two boys going barefooted so much in the summertime. She was constantly warning them about slivers. Of course, there were times when they came home crying because they did have a big sliver, which Mama carefully extracted, and then she put on the dreaded iodine. Oh, but that hurt.

The town had one elementary and one high school. All the children of the mill workers could attend. This was significant to me because I became aware that little black children did not live in the kind of homes that we had. They lived outside of town, but very close, in somewhat ramshackle homes. I never went there, but I could see their area sometimes when we were driving somewhere. I used to wonder about it.

Remember that I am still only six. I remember that a nice little black boy sat right in front of me in school. His name was William. He was very well behaved and sat up quite straight all the time.

The company also provided the town with a wonderful swimming pool. It was large enough for us to have a wonderful time. One section was for little kids who couldn't swim very well. The water came up to my waist. I learned to dog paddle with the best of them. An old fellow was the lifeguard or caretaker. He was always there to see that everyone was fine, and that we showered ourselves before jumping in the water.

I notice after awhile that there were no little black children permitted in the pool. I would ask my parents questions about this, but they gave me some vague answers, which made me, wonder all the more. My biggest revelation about where the black children went swimming was one day when we were out in the woods behind our house I could hear a lot of laughing and joyous yelling. When I looked through the trees I could see a whole lot of black children going for a swim in Squaw Creek. They were having a wonderful time. But now I wondered more. Were they dirty or something? No one ever gave me a plausible answer.

I finally graduated to the deep section of the pool which was much larger than our semi-wading pool. To show that I could hold my own, I had to show the old guy that I could make it across safely. Well, I started to dog paddle as hard as I could, and I was petrified when I realized I was in deep water, but I kept on paddling. Finally I made it. All he did was nod. That meant I could swim with all the big kids. What bliss.

My two brothers were well along in school by now. They were talking about it, so I was looking forward to starting. Well, I think my mother took me over to first grade sometime in the middle of the year. I was only five, but they took me anyway. I was all agog. I can still see the teacher giving me a sheet of lined tablet paper, and a pencil and writing my first name at the top in large cursive writing. She told me to practice it so that I could put my name on my papers. So I never took printing in first grade; I just started right in.

If anyone will think about it for awhile they will see that I had a very hard "row to hoe" with my first letter – a capital D. That is one of the hardest letters to learn because of the twists and turns it takes. Little fingers really have a hard time mastering it. I must have done ok because I don't remember anyone getting after me for not writing well.

I went through first grade and second grade in that

company-town school. I learned to read very well. However, I was always the youngest in my class because I was passed to the second grade when I was six. I didn't turn seven until the tail end of the school year. This remained the case all through my school days. Beverly was still too little to go to school so I took her with me one day. She sat in the seat with me, and snuggled up to me real close. She was very good all day. We wore matching party dresses that one of my uncles had brought to us as a present. The dresses were beautiful lime-green satin with many colored ribbons and rosettes. I am sure we looked wonderful. I didn't know it then, but those dresses would be the only presents we would ever receive from any of our relatives.

Life in McCloud was quite peaceful. We always had enough to eat, and even had new clothes that my parents ordered from a catalog because there was no clothing store in the town. I remember getting my first pair of goulashes to wear to school in the snow. The only thing was that my shoe size must have gone up a tad because when I put on the goulashes to go to school I couldn't get them off because my shoes were so tight inside them. The teacher had to let me wear them inside because it was too cold to go in stocking feet. I was only in the first grade.

So our lives moved along in a wonderful, quiet manner. My parents were always calm and supportive. I can still hear my father going off to work in the morning and saying, "Goodbye Mart" to my mother. However, I don't have any memory that he ever kissed her goodbye or gave her a hug. In fact I don't remember ever seeing them hold hands or walk arm-in-arm. Of course, I wasn't thinking about these things then. All I knew was that we enjoyed a serene family life, and felt very secure with our parents always near us. We laughed a lot, and we had lots of company. My mother's brothers and sisters came south for visits a lot. I have many snapshots of them at these times. I think my folks were good hosts. I know that my mother was a good cook, and my father loved to talk and talk. So we were growing up in a nice family atmosphere where there was no violence of any kind. I felt very protected and safe.

It was in McCloud that I first became aware of religion. We always attended Sunday Mass together as a family unit. It seems that the Catholics in McCloud had gotten enough money together to have their own church right in town, it was a lovely Church built entirely of logs. The interior was finished in polished wood. I was entranced. It was fascinating to see the vestments and candles, and to hear the music.

I became aware early on that Mama was not sitting with us in the pew. This was because she had volunteered to be the organist when the Pastor announced the need for one. I am certain she had some trepidation because she was probably not too familiar with Catholic Church music. But because she could read music like the experts she had no trouble with the hymns. She also learned how to follow the ceremony of the Mass so she would know when to start playing the hymns for the choir. This was to be her pattern for the rest of her life, but we didn't know it then. I am sure her years of playing for the silent movies paid off. Besides playing for the Sunday Mass, Mama also must have been available for weddings and funerals.

It was here in this little church that I learned about death. It seems that the tiny daughter of one of the parishioners had died. She was to have her funeral soon. Our parents asked us if we would care to go. I had not even thought about anyone dying before, so I didn't know what to say. My folks said the coffin would probably be open to view. Well, my brothers were so brave saying they weren't afraid. So I said I wasn't afraid either. I can still see the beautiful little face of that toddler. I was amazed that she looked just like she was sleeping. Several of my playmates also attended the funeral. We all agreed that the little girl must surely be in Heaven. Of course, Heaven was the place where the angels lived with God. So she is very happy now.

There was a park about a block north of our house where we spent many happy times. My brother, Bernie, did have one setback there. He fell off the swing and broke his arm. Mama said he came running home holding his arm which was bent in a strange way. Of course, he was king of the family hill for the next several weeks. I think he must have been about ten.

Walking to school each day was a treat for me because the way was so beautiful and mysterious. We had to go through part of the woods. Imagine the mosses, the little flowing creek, the pussy willows, the aroma of the pine trees, and the wildflowers. Then there were little creatures like squirrels, sometimes a deer, and unknown animals. I was usually entranced by the time I finished walking to and from school.

The days passed with the change of seasons. My Mother would look forward to each Spring. That was the time she would go out in front and plant her pansies. She just loved that beautiful little flower, and so did I. I can still see her down on her hands and knees getting the flower plot ready.

We had pansies out in front, but on the south side of the house we had a giant growth of hops. This was a very fast-growing vine that would loop itself around the strings that were positioned from ground to eaves about six inches apart. These vines would reach the top in a few weeks. I didn't know until later years that this was my father's project. He used the hops to make BEER. Now this was the time of Prohibition in our country. It was really against the law to make or sell liquor.

All over the land there were guys planting the hops, and then they would get the needed ingredients and make several gallons of homemade beer. Someone would usually volunteer the use of his bathtub, hence came the use of the description "bathtub suds." No matter where you went you would see these healthy stands of vines growing against houses in the springtime. I have some photos of relatives visiting us, and there are the hops as big as life.

Because we are living in a lumber company town there were some unique things that came with the territory.

For me the scariest was the threat of fire. We would always be warned not to light matches in the woodshed. That prospect was scary enough to a shy little girl, but the worst was hearing in the dead of night the blast from the lumber mill telling all the town volunteer firemen that they had to come at once. It was so loud that it would wake us up. And it would blast with loud blaring honks that made me shiver. I was always worried that my father would go, but he never did. I guess he didn't volunteer.

Since the town was located right in the middle of a huge expanse of pine forest we were surrounded in every direction by the woods, as we called them. This meant that when we went on picnics or rides it was always through high stands of beautiful trees. My parents were often planning a picnic out to Two-mile Flat or some such interesting sounding place. We all enjoyed the running and playing and fun. My mother was always ready to help the boys build a tepee or make something with twigs. I was still small, so I just enjoyed it all. Beverly was probably three or four. My father would smoke his pipe and look on benevolently. I don't remember that he did any particular activity with the boys. My parents had made lots of friends who were neighbors and co-workers so we were surrounded by lots of sociability.

So we had about three years of quiet living. We were all growing and happy. We spent evenings around the wonderful radio we had in the front room. It had a great big speaker on top. It was quite a marvelous piece of furniture. The seasons passed with warm summers, beautiful springs, and white winters. I was entranced by it all. Then something happened which was to change our lives forever.

My grandfather James, who still lived in Portland with

Aunt Josephine, passed away. I believe it was in 1929. I remember that we took the train up to Portland once. I fell asleep on the seat that was covered with the most beautiful velvet material – it was deep red in color. I don't remember anything else about the visit except that we were in the Gertz grandparent's home for a while. There are just little snippets of memory about this time. I suppose my father went up there to either see his father or to make arrangements for the funeral. In any case, grandpa died.

It was sometime later, maybe even a year that my parents went back to Portland. I now think that they had to meet with some lawyer about my grandfather's will. Well, it turned out that my grandfather's employers over the years had paid him with some of the stocks they owned. In fact, he had enough stocks in some of the largest companies in America that he stated in his will that they should be divided into three parts – one for each of his children. I'm not sure that my father even knew that his Dad had any assets whatsoever. In any case, my father received a windfall of ten thousand dollars worth of stocks. At least that was their value in 1929 or 1930 when he finally finished all the paperwork. What a surprise. This gift, in effect, changed any and all plans my parents had made for our stay in McCloud.

Of course, we kids didn't realize the import of such a windfall, but we were saying to one another, "We must be rich." I am not sure how my mother handled it, but she said in later years that my father didn't let her have any say at all about what to do with this sudden wealth. I am sure they had lots of talks about it, but she said he made the decisions in spite of her cautions. She said the biggest shock to her was the day he came home with a brand new car, one of the most up-to-date upscale autos then on the market.

It was a Studebaker Commander – four doors, wire wheels, trunk in back, and lots of chrome. She didn't have any say about it. It seems that he didn't pay for the car outright, but was going to make payments. We have several photos of all of us next to this beautiful auto. Since we had ridden around in rather rickety cars up to now, this was a big step up the society ladder. With all those stocks that could be cashed in at the local banks it seemed that we were on "easy street." Remember that in those days $10,000 was probably equivalent to two or three year's salary, maybe even more. I am sure my father couldn't believe his good fortune.

As time went on my parents made some very big decisions. Even though we were doing very well financially with my father working in the mill, my folks must have talked about it long into the nights. In the end they decided, or my father decided, that he would quit his job in the mill, and we would move bag and baggage.

In 1931 the land of promise had to be Southern California. This was where all the glamour was. The movies were a huge presence in the south, the climate was absolutely perfect, and the area was busy with jobs in all kinds of industry. What could be better than to get in our fine automobile and head south to the land of sunshine? I know that one factor in the whole equation was for my parents to put more distance between themselves and cold climates. No more snow.

After saying goodbye to everyone, and packing up a few things for the journey, we drove out of McCloud in June, 1931 heading south on the rather primitive highways of those early California days. We experienced no problems with our great big, brand new car; we spent each night in motels all along the way. We four kids fit very nicely in the back seat. I was seven, Beverly was five, Barr was nine, and Bernie was eleven. We enjoyed the driving each day. It was a treat being out on a "ride" day after day.

Our first stop was in Red Bluff where my mother's brother, Uncle Ray, lived with Beulah and their son Russell. We stayed with them a few days. Then we progressed further south to Oakland where we stayed awhile with mama's brother, Uncle Gus and Mary.

This was all in 1931. We stayed in Oakland long enough for us to go to school for a little while. Also, it was in Oakland that my mother decided to have all of her teeth pulled. This must have been a very hard thing for her to bear. Just the thought of having all your teeth out at once makes you shiver. I remember that I came home from school a couple of times and Mama would be sitting at the kitchen table crying real hard. Of course I would start to cry with her. She kept reassuring me that she was crying because her mouth hurt so much, not about anything else. I guess that answer allayed my fears because I would kiss her and then go out to play. In any case, in the Fall sometime we were rolling again down to Southern California where my folks had decided to live. They hadn't picked out the place yet, but we were passing through some very nice, pleasant towns along the way. They finally said that San Diego was our destination. I guess you couldn't get any further south than that. So the Saga that began in Didsbury, Alberta, Canada ended up in Beautiful Southern California.

All the while this was going on my father blithely paid all the bills with cash. When he needed some money it seems that he took one of the stocks and went to a bank and cashed it in. It is evident even from this very early time that my father was not astute about managing finances. He doesn't seem to have thought about conserving what assets we had so there were no investments made. I have letters that he wrote to the executor asking him to send the stocks immediately because he wanted to use them. There really weren't that many, but it seems as if he thought this money would last him forever. How wrong he was.

Family at Ferndale: Mama, Barr, Bernie, Doris, Beverly & Pa at far right

Family outing with the Studebaker Commander.

House No. 4 - 1932

Second Street - Long Beach, California

Now I begin the story of my life in Long Beach. We didn't immediately plop down in Long Beach the first time we went through it. I believe we stopped at the Chief Motel on Long Beach Boulevard for an overnight stay on our way to San Diego. It looks as if my parents were trying to get as far away as possible from the cold and maybe other perceived problems. Anyway, I know we drove down to beautiful Ocean Boulevard, but then moved on down the coast.

I should say a few words about the motels of the day. We didn't call them "motels" because the word wasn't common at that time – 1932. They were called "motor lodges" or some such name. There really weren't very many of them because the highways were just being developed along our way. There were many times that we had to go slowly past highway crews working on the paving or widening of the route. Of course, we didn't encounter any car trouble because we were riding in that great big Studebaker Commander. It sure filled the bill in getting us to Southern California. Ma and Pop were in the front seat. We kids sat in a nice row in the back. We were still so young that we fit fine. I look back now at how much I enjoyed seeing the sights along the way. Driving right next to the Pacific Ocean was a revelation to me. I'm sure we were all agog at its beauty, and the fact that we were here in the "land of promise" by pure chance – my father's inheritance.

We arrived in San Diego, and stayed again in a motel. I am not sure what transpired there about the plan for

our settling down. I do know that years later my
mother told me that Pa couldn't decide what kind of
work to do, so she suggested that the best place for us
to settle down would probably be "that clean and
attractive little city we passed through- Long Beach".
He agreed because we ended up in Long Beach.

This was to be the place I spent the remainder of my
childhood. We all seemed to call Long Beach our
hometown from then on.

We stayed at the Harvey Line Motel on Pacific and
Willow for awhile, and the rented a house on Second
Street. It was so wonderful to us kids. It was only two
blocks from the beach, and a few blocks from Bixby
Park. We lived there only a short while. Several
things transpired that had a bearing on our lives. It
seemed that my father was going to go into the Real
Estate business as a salesman. I don't know any of the
details about why he decided that this would be his
field. He had never dabbled in property before. Nor
did he bother to take any classes to prepare himself
for this job. I do know that from things he would say
in later years that he was "meant for a desk job, not a
laborer". How he came to this conclusion I will never
understand because his work history up to this point
was very spotty. The longest he had remained on any
job was three years. Those were the years when he
worked in the lumber mill as a laborer. That probably
wasn't what his job was called, but he worked with
all the ordinary crew. He was not behind a desk in any
capacity. I have a long photo of all the workers at the
mill. There is my Dad right in the middle of the
crowd of workers with his sleeves rolled up just like
the rest of them.

For a time my Dad had a desk in a Real Estate office on American Avenue near 5th street. I saw him in there one time when I was going home from school. The top of his desk had no papers. My mother told me later that he did not know anything about the business, but he was going to try his luck with the company that let him use their office. Of course, if he had to pay a fee for this privilege he could handle it because he still had lots of money. So our future was going to be dependent upon his good-natured persuasiveness in getting people to purchase what they wanted.

In the meantime, my parents did something for us kids that would really change our outlook on life. They enrolled us in Catholic school in Long Beach. We lived a few blocks from the parish school and church. It turned out to be St. Anthony's. One of the things I have mentioned in my narration several times is the fact that we were a devoted Catholic family. There was no doubt in my mind that that was our Religion. So when we drove up to the convent on Sixth Street we were all agog, except Beverly. She was still so young that she didn't figure in these school plans. I remember being amazed when I saw the nuns through the front window of the convent. For some reason our parents didn't take us inside. I don't know why, because we really were pretty well behaved youngsters. Behind the scenes at home we had our tussles, but we always knew that we should be polite while out with others.

I had never laid eyes on a nun before. I was instantly

fascinated. Who were these ladies? How did they get to look that strange way? I had never seen anyone dressed like that. Were they nice?

When my folks came out to the car they said we were going to attend St. Anthony's starting the next day. Whew. What an adventure. I was in third grade with Sister Miriam. Barr was in fifth grade with a nun I can't remember. Bernie was in Seventh grade with Sister Andrea. I remember enjoying each day, and especially recess because then I could play "Jacks" with my little friends. At the end of the school day we three kids would walk home where Mama was waiting with treats. If the weather was great we would all walk down to the beach for a refreshing swim.

So here we were, getting all settled in Long Beach. We lived in a cozy little cottage on Second Street. We could walk to school together, go to the beach each day after school, play in Bixby Park, and generally live a carefree existence. My father was going to his office each day.

Mama was at home taking care of us all. It was a time when we had no cares and worries to think about. We children were happy and healthy. We had some nice clothes to wear, and there was food on the table for every meal. We attended church regularly, and got settled in to a pleasant and happy routine. It was while we lived on Second Street that I learned how to ride a "two wheeler" bike. Some neighbor boy had the bike, and asked me if I wanted to try it. I said "Sure", and I climbed on. What a high it was to suddenly be pedaling along and realize that no one was helping me. I rode all the way to the end of the alley and back thrilled by the knowledge that "I could do it." I was seven years old.

One of the things that was very common at that time – 1932 – was that most families needed ice for their attractive wooden iceboxes. There were no refrigerators for ordinary folk yet. So we had an icebox.

To me, that was a luxury that we had never had before. It was customary for the iceman to come slowly down the road with his truck full of blocks of ice. He would look at the front window of each house. If there was a square card hanging from the window shade he would stop. The card had figures printed in big print on each of the four sides of the card. The card itself was probably about 10 inches square. One side had 10; the next might have 15, the next 20 and finally 25. Whichever number was placed in the top position that day indicated to the iceman how big a block to bring into the house for the icebox.

He would chop or chip off the requested amount with his trusty ice pick. Then he would carry the block of ice into the house and deposit it neatly in the icebox. Well, I didn't know of this arrangement at all. My mother hadn't mentioned to us how the iceman knew how much ice to bring inside. So, one day I was noticing the card hanging from the window shade. I was curious, so I looked at it and decided that instead of 10 at the top I would change it to 20. Of course, I had no idea what it was all about. When we got home from school that day my mother questioned us about the card. I spoke up and said I had turned it. Then I asked her what it was for. She told me the iceman brought a 20-pound chunk of ice into the kitchen. Our icebox would hold only a 10-pound block. She had to send him back to bring a smaller chunk. All day she was puzzled about the number 20. She decided, rightly so, that one of us had fiddled with the card. I don't remember being scolded, but from then on I was careful to ask questions about mysteries around the house.

Our stay at the house on Second Street was quite short, by Christmas time we had moved to House #5 on Delta Avenue.

House No 5 - 1932

Delta Avenue - Long Beach, California

I don't know the reason for our move to Delta
Avenue. We kids were disappointed because we were
now about 3 or 4 miles away from the beach. There
would be no more romping in the waves after school
on a warm day. Now we had to take a bus to get there.
But our new house was really the nicest one we
would ever live in as a family. It was located in the
Wrigley District of Long Beach that was an area
developed by the Wrigley Family of Chewing Gum
fame. They had many holdings in Southern
California, so Long Beach was one of the areas they
were developing. It was widely known that the
Wrigley Family owned Catalina Island. So our new
neighborhood was part of an empire of a very wealthy
family.

We were located just north of Willow Street. The
homes were built in the popular Spanish style of
those days. The whole of Southern California is
peppered with neighborhoods all with homes
reminiscent of early Spanish rancho and colonial
styles. We had an entrance way with arches and
enclosed patio. The front of the house sported a huge
bay window that had deep red velvet drapes to cover
it at night. It looked so elegant to me. We six
Murphys fit quite comfortably in such a lovely home.
I am still seven years old and in the third grade at St.
Anthony's.

That year was the Christmas that my parents told the
four of us that we could each choose a present that we

would really like. It couldn't be too expensive, but it could be nice. It was so thrilling to go downtown to Long Beach and visit the big stores. I remember looking and looking in the toy department of the big Montgomery Wards on Pine Avenue. Beverly, Barr, and Bernie were doing the same thing. My eye fell on a beautiful toy trombone. I was already being enchanted with music, so I thought that with the trombone having a slide I would be able to play any tune I wished. So that is the present I picked. Our presents were all beautifully wrapped, and placed under the tree in the living room. It was a wonderful Christmas in some ways, but in another way it was disappointment to me.

Here is what happened. When we all got up on Christmas morning we had breakfast, and then we were going to enjoy this wonderful day with our Christmas presents. I was so looking forward to playing my new trombone. It turned out I wouldn't be doing that. For the first time in my young life I saw a side of my father that mystified me. When I was just getting ready to go and get my present I began to hear sounds of music coming from the living room. I was wondering what it was. When I went in to look I saw my father comfortably laid out on the couch with MY trombone. He was happily playing it. Of course I couldn't go up to him and demand my present, so I just waited. After a while I had waited so long that I went out to the back steps to just look out over the yard. I was sitting there thinking about what I had seen and heard. I could not believe that my dad was not conscious of the fact that that was my chosen gift. He just kept right on playing and playing. Finally, after what seemed like an hour or two, he got tired and then put it down. He did not even give it to me.

I had a deep feeling of not mattering to him. I was so hurt that I never touched the little trombone to play or to even care what happened to it. When I would think about that day I would feel the hurt again. I was only eight years old. I count that day as being one when I saw my father in a different light than I had been used to. This was just one little incident, but I have never forgotten it.

As the months rolled by we were all happily going about our business. We kids were in school at St. Anthony's, and Bev was in kindergarten at the public school down the street from our house. Mama stayed at home, and took care of us all. Pop was still at the Real Estate office down in American Avenue. I was enrolled in the First Communion class at Holy Innocents Church. After school I got to class somehow. I think Bernie took me on his bike. He was supposed to wait for me to ride me home, but I know that a couple of times he was not out there. So I would walk home which was quite a long way. The church was located on 20th Street, so I had a good walk ahead of me. One time I was trudging up Pacific Avenue when the city bus that I usually rode was passing me. The driver saw me, and stopped. I called out that I didn't have the five- cent bus fare. He said that was ok. "Jump on." So I did.

One of the sweetest memories I have of Delta Street is the day it was pouring "cats and dogs." We three kids came home on the bus from St. Anthony's. We got off at the corner in the rain. We could see my mother standing in the doorway of our house that was about a third of the way up the block. She was beckoning for us to run home fast. What a delight it was to receive hugs and kisses, and to have her seat us at the table. She had prepared delicious hot cocoa with marshmallows to warm us up. We were all so happy laughing and talking about the day. Then my mother would sit at the piano and play songs for us that we could sing. She loved hearing Bernie sing "Trees." He did a good job of it. We were all developing a good ear for melody thanks to her.

I didn't realize it but these carefree days were almost at an end. We always enjoyed Sundays driving around in our big beautiful Studebaker. We visited many interesting places in Southern California. I have photos of our family posing beside the car in Fern Dell up in Hollywood. Little did I know that ten years later I would be standing in the same beautiful park as an IHM Postulant. We continued going to the beach whenever we could, and the most blissful trip of all was to the PIKE.

I have to tell you about the PIKE. It was a dream come true for everyone, children and adults. It was located right down on the beachfront below Ocean Avenue. It was about two blocks long with interesting shows and performing artists on each side.

There were eating places, tattoo parlors, trinket shops, and even an apple cider store that had a gigantic apple press right out in front for everyone to see. They would dump in a basket of apples, and we could watch them being pressed down so that the juice just flowed out the spot at the bottom of the press. I was always very interested in this phenomenon. However, the best parts of the whole PIKE were the rides.

Whenever I talk about these things just remember that we had just come from a very small lumber town at the foot of Mt. Shasta. My parents had spent all of their lives in the northern part of New England, the Province of Alberta, Canada, and in Portland. It must have been pure bliss for them to find themselves in what was at that time the most glamorous part of the WORLD. The movies were in their prime. Movie stars were the most famous people on earth. Here we were surrounded by all this glitter, living in a lovely home in a city right on the Pacific Ocean. There were even some famous movie stars who had homes in Long Beach down on Ocean Boulevard. It was a time of glamour; it was a place of glamour. And there we were right in the middle of it all. Added to all of this was the "glorious Pike."

Today everyone is familiar with a theme park such as Disneyland. Children, and adults, love to go there to enjoy the entire fantasy world, the beauty, and the rides. Well, that is just what we had in our front yard. The PIKE was fantastic because it did not charge any admission to stroll all along its fascinating streets. You could just go down and walk along enjoying the crowds and music even if you didn't have a nickel to spend. The most popular ride seemed to be the double Cyclone Racer.

There was the famous Looff Carousel. Looff is world famous for the beauty and spirit he put into the carving of the animals for us to ride. Beverly and I had lots of fun riding around and leaning out to grasp the steel ring that was just the thing to toss into the mouth of the big clown poster that was right there.

But, the best part of all was if you got a "gold" ring. You didn't toss it because that was the prize you would give to the attendant. It meant you got a FREE ride. What rapture. We would just laugh so hard, and be so happy. There were other rides that kept us ecstatic. Most of them charged a nickel for each ride. I can still see my parents digging into purse and pockets to find just one more nickel so we could go into the Fun House, or ride the airplanes, or drive a bumper car. Barr was always very adventurous. His favorite ride was always the Cyclone Racer. For some reason I could never make myself get on it. I had a deep fear of the heights, and the drops. Barr even offered to pay my way sometimes, but I could not do it. To this day I can't stand the sensation of falling. But Barr got a big thrill out of it. He was always ready for any challenging thrill.

The Pike and the pier and the beach were always crowded with many people doing what we were doing – enjoying the amusements Long Beach had to offer.

When we got tired of swimming in the nearby surf we would stroll up the beach to the Pike, or even go along the sand to the band shell that was built right there on the beach. It was fun to rest and enjoy the music of the Long Beach Municipal Band that played almost every afternoon. In those days it was directed by a member of the world famous John Philip Sousa Band. The director's name was Herbert Clark. I believe he played the trumpet in the Sousa Band. These concerts were also free because the city of Long Beach supported them, and still does to this day. Long Beach is one of the few cities in the US that maintains its own municipal band. Sometimes we would all sit on the benches and listen to wonderful band music while we rested our feet.

So you can see that we were living an amazingly quiet and enjoyable life. We kids had school, church, playgrounds, and neighbor friends to keep us busy. My parents were always calm and doing what seemed just the thing for all of us. The year was 1932.

One of the biggest events I remember about that year was the sensational kidnapping of the Lindbergh baby. I can remember my parents exclaiming about it when the morning paper came. That was the first time in my life that I had even heard of anything like kidnapping. Of course the drama eventually played out with the trial of Bruno Hauphmann. The little baby was found dead. I was always a little worried during my childhood about kidnappers.

Our life changed drastically one Saturday. I had gone down to Holy Innocents Church to make my first Confession. This was a great big event in the life of a small Catholic child. I had been attending catechism classes at Holy Innocents. It was always customary for parishioners to receive the Sacraments in their own parish. It is still somewhat of a rule to this day.

I was nervous about going to confession because I was trying to figure out what sins I had committed. I was ready to confess that I had fights with my sister, had not said all my prayers, etc. We had to have our sins in our mind because going to confession had a routine series of short phrases, which we were supposed to say. It always became a time of nervousness because after standing in line to wait for your turn you entered the confessional. It was dark. There you were supposed to kneel facing a little window with a thick screen over it. A little sliding door was on the priest's side. He sat between two of these confessionals, and leaned from one side to the other, sliding open the little door. He did not look through the screen. He just put his ear close to the screen so the penitent could whisper the prayers. "Bless me Father, for I have sinned. This is my first confession." Then in my little voice I told him my sins. He said the prayers of absolution in Latin, and gave me a penance. It was probably to say three "Hail Marys". I came out of the confessional happy as a lark because I was sure I was free of all those bad things I had done in the past. The best part, though, was that the very next day, Sunday, I would put on the pretty snow-white dress and filmy veil, and wear it to church for the day of my First Communion. I was ready with everything.

When I got home to our lovely house on Delta I came in the door all excited to tell Mama how happy I was. You can't imagine my shock to see my father and mother very busy packing clothes, dishes, furniture, and all the rest of our possessions in boxes. My mother looked especially harried, and didn't respond to my exhilaration. I asked her what was happening. She said, "We are moving today to a different house." I said, "What about my First Communion tomorrow?" She said we couldn't help it; we had to leave this house today. I looked out the front bay window and noticed that our car was not there. I asked her where it was. She said simply that it had been taken back by the bank. I didn't understand any of this, but I knew that we were on the verge of a big and unexpected change in our lives. I didn't realize how changed our lives would be.

House No 6 - 1933

Lime Avenue - Long Beach, California

Several things happened all at once for me. First of all, I didn't attend third grade at St. Anthony's again. Barr didn't return either. But, Bernie stayed on there in Seventh Grade with Sister Andrea. He said all the time that he liked going to Catholic School, but that Sister Andrea was real tough. I never heard any examples of what made her tough; I just know he felt that way. He must have been about thirteen.

Bernie was always a very serious boy. He was the perfect big brother. He was in charge of us when our parents were not around. As it happened, we never ever had a baby sitter. For one thing, we couldn't afford one, and for another thing we seemed to be pretty reliable children.

On the whole we got along real well. The boys were pals, and did all kinds of things that boys do. They were always together. Beverly and I were chums. We were together for most of our playtime. We would sometimes get into spats about some little nothing. Then the fur would fly. She was so wiry that I could never get the better of her. In the end these tiffs were not real serious because we always ended up playing together again.

So, here we were moving to a different house, into a different neighborhood, without a car, and it became apparent real soon that we were also without any money. It was many years later, when I was a grown woman, that I asked my mother what happened that Saturday that caused such a drastic change in our lives. She said, "The depression finally hit us."

It seems that history shows that there was a great deal of economic prosperity in our country, and maybe throughout the western world, during the twenties. After World War I our country seemed to be riding high on the stock market and banking practices of the day. There were numerous millionaires made almost overnight by speculating in the stock market, or by investing in high return deals.

The country had become very modern overnight. Long skirts on the women were gone. Also, the wonderful upswept hairdos that the women had worn for decades if not centuries were now gone. There was a sense of freedom and liberation in the air. There was also the opportunity for almost anyone to make a good living if the right circumstances presented themselves. A person was supposed to be self-reliant.

Our country was caught up in the euphoria of the times. Many young people were leaving the farms to go to the big city to find their fortunes. There was a sense of change in the air. Added to all of the mix was the wonderful invention of the automobile. Roads were being laid all over the country so the ordinary person who could get a Model T Ford for a few hundred dollars could really dream of traveling around the nation. There was real adventure in the air. I am sure my parents had the same hopes and dreams as all the young people of the day. As fate would have it, this great prosperity could not last forever for many people. There were some wealthy families who never felt the real financial pinch, but the vast majority of people were caught up in a devastating circumstance that was called "Black Friday in October 1929.

It happened that there was so much speculation in the Stock market that the whole system of using stocks and bonds for wealth was suddenly in chaos. The market collapsed almost overnight. There were fortunes that disappeared in a few minutes because the value of the stocks plummeted. Now we know that stock markets fluctuate from day to day, and they are watched very carefully, but in the twenties everything had been rolling along at such a high for so long that no one paid attention to danger signals. The stock market on Wall Street collapsed. This meant that businesses, factories, and farms all over the nation were exposed to immediate ruin. It also meant that millions of men were suddenly out of work.

Even though my father had a history of going from one job to the other after being let go, it looked like he was on the right track in starting his work in real estate. After all, he had inherited $10,000 in 1929. He came into possession of the money in 1931. And we were settling into a peaceful life in Long Beach.

Now, back to the question I asked my mother on that Saturday. Later in life she told me that Pa was always going to the bank to draw on the stocks he had deposited there. He never had any trouble cashing checks or withdrawing funds until one day. It seems that he went in as usual to get some money, and he was told that there were no funds in the account. The stocks had become worthless overnight, so the bank was not able to redeem them in any way. I am sure this must have been an absolute shock to my father because he was probably counting on this seemingly large fund to carry us through for a few years at least. My mother never revealed to us any of the conversations they had in regard to our future. All I know is that when I came home from making my first confession we moved bag and baggage to the little house on Lime Avenue in North Long Beach. It would turn out that North Long Beach would be our home from then on.

Now that I think about it I am sure my father must have been very disheartened by the terrible surprise at the bank. It turned out that the bank repossessed the wonderful big Studebaker that we had enjoyed for many months. My father probably didn't have any backup plan for supporting his family except his try at selling real estate. But, that failed overnight because he suddenly didn't have a car to take prospective buyers around. And he surely didn't have any money to pay for his desk space in the company. All in all, it was a true disaster for him, and for us. But I came to this knowledge on my own. It was really never a point of discussion among us kids.

One of the most calming things that had an effect on us was the fact that we were devout Catholics. We never missed Mass on Sunday or Holy Days of Obligation. We were faithful to all the rules about "no meat on Friday", etc. that were part of our daily life. I look back on this fact with a greater understanding of the direction my own life took, and the value I must have placed on it following the example of both my parents. Praying and participating in religious events gradually became an integrated part of my view of life. We just knew it.

I still marvel at the great faith my mother showed. Even at this stage she had not been a Catholic for very many years, but she embraced it whole-heartedly. She said in later years that it was her faith that pulled her through the hard times because she didn't have anywhere else to turn.

To show how important it was to both of my parents that we find the local Catholic Church I remember that they asked Bernie to ride his bike down to that 'little church on Market Street' to see if he could spot a red light in it. That was always the sign to Catholics that the building was a church because the red lighted candle signified the presence of the Blessed Sacrament right there. We were all excited when Bernie came back happily telling us that because the front door was locked he climbed up and looked in the window. He said he saw the RED LIGHT. So that settled where we would go to Mass on Sundays.

St. Athanasius, was too small to have its own pastor yet. It wasn't too long after that that my parents introduced themselves to the priest who came on Sunday. He was stationed in Holy Innocence Parish and was the same priest who had been instructing me for First Communion.
So everything seemed to go well in regard to our belonging to St. Athanasius.

It wasn't long before my mother heard a request from the priest on one of those Sundays for anyone who could play the organ. She promptly volunteered her services. She had played the organ in the little church in McCloud so she was comfortable with the technique. I always marveled at her ability to read the notes, play the keys, and pump the two pedals for the air needed to make the keys sound.

She was just the BEST in my estimation. It proved to be the one thing that sustained her in so many ways. She was there for the 10:30 Mass every Sunday, and so were we.

She played for the regular Wednesday night devotions. We also went. So the routine of Church services was a very regular part of our growing up. Of course, both of the boys became altar boys. They looked so grand up there on the altar with the priest during Mass. They seemed so smart to me because every response they gave to the prayers of the priest was said in LATIN. I always marveled at that. Also, they looked so wonderful all dressed up in the black cassock and pure white surplice neatly ironed.

My father was an Usher at all the services we attended. He belonged to the Holy Name Society, and the Knights of Columbus. I don't know how he paid his dues, but he was a member all through my childhood. And that left my sister, Beverly, and me. There really wasn't anything for little girls to do that was special so we sat downstairs in the pews until we were old enough to sing in the choir.

One of the first things that happened in our new home was the preparation for me to make my First Communion. My mother had gotten a very pretty little white dress and a veil for me to wear for the big day. It must have been a revelation to Mama because she had prepared my two brothers for this event, probably in McCloud, but I was the first daughter to be dressed so fine. I was thrilled with it all. I was already beginning to feel a close affinity with spiritual things.

There is a photo in the St. Athanasius Parish Memory book that shows the picture of my First Communion. Considering that the book was commemorating the 50th anniversary of the Parish it was singular that that photo would be the one chosen.

We settled into life in our little home. Bernie continued on at St. Anthony's in Seventh Grade. He rode his bike to school some days. It was a trip of about six miles. Some days he could ride the bus if we had any money. It would stand to reason that the first thing my father would do was to pound the pavement in search of employment. Maybe he did, but he never seemed to find any.

I want to point out here that we were not living in a severely depressed area such as the "Dust Bowl" in the Midwest or the failing farms of Oklahoma. In fact, California was the place where all those people headed for because there was work to be had. Long Beach was a Port city with two large shipbuilding piers. It also boasted of one of the largest and most prolific oil fields in the world at the time – Signal Hill. Then there was the motion picture industry just a little way up the street in Hollywood. We were surrounded by truck farms and orange groves as far as the eye could see. All of this was true clear through the 'Depression'. In the light of all this I do wonder why my father never seemed to connect with some means of supporting us.

Consequently, we were on the verge of poverty before too long. We did have some support through those years. It seemed that when President Roosevelt was elected there were so many people in the country who were in dire straits that he got Congress to enact a bill of Relief. My father must have applied for Relief because we did get a check every month for $53. This saved us from starvation, but it wasn't enough to provide very much. Half of it went for the rent on our little house. That left about $26 for the rest of the month. This was a meager amount to provide food and everything else for a family of six. It was common for us to run out of money before the end of the month. On those days we had very little to eat. So you can see that the hopes and dreams of my father were smashed in the world of reality. My mother always tried to help. She went out and cleaned people's houses for money or a bag of groceries.

One of the things I will say about all of this is that I was looking at the situation from the viewpoint of a young girl – nine, ten, eleven years old. So many people my age talk about the Depression and say, "We were poor, but we didn't know it because everyone around us was poor." Well, I never have said that because I knew we were poor. Every day at lunch I would have a very simple piece of bread while my friends were sitting there and looking at their sandwiches, and saying such things as, "I don't like cheese sandwiches." Or, they might say, "I wish my mother wouldn't put so much butter on my bread. I don't want that much." It was evident to me that we were different.

In later years, when I was thinking about those days, I recalled that there wasn't one single playmate whose father didn't have a job somewhere. I really can't say what the problem was. My dear mother never made any reference to it in later years, but I'm sure it was very hard and disappointing to her to see us in such straits for so long. I can't say anything about what my father felt because he never said anything about it. So much for the hard times.

I don't want to tell my story as if it was terrible. In reality, we were a very resilient family. As I have said, my parents were kind and mild-mannered. For this I thank them both. My father was a great 'talker' who loved to converse with anyone. He could go on for hours at a time. My mother was always very nice to be around. She kept us kids laughing even when times were hardest.

Barr, Beverly, and I started to school at US Grant Elementary. It was exactly twelve short blocks from our home on Lime Avenue. I was in the third grade. I think Beverly was in first. Barr must have been in fifth. My teacher was Miss Libby. She was very nice to me. Bev and I would eat lunch in the school auditorium, which had a beautiful deep red velvet stage curtain. I can still see it in my mind. Sometimes we had to leave for school without any lunch because there wasn't anything. My sweet mother would later come trudging across the fields with a bag, waving to us and laughing. She would have gotten together some bread, and spread it with lard and salt and pepper. She would say what a treat it was. Of course, we went right along with her. How could we not because she was trying to be so positive?

Soon, after the summer, I was in the fourth grade with Miss Gale as my teacher. It was that year that I discovered that I could not only carry a tune, but I could hold my own in harmonizing. The music teacher would go around the room listening to us sing. When she tapped me on the shoulder I was ecstatic. It meant I would get to sing in the chorus for the Christmas Play. What a treat for me. I liked school, and tried to be a good student, but I was very shy. I don't think I raised my hand to answer a question the whole year. Consequently, my grades were just so-so except in music, art, and conduct. Bev and I walked together each day. Barr had his own agenda. He always did. He was quite a mischief all the time.

It was during my fourth grade year that we experienced a humongous event – The Long Beach Earthquake.

I still look back and say that I have never felt anything like it since. We were all sitting around the kitchen table starting to eat dinner when we all looked at each other. We could hear a deep rumbling sound coming closer and closer. We also began to hear wrenching wood. It sounded like it was splintering all over the place. The sounds got closer and closer. Suddenly the whole house began to shake tremendously. We were screaming at each other to get outside in the backyard. We all jumped off the low back porch and ran to the middle of the yard.

When the shaking finally stopped we found ourselves looking bewildered and standing in a circle all holding hands. At least we had each other. Then, still dazed because we had never experienced such a thing before, we followed my parents and went back into our house. We walked straight through it and out the front door.

What we found in the house was everything in the kitchen cupboards all over the floor. There were broken dishes mixed in with broken jars of food. Our canary bird's cage was tipped over, but the little bird was ok. The front room was one big mess of overturned furniture. Our big overstuffed couch and chair were both tipped completely over. I was amazed. We ended up out in the front yard. When we looked around we saw every single one of our neighbors also out in front. Everyone had a completely dazed look. Mrs. Sutton on the corner was screaming. Mama had a sprained ankle, which happened when she jumped off the back porch. By now everyone knew it was an earthquake. We had never experienced one before. The date was March 10, 1933, and the time was five minutes to six.

Before we knew it there was an aftershock which felt as strong as the first one. We saw that some of the houses were moved a bit off their foundations. We had aftershocks about every half-hour for the rest of the night. It scared us all to pieces. We all were afraid to go back into our homes because of the quakes, so several families decided that we would all stay outside for the night. The brave ones ran into the house and brought out mattresses, blankets, and pillows. Some of the men got wood somewhere and built a nice fire. We were on the curb lawn at the corner of Lime and 60th Street. In between shakes and the advance of night it was a very eerie kind of adventure.

What an adventure it was indeed. There we were all together in groups. The children were all quiet and probably scared. The adults were sitting by the fire all talking in very subdued tones. They were saying such things as, "Will our houses fall down?" or, "Do you think we will have a bigger earthquake?" or, "Is anyone killed downtown? To add to the surreal quality of the night we heard and saw a constant parade of ambulances and fire trucks going up and down Atlantic Avenue. Then, very gradually, the moon was covered with clouds, and we were enveloped by very thick fog. I can remember hunkering down into the blanket with Beverly. We were warm, but every so often we could feel the ground beneath us start its shaking. Then we would hug each other so we wouldn't fall off anything. We could overhear the adults talking about the danger of a tidal wave. There was a lot of conversation about it. I was very scared because the grown-ups were so serious about whether or not we were far enough from the ocean so we wouldn't be in danger.

The night grew colder and more eerie. Then, the quiet talk was interrupted by the terrible sound in the distance of a woman screaming. She was crying out, "Help, help". Instantly all the men looked at each other to see what to do. After some time a couple of them decided to go and investigate what was happening. But I could tell, even as a nine-year old that they really didn't want to go away from their families, the fire, and the protection of the group. I was watching it all because I was petrified by the scream. Off went a couple of guys into the dense fog. It now seems like a movie. I didn't know if we would ever see them again. My father was not one who volunteered.

Several days later, when things were quieting down, I asked my mother what it was all about. She said that a man and woman in the local beer joint about a block up Atlantic Avenue were in a fight. No harm came to the woman, but she and the man were drunk, and couldn't figure out why the building was shaking so much. She kind of chuckled at it, so I felt a little better.

The earthquake devastated the whole area around Long Beach. I have been in many quakes since then, but I have never felt one so strong, or one that had so many aftershocks right away. They must have occurred every half-hour or so during the whole night. By the next day things had quieted down. When we ventured forth from our corner with all the other people we realized we couldn't go back into our homes. The gas and lights were all disconnected. Some of the homes were unstable. Ours seemed to be ok, but we were afraid to go inside. So my father did what many of the fathers were doing – he constructed a kind of lean-to tent on our front lawn with blankets and sheets. He got a small steel container to make a fire. It had places for us all to lie down on blankets to sleep. So my two parents and we four kids had a snug place to stay.

We were not alone with this arrangement. When I looked up and down the block there were many more makeshift tents. The families all stuck together. The men couldn't go to work because they couldn't travel anywhere. The Naval Police closed all the big intersections to local traffic. They were called in to protect the city. They carried rifles, and looked very sharp. We felt well protected. I don't remember hearing about looting or other kinds of mischief. I think the whole populace was in a state of shock because the earthquake had caused so much devastation.

For about a week or ten days we all lived outside on our front lawns. I was fascinated by everything. Every day a big truck would come down the street with a load of coal, which a helper would distribute at each little encampment. So we had warmth that was provided for all who needed it. Then, the best part was the help of the Red Cross. Right away everyone was told that because no one could really cook on the little coal stove, or go inside to the gas stove, we could just walk up to Houghton Park three times a day and the Red Cross would provide a nice meal for anyone who came.

What a treat that was for me. We all went up there with our neighbors and lined up. There were cauldrons of food of all kinds. It was not only delicious, it was plentiful. You could have as much as you wanted. I still remember the luxury of sitting down and eating until I was really filled up. This lasted until the city inspected each street and turned the gas and lights back on. My memory wants to say it was about two weeks. We finally felt safe enough to go inside our house to stay. Life settled down again.

The biggest change for us children was that we didn't go to school for about a month. This was because every single public school in Long Beach was so badly damaged that all of them had to be torn down.

The school district finally figured out a way to take care of us. They erected bungalows on every school playground. These structures were quite flimsy. They all had a wooden floor and sides of wood planks up to about four feet. Above that configuration there were hung canvas flaps that could be rolled up in the warm weather or rolled down to protect us from the cold and rain. The roof was either canvas or wood. Each bungalow was large enough to hold one class full of children with a little space for the teacher. The district solved the problem of having to take care of so many students by dividing up the whole student population into two parts.

Each child was told that he or she would attend school for only half a day until the new schools could be built. If you attended school for four hours in the morning for one semester you were assigned the four afternoon hours for the second semester. Sometimes we would be split up in our time as a family. Barr was attending school in the morning while Bev and I went in the afternoon. All in all, it was a great adventure. This procedure didn't go on for just a few weeks; it was the way I went to school for the rest of fourth grade – April, May, and June – For all of fifth grade too. It was in sixth grade that we began attending all day as usual, but we were still in the tent bungalows. I didn't have the luxury of going to school in a regular school building until I was in the eighth grade. This gives one the idea of the immensity of the damage caused by the famous Long Beach earthquake. I learned later that there were about one hundred people killed, but our parents never scared us with tales of such things.

So we settled back into life on Lime Avenue. My father didn't get employment with any of the many cleanup crews that must have been numerous in the devastated part of downtown Long Beach. We kids went along happily to school each day. We spent a lot of time playing with our friends up and down the street. Those were days when there wasn't entertainment at our fingertips, so we made our own fun. "Hide-and-seek" was a favorite game that we would play all over the neighborhood. Another one was "Follow the Arrow". Our favorite, though, seemed to be "Kick the Can." We would play it until it got too dark to see the can. By then Mama would be calling to us to come in for the night.

As I have said before, we had a pretty serene family life. There was never any harsh talk or violence of any kind. My parents were always comforting and made us feel safe. I don't remember ever having doubts about it. The evenings were always spent together. My father would sit and read something and smoke his pipe. Sometimes he would smoke cigarettes that he rolled himself. He didn't have the money to buy a pack of machine rolled cigarettes so he bought the cheapest kind. It was called "Bull Durham" and it came in a nice little cloth bag with a little string tie. On the outside would be printed the logo.

Attached to the bag would be a small packet of about 20 pieces of very thin tissue paper cut just the right size for a cigarette. He would take one of the tissues and hold it flat in his hand just right. Then he would sprinkle a small amount of the tobacco onto the tissue. He then proceeded to roll it up and lick the edge to attach it to the other edge. He ended up with a cigarette that looked just like the others, except you could tell it was Bull Durham because the end would have a little twist in it instead of having a sharp flat end.

Often we would all gather around the radio to listen to our favorite programs. In those days the radio had the same powerful attraction that the television has today. We heard all the latest news – which wasn't too good in those days – and listened to soap operas, or music, or comedians. It had everything. So during our evenings we would all be together around the dinner table to eat whatever my parents could provide for that day. After dinner we would go to the front room. Pop would be sitting benignly smoking and reading, but we kids would get into a game of marbles. Believe it or not the biggest instigator of these entertainments was my dear Mama. She would get right down on the floor with us and play her turn. She never showed any partiality so we kids were very contented. These were always happy moments. Sometimes she would sit at the piano and play all of our favorite songs. We turned into very good singers. Maybe that is how I acquired the ear for harmony. Of course, our voices were developing also.

Another big event happened while we lived on Lime Avenue. At the age of thirteen or fourteen Bernie begged my parents to let him go to the seminary to study for the priesthood. It seems that he was impressed with his experiences close to the priests in our parish and at Catholic school. He wanted to be the same. I don't remember hearing my parents discuss this with Bernie, but in September we took him to the Claretian Seminary for high school boys.

We had acquired an old Model T Ford somewhere so we had a way of getting around. We drove Bernie up to Pomona to a nice ranch-like school called Silver Peak. It was for boarders only so he was going to live there. What a mystery it was for me to see my big brother leave us and go to another life. My father was immensely proud that his oldest son would be a priest and serve God. My mother was very proud too, but because she was a convert I'm sure she was wondering what it all meant.

As the years passed Bernie seemed to thrive there, and finally graduated from high school. He chose to continue on as a Novice in the Claretian Order so he was transferred to Dominguez Seminary, just two or three miles from where we lived. Once a month for five years we would all get into whatever old car we had at the time and go visit Bernie for the afternoon. I would always look forward to these visits.

I admired Bernie so much. He seemed to enter into his vocation with his whole heart. Even when he came home for the summer he would spend most of the time helping Father O'Sullivan at St. Athanasius. He made the whole family proud of him.

I especially began to wonder about the way some young people would promise to serve God. It fascinated me when I would see them. Of course, I wasn't around nuns. I had experienced only about two months of their teaching at St. Anthonys before we moved to North Long Beach. But I could tell I was interested in the whole idea. This interest developed very gradually. Being around religious events and people was an integral part of my childhood, so I was comfortable with what I was observing. The experiences I had with religious people were all positive.

In a sincerely Catholic family it was understood that the children would be brought up as Catholics. That was just exactly what my parents did. My mother, as a convert, entered into the spirit of it all. I was always aware of her generosity in serving the Church in whatever way she could, which just happened to be playing the organ for 35 years in St. Athanasius Parish. When we were growing up she told us that we were to attend Catechism classes at our church every Saturday morning rain or shine. So that is what we did.

The three of us would traipse off to Market and Linden Avenue and spend an hour reciting all the lessons we were supposed to memorize from the previous week. The way the Church took care of our schooling in the Faith was to provide lay people to be our teachers on the Saturday mornings. These persons were usually very devoted and generous Catholics who probably did it for love of the Church. How Beverly and I would study. Barr was ahead of us a little so I don't know how well he was doing. All I know is that he was always very cheerful and laughing at us for working so hard. We would ask each other the questions on the way to the Church.

It is amazing to me now to sometimes pull out of my memory the questions and the answers as if I had recited them yesterday. Father O'Sullivan, the Pastor, would sometimes question us. We would be so pleased if we could rattle off the answers, which were quite long sometimes. As each year passed we would be promoted to the next highest group until we reached the last one. By that time we would be around fourteen. That was the age for receiving the Sacrament of Confirmation. Actually, twelve was a permissible age for this.

We three children attended religion classes for at least six years. Bernie was in the Claretian Seminary. My parents were very faithful in their attendance, with us, at all the Catholic ceremonies they could. So, all in all, I grew up in a home that respected the Faith. We could experience the strength that it could give us. I am sure that all of this was a stepping stone to my own appreciation of things religious.

During these years, even though we were in a state of need most of the time, we were always able to put our best face forward. My parents had a certain dignity about living that made us put our best face forward as well. We never told any of our playmates that we were hungry at times. We never alluded to the fact that my father did not have a job. In fact, I didn't think about the 'why' of our circumstances when I was a child. It was only when I gained maturity, and began wondering about it, that I came to the conclusion that he must not have looked very earnestly - everyone else's dad had work somewhere.

What we did was make the best of it. I know it was

my dear mother's outlook on life that carried us through. She made us laugh at everything, even the most difficult. Beverly and I found our enjoyment in things that did not cost anything. For example, we would go over to Houghton Park after school and on Saturdays for drama lessons, tap dancing, and just playing with the equipment which the Recreation Department provided free. You just had to return it right after you were finished. I remember how proud I was when the director of the park gave me the job of checking out the bats and balls, horseshoes, croquets, etc. to all who came on a Sunday afternoon. This was my first taste of being responsible. I must have been about eleven or twelve. I can honestly say that every single item I checked out to anyone was returned before the day was done.

Because our parents never gave us any spending money, Bev and I learned early on that we could earn some by collecting glass milk bottles which were the common container of that time. It was customary to return the bottles to the grocer for one cent apiece. By searching in the trash up and down the alley we would collect at least five, but sometimes more. If we each had five we would take them to the corner grocer. We would just be jumping for joy and laughing because now we had enough. The grocer would give us each a nickel.

That was the biggest treat for us because then we could go to the Saturday matinee at the LaShell Theater down on Market and Long Beach Boulevard. It cost only five cents for two cartoons and two features. We went to the movies every Saturday for several years – and paid our own way. If by chance, we found more bottles we could cash them in, and take the bus down to the beach. Believe it or not, the fare was only a nickel each way. The bus drivers were always very nice to us. We never had any trouble even though Bev and I were going downtown alone. We even went to the Pike sometimes. If we had collected enough bottles we could take a ride on the merry-go-round. It all depended on how lucky we were. There were times when we couldn't find enough bottles so we would go around to people's yards and pick some flowers to sell as little bouquets. When I think about it now I just wonder how we gave each other the nerve to do some of those things.

Anyway, we did it. Bev and I were great chums all through our childhood. You can see that we had a rather carefree existence. My mother did not go with us on most of these forays, so we were on our own. We were lucky that at that time there were not dangers around every bend, at least for us. No one ever bothered us or scared us in any way. I can thank God for it all.

Our brother Barr was always a step ahead of us. He showed a great interest in fixing things. Mama said Barr could take the car apart and put it back together again. I believe her because he was always out there with his head under the hood doing something that looked hard to me. Bev and I traveled in a different orbit than Barr. He was very good-natured.

Sometimes I would feel sorry for him because of the way my father treated him. I don't know what the trouble was but Barr was the one in the family who got blamed for everything. If something broke it was

Barr's fault. If something was missing it was Barr's fault. If he was working out in back with my father hoeing the few little vegetables we had, or putting the few chickens up to roost we would sometimes hear my father scolding Barr for some mistake or shortcoming. I have heard that many times there is one child in a family who becomes a kind of scapegoat. I am sure my father didn't mean to make it seem that Barr was the only one who messed up, but he did make Barr's self-image plunge to the ground I am sure. But, I have to hand it to Barr because through it all he maintained a very cheery demeanor. He was the first to laugh at hardships. He was able to make do with fun activities when Bev and I were hard- pressed to come up with anything. He was always running and jumping and helping. In a word, he was a very active boy who seemed to be trying to make the best of his life.

So you can see that our life on Lime Avenue settled into routines that included church, school, and home evenings. My parents continued to be calm about things outwardly, but I am sure that they must have had words about the situation. My mother was especially good about seeing that we children were not worried about anything. She and dad never spoke of his circumstances, but she didn't have to. We were able to see that 'something was wrong with this picture.' I used to wonder why it was that we kids didn't have nice things and enough food to eat while all the other kids we knew had all of this. But, again, we seemed to take what was happening in stride mostly because my mother was so stable. She never let us down. One of the nicest things she did for each of us was to treat us to a trip to the Pike with her. The best part was that she took just one at a time. What fun that was. I was in the fourth grade when it came time for me to go with her. When I got home from school she was waiting. I wondered how she had the money to take me on such a treat. I realized how she did it when we got on the bus. She pulled out of her purse a handkerchief with a knot in it. Inside were only coins – nickels and dimes. She had saved them little by little until she had enough for our bus fares and the rides at the Pike. If there were enough nickels maybe we would have an ice cream cone. What bliss. I was ecstatic that day. In fact, it was so delightful that I have never forgotten one minute of our treat downtown. I can still see her pulling out the handkerchief, and the delight I felt that we were really going on a toot. As fate would have it, that was the only time she ever did that. Of course, my mother was eminently fair. Both Barr and Bev had their day of fun with Mama. This gives another insight to the sweet character of my mother. She loved us all with her whole heart.

I have spent a lot of time telling the story of our life as a family. We made do as best we could, and time marched on. After about a year living in the little house on Lime Avenue we moved again. This time we ended up on Ellis Street just a few blocks from where we were living. We moved into the very same kind of house.

House No 7 - 1934
Ellis Street - Long Beach, California

This was the year I entered fifth grade. It was 1934. Because we moved from Lime Avenue we kids had to be enrolled in a different school. So I left US Grant School and enrolled in Jane Addams in Long Beach. I attended fifth and sixth grades in a wooden bungalow. I don't remember my teacher's names, but I do remember that they were very nice to be with. In fact, all through my public school days I enjoyed being with the children and teachers. At that time we students were always well behaved. I don't remember any time when a teacher had to reprimand us sharply for anything. We seemed to take pride in doing the right thing. It was also around this time that I realized how much I loved to read. I would check out ten books at a time from the library and get them all read in two weeks. Bev and I would do the same thing. After school I would read instead of playing. Of course, this wasn't all the time, but it was often enough for me to read some wonderful books over the next few years.

Even though I was a very good reader I wasn't an outstanding student. I had always been shy and by this time I was self-conscious about my appearance and looks. Our clothes were hand-me-downs but always clean. I was developing into a gangling girl. I didn't like my hair because it was straight. I did so dream of having curly hair. My teeth were crooked so I didn't want to open my mouth in class. All in all I was just shy.

However, I was a good listener and absorbed everything I could. It was always fun to go to school. We never ate in the cafeteria, but took a lunch. Sometimes there wasn't any lunch so we would walk back home at noon for something. My mother always came through.

Well, this house turned out to be exactly the same as the one we left. It was warm and snug for the five of us. Bev and I always slept together. Barr had a place on the couch. My folks always had one of the bedrooms. We continued on with our usual adventures, except that now we were a little older. Barr was going to Junior High. Bernie was doing well in the seminary. Bev and I were at Jane Addams. We continued spending our evenings together enjoying the radio, or marbles, or playing cards. One night a week we all went down to St. Athanasius for devotions. I soon was allowed to sing in the choir. I just loved to be up there with mama. I learned to sing all the hymns, even the ones in Latin. I could also harmonize if need be. Bev sang too, but she came later. She and I would often spend an hour or so on a rainy day leafing through the old St. Basil's Hymnbook and sing absolutely every song in the book.

When we lived on Lime Avenue we would sometimes go next door to the Spauldings and sit in their swing. We would start singing all the hymns. Mrs. Spaulding told my mother that she thought we were so wonderful just singing away. She loved it, but she never told us. I suppose she thought we would not come back. Well, we did it many times. Sitting there with Bev and singing is one of the sweetest memories of my childhood.

We are still not on our feet financially. I believe we are still on relief. I remember that one of the Christmases we had nothing to eat so my mother took Bev and me with her to the Salvation Army office. I don't remember how we got down there, but we did go. In a way I was mortified, but I kept looking at my mother. She held her head up, and spoke to the kind lady in a soft voice telling her we really needed some help. Well, to this day I remember how very kind the Salvation Army woman was to my mother. She got a couple of big bags of food together and gave them to her. Of course, we helped carry this manna from Heaven. I am not sure where my father was that day because he did not go with us. We had a wonderful filling Christmas dinner that year. Even to this day I never pass by one of the Salvation Army Christmas kettles without putting something in it, and saying 'thank you' to whomever is ringing the little bell.

Things went on as usual for about a year. We had a serene family life thanks to the fact that my parents set the tone. They never squabbled in front of us. The only thing that made life hard was that we were so short of money. My father has still not landed a job anywhere. I don't know how hard he looked.

I got one clue in later years when I was asking my mother about those days. She said that Pop was a good man, but he had grandiose ideas of what he could do. He obviously wasn't a success so far in his working life. He just wasn't realistic about how to get us out of the predicament we were in. She said that some of our good neighbor friends, the men, would sometimes tell George about an opening in the oil fields or at the port. The job would not be a high level one, or a desk job, which is what he wanted. Mama said that he would turn down these opportunities because he didn't want to do a lowly job.

I am sure they had many a word over this, but in the end he never ever got a job.

Consequently, I have not one single memory of him coming home in the afternoon carrying a bag of groceries, or handing over money he had earned to my mother to pay bills. He just never ever earned anything. If he did it was not enough for us to even know about. I don't know where he went every day while we were at school. We kept up a good face thanks to the fact that my parents never discussed our plight in front of us.

I knew by now that something was wrong because all of my playmates and school chums had fathers who had work somewhere. Add to this the fact that we never once got any new clothes, just socks or panties. The shoes we wore were of the cheapest kind for that day – blue tennis shoes. I was the only student at Lindbergh who wore them. I was sure every classmate knew that I was poor.

One of the most cherished memories I have is of my mother going down to the Carlson's house to do housework for them. The Carlsons were nice people who happened to own a grocery store. They paid mama in cash or in bags of groceries. I went with her a few times, and I could see how hard she worked.

Seeing my mother do this made a lasting impression on me. However, I was a young teenager so I was mortified to have my mother do that because I went to school with the Carlson kids. It didn't seem right to me that my dear mother was their servant. The Carlsons never said anything to me, but when you are that age you don't need anyone to say a word. You know what the lay of the land is.

Every so often we would have company. What a revelation. We saw some of the relatives we hadn't seen since we left McCloud. It was nice that our Gertz relatives seemed to keep in touch. We had visits every so often, sometimes from Uncle Gus, then another time Aunt Hilda would come for a few days. Aunt Edith and Aunt Hannah also touched bases with us. Even Uncle Ray and Uncle Walter were down for a few days. All in all, my mother's siblings did look in on her. However, her parents never once came to visit us in Southern California.

Consequently, I never got to know them at all. They just knew me from infancy and very early childhood, so I didn't develop any sense of what a Grandma and Grandpa could be. I am sure that these visits were really not welcomed too much by either of my parents. This was not because Mama didn't like her brothers and sisters, but it meant that they could see that we were worse off than when we lived in McCloud. They probably were very curious about what happened to the ten thousand dollars. It is doubly interesting to note that neither of my father's sisters ever came for a visit. I never ever saw them. I think that they and my dad might have been estranged for some reason. My father never mentioned anything about it. I wouldn't be surprised if it was over some disagreement about the inheritance, or maybe the care of their elderly father. I will never know because, as I said, my father never spoke about it.

It was while we were living on Ellis Street, around 1936, that my folks hatched the idea of going into business for themselves. What a wonderful idea it was. They came up with a plan to open a dry cleaning shop. After all, my mother was a very fine seamstress, and dad knew how to press suits. The only thing they needed to get started was some capital to purchase the press and the water tank that produced the steam. Wow. We were all excited about our fortune changing. The whole idea fit in with my father's view of what he should be – a businessman. He was elated. So was mama.

Here comes the good part. After explaining to Father O'Sullivan what they were prepared to do my parents borrowed four hundred dollars from him. He gave them the money to get started. I will always have admiration for our parish priest who certainly helped one little family in his parish.

The plans developed very well. My folks found a store front on Atlantic and South Street, not far from where we lived. We had acquired an old Essex automobile that would be perfect for the business. They set up shop at 5729 Atlantic Avenue. Their slogan was "We pick up and deliver." They found a jobber who would do the actual cleaning of the suits and dresses for a small fee. He was located down on Long Beach Boulevard and Willow. Before long everything was in place, and we were soon off relief.

Of course, we kids didn't know the ins and outs of getting set up in business, but we could tell that my parents were elated about this whole thing. They worked together as a team. This was the start of Atlantic Cleaners.

We kids would often go to the shop after school. Sometimes we would help out by sweeping, or applying the identification tags to the garments, or just visit.

Sometimes I would be recruited to tack up each cuff on the men's pants. In those days they turned up the bottom of the leg about one inch. A little tack of thread had to be made on both sides of each leg or the cuff would hang down. This wasn't considered stylish. I used to wish that my father would give me a penny or two for each leg because Bev and I were still looking for milk bottles in the trashcans. For some reason he never saw my side even when I would ask. By now Barr was around sixteen. He knew how to drive very well, so he would be recruited to pick up and or deliver. Sometimes he liked doing it, but sometimes not.

By now I was in Lindbergh Junior High. So was Barr. He must have been in the ninth grade. When I got to Junior High I was assigned to class number 2. So I was 7B-2, then 7A-2, etc. There must have been about twelve or so classes of one grade level. All through my public school days I remember taking tests many times. I always felt good about the reading parts because I had spent so much time enjoying those library books. I am sure these tests were used to place the kids. The teachers never told us what the test results were, but you were just put in the group where they thought you could function best. I could tell that as the class's homeroom numbers rose the kids seemed to be more and more behind. This kind of segregation would hardly be permitted in these times, but it was thought that children should be put with those around them who could accomplish the same amount of schoolwork. Of course, I didn't think about it at the time. I just knew that I could hold my own with the group I was with.

We stayed together as a class for the entire three years of Junior High. There was one big flap when I was in the ninth grade. It seems we got a new Counselor who administered the usual tests. Well, it was soon announced all around the school that all the students were going to be placed with updated level numbers. We were all in an uproar because we just did not want to be separated from the friends we had made during the past two and a half years. Well, when the list came out I was assigned to 9B-1. A couple of my friends were also assigned, but we just didn't like the idea.

The whole student body was in a tizzy about it, and many were objecting very loudly. The Principal and Counselor must have been unnerved to have a usually placid student body become very verbal about this change. So we were told that if we wanted to remain in our former group all we had to do was go to the Counselor and say so. Well, a couple of friends and I promptly went to her and asked to be returned to our real class. She didn't make any big to-do about it. So I finished my whole three years at Lindbergh as a 2, .I could have been a 1 but I didn't really like the kids in that class. They seemed, as we used to say, 'stuck up'.

They probably weren't. We were so immature that we would talk like that. You know – teenagers.

We were growing up. Bernie was still at the seminary. He seemed to like it a lot. He was a young man now, and was becoming handsome. He had a great big smile. We still visited him once a month at Silver Peak. When I would see Bernie preparing for the priesthood I became more and more fascinated with the whole idea of serving God. I seemed to find contentment in the religious ceremonies of the time. I liked being a part of it all. Barr was going on to Jordan High School. He was also becoming a young man. He was very resourceful in so many ways. He could repair anything. He was a happy-go-lucky kid. He was becoming quite handsome. The most fortunate thing that he did was getting a part-time job in the meat department of the Dollar Market across the street from the Cleaning shop. He worked there for a couple of years. This meant that he had a little bit of extra money, but I never saw any of it.

When I was going into the ninth grade at Lindbergh we moved again. This time we ended up on Olive Avenue just a few blocks on the other side of Atlantic from where we now lived. I can remember being bewildered about moving because we always stayed in the same neighborhood and Parish, and we never moved into a better house than the one we had left. My parents never gave a reason for the move. We just packed all our belongings and went to the next house. I now suspect that we had to move because we did not pay the rent for a few months. The landlord probably told us to just move out. So we did.

My mother did the usual thing. She was on her hands and knees scrubbing the hardwood floors of the whole house before we left. My father took care of getting our belongings off to the new house. I can still see my mother down on the floor working so hard. She said she didn't want the landlord to think we were just slobs. My parents always gave us the lead in holding up our heads. We had a certain dignity. We still did not ever talk to our friends about our circumstances because we wanted to maintain that dignity. It is funny but my folks never instructed us not to say anything. We just followed their lead. They always put on a good front.

Off we go next to Olive Avenue.

House No 8 - 1937

Olive Avenue - Long Beach, California

Once again we have moved to a nice house on Olive Avenue. It was compact and comfortable for our family of five. Now, I want to relate some of our adventures as we grew up in North Long Beach.

I was now in the ninth grade at Lindbergh Junior High. I still enjoyed school a lot. I was getting pretty good grades, but I was still very shy about raising my hand to answer. If the teacher called on me, I was ok, but otherwise, I kept my thoughts to myself. I made several friends, and joined in on any activities that didn't cost any money. All in all, the kids were nice to be with. They didn't say nor do anything to make me feel too bad about not having new and up-to-date clothes. I began to feel good about my classes, and hoped that I would do well in high school. I thoroughly enjoyed chorus and art classes. The heavy courses were always a part of the day, but I reveled in the freedom of creating color and form and in singing beautiful pieces.

It was during this year that Lindbergh Jr. High installed the bronze panel that still rests above the school entrance on Market Street. Our teachers got the entire student body to line up on the front lawn and watch the unveiling. It turned out that this was done to commemorate the tenth anniversary of Charles Lindbergh's solo flight across the Atlantic Ocean. To us it seemed like a long time ago, but in retrospect it was just yesterday. Every time I drove past the school, I remember that event.

I liked Junior High. I had some good chums who were assigned to my same class. We would pal around together, eating lunch, going to our lockers, singing in the chorus, etc. I was elected secretary of my class each year. I could take good notes and read the minutes very well even in those days. I was still very shy about getting up in front of the class. I know it was because of the way I was dressed and the way I looked. My clothes were still out of date and worn. My shoes were never the style – just those 99-cent blue tennis shoes. I must say though that the kids never seemed to make anything of it. I was usually friends with them all.

My teachers were all good. They kept us working. My favorite teacher was Mrs. Wick in Social Studies. She treated us so well. We tried to please her in every way. Even the boys were very well behaved in those days. We were teenagers, but we had a great respect for our teachers and school.

The only time I was made to feel bad was by an inadvertent remark by one of my teachers. I was about 14 and in the eighth grade. The winter had continued to be extremely cold that year. I can remember walking down to Lindbergh, hugging myself in a thin coat, and wishing I could get to school faster so I could enjoy the warm classrooms. The sky had a very dark cloud hanging over everything. The cause of this was the smudge pots. There were millions of orange trees for miles in every direction. In those days, when the temperature got down to freezing, the rancher's way of keeping his fruit from being destroyed by ice was to burn oil in large pots that were placed in strategic places all over his orchard. The end result was a black sky and oily residue on everything under the cloud. You can imagine how everything looked.

I finally got to school. We kids were pushing our way around the teacher's desk before class started. Everyone was saying how cold it was this day. I happened to say it was so cold and that my feet were freezing. At that, my teacher looked down at my blue tennis shoes and said, "Why don't you wear better shoes?" I just looked at her and turned away. This was the only time anyone ever made any kind of remark about my clothes.

Sometimes people say things that make lasting impressions. We just never know, do we?

I took all the usual classes in junior high. I tried to include art somewhere. I really loved it. I learned some things from my art teachers, but I was always yearning for more. One of the extra classes I signed up for was right down my alley – library aide.

In eighth and ninth grade I was a librarian helper for one period a day. I just loved being around the books. I learned all about the Dewey Decimal System and how to shelve the books in their proper places. I did feel so grown up and responsible. It was one more step in my journey from childhood to young teenager. I can trace my deep interest in the earth and its sciences from those days. I just simply devoured every one of the National Geographics that appeared on the shelf. I read all the travel books, both fictional and non-fiction. My interest just seemed to be intense whenever I would come across one of these books. I found that so much of the information about the earth just seemed to stick in my mind. I dreamed about traveling to faraway places. It was going to be many years before I could pursue this interest in depth. That story will come later.

One part of the day at school that I especially liked was lunchtime. When I had a sack lunch with a sandwich and maybe a cookie I would join my friends out on the lawn under a shady tree. There we would talk, and laugh about everything, and we seemed to frequently discuss 'what we were going to be.' It was interesting to hear the ideas each one had. When it was my turn to say, I can remember telling them that I was thinking of five different things to 'be'. These were the options I thought were possible. First, there was getting married and having children.

Then, I said that being a nurse was pretty exciting. Third, I mentioned that maybe I would do well as a teacher. Fourth, the life of an opera singer was very appealing. I could sing pretty well by then. But last I would say that becoming a nun would be something I would like to do. I can remember the silence, stunned silence; this last choice was met with. Most of the little circle of friends were not Catholic, so I am sure they couldn't even comprehend how anyone could even think of such a choice. Well, I was thinking of it, but I had not the slightest idea of how I was going to do it. I just let it lie there in my mind with the other four possibilities. I was only about fourteen at the time.

Our family life continued to go on as usual. We all got along very well. The usual tussles were part of the scene, but there was really never any harshness shown. My mother was so very loving and supportive of each of us. My father was calm and noncommittal about things. In a way this made me feel secure. The evenings were always the same – radio, marbles, homework, reading, laughing. And sometimes Bev and I would put on a show. We had been going to dance and drama classes at Houghton Park for years. The classes were free, so we could attend. Bev and I loved to do little skits with dialogue, which we made up, and sing, for anyone who happened to be visiting. Our parents seemed to enjoy what we did because they never told us to stop 'taking over the stage.' We did a lot of laughing and joking about it. Barr seemed to be already running in his own circles. Most of the time I didn't know where he was, but he always showed up at home eventually. He and my father were not getting along very well. I think my father's lack of acceptance of Barr had a lot to do with Barr's later life. Of course, the source of great pride to my father was Bernie. My father played favorites, and it was very apparent that Barr was not included. Neither was I. I coped by just going right on with my life, and counting on the warmth and love I received from my mother. That saved the day. She gave me a great sense of worth.

There was one great scare thrown into our family one evening. It had to do with Beverly. She was 11. She and I had been going over to the local YMCA in the early evenings with the neighbor kids. We didn't have any adults with us, but we seemed to get along fine. We would go upstairs in the gym to sit on benches in the balcony that ran along one of the upper walls. There we would sit to watch older teenagers and adults play volleyball below. We weren't particularly interested in the game because we hadn't played it very much. We just liked being out after dark, and around a lot of yelling and cheering – just excitement. Our parents didn't worry about us. They were at home resting after a long day's work in the shop.

On this particular evening Bev and I met our friends, who lived down the street. We ran over to the YMCA to enjoy ourselves. We were very good at finding entertainment that didn't cost any money.

During the course of the evening Bev was doing what she was so good at – jumping around and swinging in the balcony. The only problem was that she jumped up off the bench to reach the rafter that was one of many just above our heads. She was having a grand time reaching up and swinging her legs back and forth, laughing all the while. She was always so energetic, athletic and daring far more than I was. One of my friends jumped up and started swinging too. The drop to the balcony floor was not very far, maybe about two to three feet. We kids didn't see anything wrong with that, and there were no adults upstairs with us to say, "Stop it."

The accident happened like lightening. Beverly was swinging. One of her hands must have come loose because she lost her grip and was falling the short distance to the floor. But, as fate would have it, she swung a little sideways so that one foot hit the bench below. This swung her body sideways and down so that she hit the floor full force on her head. I turned just in time to see her feet up on the bench and her head on the floor. Her eyes were staring. Then I was horrified to see a great gusher of blood come out of her nose and shoot across the floor. We all began screaming. I leaned over the railing and yelled to the people below, "My sister is hurt, Please come help us." I was terrified that Bev was dead.

In the next instant I dashed down the stairs and ran out into the night. It was probably about three blocks to our house, but fright gave wings to my feet. I burst into the front room and yelled out to my parents that we were at the YMCA and Bev was hurt. They both jumped up, Pop grabbed the keys to our car, and we all drove quickly back to the 'Y'. What a scene greeted our eyes. There was a very large crowd standing out in front. People had heard the ambulance siren, and came running. They were all asking, "What happened?" Mama ran into the building with Pop. I was left standing out in front in the crowd. My knees were shaking so hard I could hardly stand. Soon the ambulance orderlies came out rolling Bev on a gurney. Mama and Dad were right there with her. Bev didn't move. Her eyes were closed. She looked so pale. I was sure this was it for her. Mama went with Bev into the ambulance. When they left my father and I jumped in our old car and started out to go to St. Mary's Hospital in Long Beach. On the way we stopped by the rectory of St. Athanasius to tell Father O'Sullivan what happened, and to ask him for prayers. My father was very worried.

We ran over to the church to say some prayers, and then hopped in the car to drive the seven miles to the hospital.

On the way my father never said a word to me. This
didn't surprise me because he hardly ever spoke to me
directly. I was very aware that he favored Beverly and
Bernie because he said so right in front of us, but he
never used any harsh language toward me. I just felt
left out. When we got to the hospital we went to the
emergency room where they were helping Bev. She
still seemed out of it. She had blood all over her
clothes and body. Pretty soon they had her ready and
took her up to a room. Evidently they saw no broken
bones, especially a fractured skull. Mama and I went
up to the floor where they took Bev, and we sat on a
bench at the end of the hall. Mama began to cry
uncontrollably. I was trying so hard to comfort her.
She said she wasn't sure Beverly would make it. She
gradually stopped. Then she told me to go find Dad. I
found him down at the front office talking to
someone. I think he may have been telling them he
had no money to pay for anything. Later we all went
home and prayed. Barr was home from work at the
meat market.

We visited Bev several times a day for the next few
days. It was there that I got my second look at nuns.
The Incarnate Word Sisters were in charge, and still
are to this day. I noticed that I was fascinated with
them, how they looked, how quietly they went about
their work, how pleasant they were to us. Now I know
that they were, and are, truly dedicated to serving the
sick and the poor. They were especially kind to my
parents, and to Bev. After several days the doctors
said Bev could come home because there seemed to
be no more danger. We were all so very relieved. She

recovered completely. We never returned to the YMCA. I don't know if or how my parents paid the hospital bill. The dry cleaning shop was not giving enough return for us to be living comfortably. In reality, we were still in trouble.

It was while we lived on Olive Avenue that I became aware of helping around the house.

I wanted to help my mother who was working so hard in the cleaning shop. I remember that on Saturday I would come home from catechism class and start right in cleaning the whole house. I don't know why I did this because my mother never told me to 'do it.' I just felt that it was something I could do to make our house a home. I would start in the bedrooms and end up in the kitchen. After a week of living in it the house needed lots of things picked up, and lots of dusting and sweeping. It would take me about an hour or so to do everything.

It was while I was doing this task that I began to listen to the radio broadcast of the Metropolitan Opera from New York. For some reason this appealed to me. I couldn't understand the words, but Milton Cross, the narrator, explained all the plots pretty thoroughly. That was the beginning of my love and appreciation of classical music.

Every Saturday in Opera season I would listen in. In between times I would sing all alone. Bev and I had been in a lot of plays and mini-musicals at the park so I was used to singing. I also was now singing in the choir at St. Athanasius. I could tell that my voice was containing some resonance that hadn't been there when I was younger. So, I was beginning to feel the stirrings of beautiful music that have never left me. To this day, I love to relax in the midst of beautiful sounds produced by the great composers. And I find it a treat when great singers perform.

It was while we lived on Olive Avenue that one very humiliating experience happened to me. We had always put our best foot forward to the world. It was evident that we were not real well off, but we maintained a dignified front.

On Sundays when we went to church we looked our best even though we were wearing the same clothes for a long, long time. My father always wore the blue suit he bought when he first started his attempt to be a real estate agent downtown. It was getting gradually shinier and shinier. But he always looked dressed up to do the ushering at church. Mama wore her hat in a perky and fashionable manner. Her clothes were becoming pretty worn. The worst part was that women wore silk stockings. No one would think of having bare legs. Silk had the propensity for runs up and down the leg. My dear mother would just put on the hose, runs and all, and go bravely to church and up the stairs to the choir loft.

She would play the organ so beautifully. She knew all the cues for the hymns perfectly. She seemed to revel in the beauty of the ceremonies. Over the years she would sometimes just go down to church in the middle of the afternoon. She would say, "I'm going to practice for Sunday." She told me later that in reality she would be feeling low about something, and playing always seemed to uplift her spirits. Often Father O'Sullivan would come into the church when he heard her playing. He would pace back and forth reading his Breviary, which he had to do every day. I guess he found the music perfect for meditation. It turned out that he was a really good friend to our family. He was especially kind and generous to mama. She was so faithful in being the organist at services at least twice a week that he would give her a check every so often. She was really a volunteer, but he did appreciate her.

It was always a big event when he would give her what we called 'the blue thing.' We would all get very excited when she came home with the blue check for a couple of hundred dollars. It was like manna from heaven. I know that mama used the money to pay people back who had given us credit for groceries or other needed items. This happened once or twice a year. Mama deserved every penny.

It so happened that I had joined the Junior Catholic Daughters. I am not sure how I paid my dues, but I suspect that I searched for more milk bottles or maybe mama had a quarter or fifty cents for me on a given day. We would have our meetings at someone's house. All the girls were friends I knew from school. I had never told anyone of our financial struggles, but it was surely evident from the way I was dressed and from the kind of lunches I had.

On one Saturday afternoon I had finished doing all the housework. Everything was spotless and neat. I had just seated myself in my favorite armchair to read a book. While I was sitting there I was aware of someone on the front porch. Before I could even get up and look out the window the door burst open. Coming into our living room was a group of Junior Catholic Daughters all laughing and smiling at me. They said "Hi", and then I noticed that they were all carrying bags of groceries.

They marched right into our kitchen and put the bags on the drain board. All the while I was still sitting in the chair looking at them with my mouth open, in amazement. They didn't give me a chance to say anything. They all seemed so pleased with themselves. I am sure that the group leader must have encouraged them to think of the poor. Somehow my name must have come up. I can imagine the conversation. "Doris looks poor. Why don't we give the food to her family? They probably need it."

Well, thank God in Heaven, the house was spotless; the kitchen didn't have a single dish out of place. Everything sparkled. I am sure that afterwards someone would say, "Her house didn't look so poor. Why did we take the food there?" It was true. We lived in a nice little cottage, and the Murphys did have a lot of pride. It was never a dump.

When my parents came home from the shop I showed them the bags of groceries. They didn't say anything. Mama just put the groceries away. I could hardly look at any of the girls when I went to school on Monday. It is hard for a teenager to know that others have talked about her behind her back. Their gesture of kindness I took for pity. It was so humiliating. To this day I can still feel the embarrassment in realizing that they knew. I have often thought that my parents must have felt the same way. I do wonder what my father thought about his failing efforts to provide for us.

I think this is a good place to talk about the shop. What a good idea it was. Both of my parents were handy with fixing things. My mother was a very good seamstress. One of the real treasures in our house, no matter where we lived, was the Singer sewing machine. It was electric. It was one of the purchases my parents made when my father got his inheritance. I first saw it in McCloud. What a great machine it was. There was a beautiful burnished wood finish on the whole thing. It was a very attractive piece of furniture because when it was not in use it would close up and become a nice side table. For some miraculous reason the sewing machine followed us wherever we moved. It was one thing that my mother would never give up. To this day I am sentimentally attached to it as it resides in a place of honor in our dining room. Even though the motor doesn't run very fast any more it is still a thing of beauty.

So to get started on their grand idea my parents consulted with the parish priest, Father O'Sullivan, gave them four hundred dollars to finance the purchase of the press and water tank needed to supply the steam. This is one good example of a parish priest really looking out for his parishioners.

My folks looked around for an empty store somewhere in the neighborhood. They found a small place at 5729 Atlantic Avenue near our home. They started the shop when we were living on Ellis Street. We were all excited about the whole thing. We had been living in North Long Beach for about three years, and in all that time my father had not yet landed a job anywhere. I believe we were still on relief.

When my parents had everything going they opened the shop quietly. People coming by could see that it was a cleaners because my father had a man paint the name of it on the window, "Atlantic Cleaners".

Were we ever proud as kids because now our circumstances would be better in every way. We could now tell other kids who asked what our father did that he was the owner of a dry cleaners. Even in school when I would be filling out the identification papers at the beginning of school I could fill in 'father's occupation' with 'owner of dry cleaning establishment.'

It was clear that my mother would take care of all the women's clothing, and my father would press the suits of the men. It seemed to be a fine arrangement. They both went off to work each day looking very happy.

In order for everything to run smoothly they had to procure the services of a company which would do the actual dry cleaning. That is what is probably done even to this day. They obtained the services of a man who had his establishment down on Long Beach Boulevard and Willow. When people would bring in their suits and dresses to be cleaned my parents would write up a receipt for them. A suit cost 80 cents for cleaning and pressing. I am not sure what my mother charged for alterations, she was in charge of all alterations on both men's and women's clothing. She was very good at it. The customers were always smiling when they left with anything she had done. The same can be said of my father's work. The suits looked just perfect when he was finished.

The routine was fairly simple. When a suit was brought in the name of the person was written on the receipt. This receipt had a number on it. All the clothes were put on a long table in the back of the shop behind a partition. Then a small tag was attached with a little metal fastener to an inside seam of the pants or dress. Before being attached someone had to copy the number from the receipt in India ink. It was jet black. I soon learned how to do this task and several others. I have already described the tacking up of the pants cuff on the men's suits. I sometimes stayed at the front counter and took in the clothes that people brought in to be cleaned and pressed. I felt so grown up and capable when I got to this stage.

Through all of these days, though, I did not get any kind of allowance. I am sure the bills were bigger than my parents had expected, so there was not anything much left over.

We three kids were rapidly growing up. Barr was always a go-getter. When he was only about ten or eleven he became a salesman for the very popular "Liberty Magazine". He had a canvas bag provided by the magazine lady, (that's what we always called her), which he crossed over his shoulder. She would provide a certain number of copies each week. Barr was expected to give her the wholesale price for each one, and then he could keep the rest as profit. I'm sure it was the usual business transaction.

Barr would go from door to door every so often and sell his magazines. Sometimes he would make me help him. I really didn't want to do it because there was something about it that I just didn't take to. I hated selling, and I still do even to this day. He would threaten me as a big brother and say he was going to beat me up. He never ever did hit me or anything, but I wasn't altogether sure, so I would go from door to door too.

In later years we were laughing one time about this time in our lives. I confessed to him that I disliked ringing doorbells so much that I would go down the side of the street across from him on purpose. When I would approach a house I would look over to see where he was. He was so intent on doing his job that he didn't notice that I was not really ringing the doorbell. I just put my finger on it, and then waited an appropriate amount of time. Then, I would leap down the front steps and go to the next house, all the while telling Barr the people weren't home. In this way I got through the job. Now I feel bad that I didn't try to do more, but when you are only ten or eleven you don't think of that.

One of my most poignant memories is of Barr coming home from selling, and handing over to Mama the few nickels he had made. Sometimes that was the only money she had for buying necessities at the corner grocer. Of course, there was always the day of reckoning when the 'magazine lady' would come to the door for her part of the sales. How embarrassed we would all be when my mother would have to tell her that we didn't have it right now, but 'come back in a couple of days.' My mother always held her head up and somehow came through. After awhile Barr didn't sell Liberty anymore. But I can still see him walking up and down the neighborhood streets trying to do his part. He always had a twinkle in his eye. I don't think that too many people could resist him.

When he was around ninth grade he got a job at the Dollar market across the street from the shop on Atlantic Avenue. He worked in the meat department behind the scenes. Every day after school he would go over there and do whatever they asked him to do. The boss was a very nice gentleman.

Barr was really growing up into a handsome young man. He was having a shaky time in school, but I think it was because he couldn't keep interested in what they were expecting of him. I know now that he was very intelligent, but he never seemed to be anxious to go to school as I was. He had the knack of getting into dutch every so often. My folks always said that Barr was the most inquisitive one of all of us kids. He was the one who would see something interesting, and then head in that direction even if it was a little dangerous. As a child he would scare my mother when we would go out on picnics in the woods near Mt Shasta, or near a river. Barr was always trying to get across, or up, or over, or into whatever obstacle was there. He was also showing a marvelous amount of dexterity around machines. He especially loved to tinker on the old cars we had. Sometimes my father would be working on the motor of the Model T or Essex. Barr would go out in the backyard to help him. They would be working side by side for awhile. Often whatever was wrong would be fixed fine. I am sure my father was showing Barr the different parts of the engine. However, I know that my father was not a very great mechanic, so I think that as Barr grew older into his teenage years he began to know more about engines than my father did.

My mother was especially proud of Barr's abilities. One day I was with her when the funniest thing happened. She and I were at church. It was a Saturday morning. When we came out from Mass my mother was talking with a lady friend. The topic of Barr came up. My mother was telling this lady that Barr was getting very good at mechanics. She said, "He can take the engine apart, and put it back together again without any trouble."

She was so proud. Just at that very moment we looked up the street. Who did we see but Barr driving our car down Linden Avenue toward us. As he got to the corner of Market he decided to turn onto Market Street. We were standing there staring at him because he shouldn't have been in the car at all. He didn't have a license yet. Just as Barr turned the corner waving and laughing – the rear wheel fell off. We gasped. The car came to a screeching halt. He wasn't hurt and neither was the car, but I'm sure his face was as red as a beet. My mother just stood there staring with her mouth open. Then she and the lady started laughing and both saying they hoped Barr could put it all back together again. He did. I don't think we ever told on him to the rest of the family.

Another time Barr had a problem was when he was in Junior High at Lindbergh. My mother said later that she got a call to come to see the Principal because Barr was in trouble. Well, she went to school. The trouble was that some kids had been teasing Barr. I think they were girls. This was probably their effort to make him notice them. He paid them back by picking up the nearby lawn hose, which was running, and spraying them. They all ran away giggling about it. The only problem was that when Barr turned around to spray them he sent the water into the Principal's office right onto his desk. And the Principal was sitting there. You can imagine the ruckus this raised. Mama said that when she got to the office there was Barr sitting with his head down not wanting to look at her. They talked to the Principal. He decided that it was really an accident, but that Barr should think before he acted. Mama said that she and the Principal were both laughing when Barr wasn't looking because it really was funny. It seems that through all of this my father never really said too much. In fact, he was never complimentary to Barr. I don't think he gave Barr any direction or advice so Barr had to make a lot of decisions on his own, and these were not always wise. This is the case with any young person who is ignored by parents.

The light of my father's life was Bernie. He is still in the seminary up near Pomona, and seems very happy with his decision. By now he has grown into a handsome young man of eighteen or nineteen. We still would go up to visit him one Sunday afternoon a month. It was always a highlight to see him thriving so well. Of course, we did not let him in on any of the hardships we were having. My father would have a few quarters to buy the gas. It was about thirty miles up there so we could make it up and back on about two or three gallons. Gas was 19 or 20 cents a gallon in those days. Our car would go about thirty miles an hour, so it was an hour up and an hour back.

I especially liked the atmosphere. Besides the classrooms and the bedrooms for the seminarians there was a beautiful chapel. We always closed our visit going there with all the other families and seminarians for Benediction of the Blessed Sacrament. This was a short ceremony with hymns and prayers honoring Jesus in the Eucharist. There were candles lit, and incense burning. We all sang the hymns in Latin. The priest was clothed in a long cape that was called a 'cope'. It had intricate embroidery in very beautiful designs. The ceremony was always the same, and lasted about twenty minutes. I just loved it. This was the same thing we did at home in our own parish every Wednesday night. We called it devotions. My parents always took us kids. Barr would be an altar boy. So was Bernie when he was home on vacation.

Bernie spent a couple of the summer months at home, and a week at Christmas time. One of the Christmases we went up to get him in our old Essex. As usual we were living on a shoestring, but my folks were putting their best foot forward as they always did. We three kids were doing our part too. We attended Midnight Mass with the boys and their families. After Mass all the seminarians could go home with their families for their vacation. As luck would have it, when we all piled into our old car my father couldn't get it to start. I don't know now what the matter was but it must have been somewhat terminal, or maybe something simple like no gas.

Just to show what a good talker my father was he cajoled one of the other fathers of a seminarian to PUSH us all the way home. Remember that it was thirty miles. There was no question of going into a gas station garage because it was Christmas Eve and no place was open at one-thirty a.m. You can imagine our total embarrassment. My father never showed any kind of chagrin. Maybe he felt like it, but he was laughing. The poor man who was pushing us had a carload of boys who lived in Long Beach so he was going our way. I don't know what my father said to him, but it is an example of his power of persuasion that the man did it.

When we arrived home and rolled into our driveway on Olive Avenue all the boys jumped out of the car and came into our house. You would have thought we had done them a favor. Well, my parents were very appreciative, and expressed their thanks a million times. My mother passed out the delicious date sugar cookies she had made for our Christmas treat to all the boys and their parents. Of course, it was a kind and gracious gesture on my mother's part. They had done a wonderful favor for us.

We kids were standing in the background eyeing the tray of disappearing cookies. Those were the only cookies my mother could make for us. Whenever I think of those cookies I think of that strange ride we had being pushed for thirty miles by very kind people. I don't remember my mother ever baking those special cookies again.

Beverly too was growing up. She was just in the pre-teen years, and had completely recovered from her accident at the YMCA. She was so wiry and active. Running was her usual mode of travel. I tried to keep up because I was pretty fast myself, but she always had one more bit of energy. She and I continued having fun with the drama and dancing classes we took at Houghton Park. One time the funniest thing happened to her. We were taken by bus down to Poly High School to be in one of the productions. We were always part of the dancing crowd. The Recreation Department of Long Beach provided all the costumes. Beverly had worn a pair of brown slacks that day. After the production we were told to be on the bus in ten minutes. Poor Bev. She still had on her costume that was something like a clown suit.

When I found her to take her to the bus she was in a state of panic. I ran out to the bus to tell them to wait for us. For a little bit I wasn't sure they were going to do it. I pleaded with the head lady to come help my sister find her pants. She finally did help us. After searching everywhere the lady said, "Let's look in the costume trunk." Beverly started searching through the costumes like a maniac. Sure enough, there was her pair of pants all rolled up and wrinkled. Someone thought they were a costume. I can still see Bev grabbing them so fast and putting them on. We were both stressed out so bad over this incident that we got on the bus crying. Part of our fright was that of being left behind. We had no money, and it was about eight miles to our home in North Long Beach. What a long walk that would be.

Our lives continued to be full of school things, homework, friends, playing with neighborhood kids, going to the park, and going downtown to the beach to swim or visit the Pike, and always on Saturday it was catechism class. After several years of these lessons we kids could answer every single question posed to us. Even to this day I can get on a roll and go through some of them. Most Saturday afternoons were spent at the movies. My parents were busy in the shop, and we helped in small ways.

But, all was not going well. I had gotten older as had Barr and Bev. I was beginning to wonder why we were still in dire straits when it came to money. My folks were busy every day, and I am sure they had to pay the rent up front. Then there was the cleaner who gave credit, and came to collect every Saturday afternoon. Then the upkeep of the car had to be taken into major consideration. After all, the slogan my father had invented for the business was "We call for and deliver." He even had signs painted that could be placed on the inside back window of our old Essex that made the car look very official. This meant that the car had to be in good running order. Then, of course, there was a family to be taken care of. There was the rent. We did have food, but it was not plentiful. We never had new clothes. There were times when my shoes would wear holes on the soles. If no new shoes were forthcoming I would have to make-do by putting cardboard inside the shoes so that my feet would not be touching the bare ground. I sometimes repaired the holes in the heel of my socks by cutting a patch of material from some cast-off shirt or dress. Then I would carefully sew it in place, using the appliqué method. I couldn't help it if the sock was red and the patch was white. I just wore them anyway, all the while holding my head up in front of my friends at school.

I learned by the time I was in seventh grade that if anything cost any money I could not go, or sign up, or buy whatever. I became rather resigned to this because there was no way I could earn any money. Boys had the paper routes. Barr worked in the butcher shop. Girls my age didn't have any way of earning anything. Even babysitting was not considered a job because you did it for nothing to help out a neighbor or family friend. Bev and I collected milk bottles so that we had the nickel for the Saturday movies.

I did not like to babysit. My dear mother would offer my services when my folks and some other couple were planning to go to some Church affair, or some such thing. She would tell them right in front of me that 'Doris will take care of your children.' My heart would just drop, but I couldn't disappoint my mother. The big problem with this arrangement was that I really didn't know how to take care of little ones. I had never been around small children and infants so I was not in on what were the things to do to keep them happy. My mother never gave me any directions or hints, so I would go to the house with a lot of trepidation hoping that I would do ok.

There was a young couple down the street from us who asked my mother if I would watch their children on a given evening. Once again I was just petrified doing it, because I didn't know anything. And as fate would have it, when I arrived, the smallest child, a little two-year old boy, saw me come in. He immediately began screaming at the top of his lungs. He was already in his crib. His parents tried to cajole him, but he would just look at me and open up his mouth and scream. This couple always told me the time they would be back. But, I babysat for them a couple of times, and I found that they would be at least two hours after the time they had set up for their return.

One of those times I had finally gotten the three little ones to go to sleep. I was sitting on the couch in the living room reading whatever was there. It was probably around midnight, I was always very uneasy. Well, I became aware of a sizzling or swishing sound. It wasn't loud, but it was persistent. I was mesmerized with fright because I had no idea what the sound was. It seemed to come from the hallway or the bathroom. Of course, we didn't have a telephone so I couldn't call home for help. That made me even more scared. I finally got up the nerve to go to the hallway and see what was there. When I turned on the light I could tell the sound was coming from the bathroom. I gingerly opened the door and turned on the light. My heart was pounding, and my hands were shaking. There under the sink was a steady spray of water coming from a burst pipe. If you know what panic means you know how I felt. I did not have the slightest idea what to do. I had never been around a broken pipe before. The floor was beginning to be flooded. I started crying to myself because of the pickle I was in. I happened to glance up at the window in the bathroom. I saw that the neighbor's light was still on. Even though I didn't know them very well I raced out of the house, ran next door, rang their doorbell, and blurted out that there was a bad leak in the bathroom. How wonderful it was to hear the nice man say he would come right over with me and see what was wrong. Of course, when he saw the gusher he just leaned over and turned the handles on the water pipes under the sink. The water stopped immediately. He even helped me sop up some of the water on the floor with the towels that were hanging there.

The couple finally came home about two a.m. It was two hours after the time they said they would return. I explained to them what had happened. They were matter-of-fact about it all. The man thanked me for staying with the children, gave me a quarter, and showed me to the door. I was once again petrified. Here I was about a block from my house at two in the morning. The man didn't offer to see me home safely. I was afraid because it was the time of night when the dogs would start barking if they heard a sound. I walked right down the middle of the street as fast as my feet would take me, looking over my shoulders in all directions, and burst into my own house. Everyone was asleep. My experience was so harrowing to me that the quarter didn't help at all. After all, we usually didn't get any pay for the job. You were expected to do it as a favor for a neighbor. My only problem with that is that I was the one who had to do it. I don't remember Barr or Bev ever being called on. I can say now that I hated to do it because I usually ended up being frightened by something, mostly frightened that I really didn't know what to do.

It was around this time that another financial catastrophe was to hit our family. I don't know what happened because my folks still did not say anything to us about it. I just knew that even though we owned a business there still was not enough money to pay all the bills. It was evident when I would come home from school and the lights would be turned off.

Sometimes the gas would be off. Sometimes both of the utilities would not turn on when I touched the switch. Of course, I was old enough to know that this didn't happen unless the bill was not paid. When my folks came home from the shop my father would sometimes put a penny in the fuse box so that the lights would go on. If the gas was off we just had to wait until my parents 'took care of it.' This happened a number of times in all the houses we lived in North Long Beach. It would sure be embarrassing if I happened to ask a friend to come over to my house after school to study or play. I never knew what to say, but I am sure I tried to cover it up somehow. Eventually everything would be turned on again, but it was always a possibility that we would not have lights or gas.

One day, the unheard of happened. I came home to find my parents packing once again. I asked what was going to happen. My mother said we were moving to some lots that my father had somehow acquired on 72nd Street. That was about a mile or so north of our house at present. I was old enough now to suspect that the real reason we were moving for the fourth time in just a few years was that the rent was not being paid. No one said it, but I began putting two and two together.

I felt sorry for my folks, especially my mother, because nothing seemed to be working. My father never gave any excuses or explanations. Now I am sure that he was realizing that he was never going to have anyone hand him a job or help him to be successful. He just had to do it on his own. What a predicament we were now in. Imagine my overwhelming surprise when I asked what kind of house we would live in and my mother said we were moving up to the lots and would be living in a TENT. I could not believe my ears. Here I was fourteen years old. Barr was sixteen and Bev was twelve. We were all going to live in a tent like homeless people. I just can't imagine what my father felt about all of us. He must have realized that we were not little kids anymore. We could catch on to what was happening. He never talked to us about it. My mother just went along with it because it was all she could do. To this day I can still feel the embarrassment of driving up there.

House No. 9 - The Tent
Long Beach, California

To this day I do not know how my father came into possession of the two lots. I do know that he was a very persuasive talker. He was basically a good man so others trusted him, but he had a history of not paying bills that came due. Now I see that this is a trait that he must have had even when my mother married him. She, of course, was the opposite. She was very conscious of making good on any purchases down to the penny. All of the years of unpaid bills must have been extremely hard on her, but it seems that she just couldn't influence my father to do the right thing regarding creditors. I suspect that they may have had many sessions of disagreement about it, but they never ever aired these episodes in front of us kids. Consequently, thanks to them, we were not in a continual state of fright because of hearing our parents fight over something. Maybe one of the best things about all of this is that I inherited the genes from my mother that make me need to pay what is due and to maintain an even temper about life.

We arrived up at the tent with our beds, carpets, couch, table and chairs, clothes, various things like lamps (which we couldn't use), and a few boxes. Who would have thought that in a relatively short period of about six years, we would go from being well-off, owning a Studebaker Commander, living in the Wrigley District, and having ample money to live on to this sorry old tent that my father borrowed from our good friends, the Mallons. I don't know what he said to them about needing the tent for us to actually live in, but I'm sure he said it was only for a short time until he got the house built. They must have wondered what was going on. Both of my parents told us that the plan was to live in the tent, rent free, until our house was built. We soon found out that not a single thing was on the lot except weeds. There was no sign of a house going up. I was in a state of adolescent panic. What would I tell my friends? I decided then and there that I would never breathe a word of it to anyone. I would just have to wait and see what would happen. I was following the lead of my mother. She always kept a good face on and held her head high. I did so admire her dignity, and now I see how loyal she was to my father. She never ever bad-mouthed him to us in any way. But I suspect that she was also panicked and disappointed by the course of events.

Our first night was awful. Mama, Bev, and I slept in one bed. Barr and Pop slept in the other. We laid the carpets on the ground so we weren't walking in the weeds. We had to use kerosene lamps for light. There was no heat. And worst of all we had no bathroom. I just could not imagine what we were going to do. I knew that Barr and Pop could go out to the weeds when they needed to, but we just couldn't do that. So, it turned out that every morning we all got up early, got in the car, and went down to the shop to go to the bathroom and wash up. Then we kids would have something to eat, and go off to school. I was in Junior High. After school we came to the shop and stayed there until it was time to close up and go home. We would all go right to bed because there wasn't anything else to do. What a way to live. I wondered how on earth we had gotten to this point. I was about fourteen years of age.

One night there was a terrible storm. It was pouring outside. Puddles were getting bigger and bigger. I was worried that we would be flooded out of our tent. Then the wind began to blow. Our tent began to sway. I thought that in a minute it was going to be blown completely away. My father and Barr went outside in the pouring rain to reinforce the pegs holding the ropes of the tent. Mama, Bev, and I were inside praying that they could save the tent. I could hear my father yelling at Barr, and Barr yelling right back at him. After awhile they both came in soaked to the skin. There wasn't anything to do but go to bed. We all spent the night shivering. Today I wonder what my father was thinking about how he had provided for his family. This was a very low point in our saga, and I'm sure in his.

It wasn't long after this that things did begin to happen. The first thing that occurred was that a big cement truck came rolling into the yard. Some men had already laid out the dimensions for a foundation. The truck was one of those big round mixers that kept on revolving as it drove to the place to be poured. That day the foundation was laid for our new house. I couldn't believe my eyes. I didn't know where my father got the money to have this done. It seemed still as if the shop was not bringing in very much extra because we never saw it. I was ecstatic. I am sure the whole family was.

After the cement set the next thing that happened was the arrival of a truck filled with lumber. The tent was still our home, but there were men around putting up the house. In reality, this was not really supposed to be a house. It was only going to be our home for a very short time. At least, that is what my parents said. The cement that was laid was really the slab to be used for the garage floor in the future. It was laid out for a two-car garage size. How's that for dreaming big? The structure going up would serve as our home until the house was built right next to it. Such dreams.

The house had a living room that took up one half of the space. The other half was divided into one bedroom, a kitchen, and a bathroom with a shower, no tub. The outside was built very neatly of lumber that was painted white. The interior was a very attractive knotty pine. It seems that the pine supply ran out before the bedroom could be paneled, so it was left in its raw state with the beams and two-by-fours all showing. Because I still, to this day, do not know where my father got the money to provide such a home, I am presuming the man who supplied the wood was not paid, so there was no way for my father to get more. Consequently, the bedroom was just left unfinished. Thus, we had a home of our own.

I can truthfully say that the weeks we spent living in the tent were the hardest for me. One reason was that for a young adolescent it was shocking. At that time in Long Beach there wasn't anyone anywhere living in a tent. I didn't want any of my friends to even know where I lived because how was I to explain it. I couldn't.

Our neighbors up and down 72nd Street must have wondered what was going on. I sometimes would spend some time there on a Saturday morning, probably straightening up. Now I thank God for watching out for me because at no time did anyone bother me, or scare me. I was alone out there. When I remember those days I begin to feel intensely sorry for my mother. She must have been in a state of despair over the lack of ambition in my father and over his lack of success in anything he undertook. On top of it all remember we did not have a bathroom, no place to take a shower. The little sink in the shop was used for cleaning up. I do remember one time that we all went over to the Mallon's house for a bath. I'm sure those nice friends must have asked my parents if we wanted to do that. I was totally embarrassed, but did it ever feel good to be in a nice warm bath. Even today I can feel the luxury of it.

Well, now we were settled in our house. It was warm and snug for the five of us. I am not sure where everyone slept, but I remember I slept on the couch. It was ok until I grew so much that I didn't fit. I couldn't stretch out. I was just so happy to be out of that awful tent that I didn't mind where I slept. At least it was under a real roof. I often went to sleep saying the rosary.

Several things were going on during these times. It must have been around 1938 and 1939. One of the most surprising events was that Bernie came home from the seminary for good. We had been faithfully visiting him every month for five years. By now he was a novice in the Claretian Order at Dominguez Seminary. We were all so proud of him. He seemed to be happy in his choice and was thriving. He had a bright future. I am sure my father especially was very disappointed. We all were for that matter. But home he came. He had lived away from us for the last five years so he did not experience the hardships and reversals of fortune that we were having.

We still never breathed a word to anyone about trouble. Our parents never told us not to say anything, but we just had a certain sense of pride in not letting anyone know. As far as Bernie was concerned we always were up-beat when we saw him. The whole family was proud, especially my parents. I am sure that Bernie soon became aware of the real state of things. It must have been a shock to him when he realized that we really weren't improving our lot.

Bernie was a fine young man by now. He was around 18 or 19. He was handsome and had a beautiful smile. I truly believe that he did wish to continue on. But, years later, I asked my mother about this decision of Bernie's. She told me very sadly that he decided to come home after one of our monthly visits. He told Ma that we all looked so poor in the same old clothes he had seen for months and months, and the same old car. We didn't look like we were prospering like the other families who came to see their sons. So, he decided to give up his dream of the priesthood and come home to see if he could help. That was a tremendous sacrifice for him to make because it would take him in a totally different direction than the one he loved so much. After all, if he could help us get on our feet maybe he could return and continue his studies. He still had about seven years to go.

So my parents received a call from the Seminary to come for Bernie. I was so shocked when I walked in the door and he was there. Of course, I was very glad to see him, but I was mystified. He said that he just got tired of being a seminarian. I took it at face value never guessing the real reason until my mother told me years later. I suspect that my father may have guessed the real reason for Bernie's return, but he didn't show any chagrin. He just put on a good face and continued on the way he always was.

Bernie set about making a new life for himself. The very first thing he did was to go out looking for work. As a young adult with no work experience he found it hard, but soon he was coming home just jubilant because he had a job in an office downtown as a secretary. He said it was for a company that collected scrap metal, especially automobiles, and compressed the metal into cubes to be sold overseas or to the steel mills in the USA. He didn't make very much but it helped a lot. I wonder now if my father noted that Bernie got a job right away even with no experience. Like the rest of us, Bernie had only the clothes he was wearing when he came home. So off to work he went each day dressed in a white shirt and tie, and a black suit. I wonder if he told his employers what school he had just finished. He had dignity and honesty. What else is there?

Another event took place just before Bernie came home. It had to do with Barr. By now he was around sixteen or seventeen. He had never been fond of school, and was not performing up to his ability, I'm sure. All in all, he was rather adrift. I noticed that Barr did not get any encouragement from my father for anything he did. They would often have disagreements. Barr could now drive, and he would be the one who would deliver the suits and dresses when necessary. He was busy at the meat market, and had a

social life that sometimes included me, but most often
not. He was always cheerful with us, but I could see
that he was not planning anything for his future.
Before long he announced that he was quitting school.
It was legal for him to do so, but it was disappointing
to me. I am sure my mother talked to him about it, but
he just wasn't doing well at all.

For the past five years he had Bernie as a kind of
impossible model. I am sure that Bernie talked to him
about things, but Barr just decided to do his own
thing. So, that was that. The biggest danger with all of
this was that Barr had no direction from his father,
and Mama couldn't persuade him to stick with it and
finish school. So he did what so many young people
do who have no real guidance. He met up with some
friends who were known in the neighborhood as
unsavory. They were older than Barr, probably about
nineteen or twenty. Barr was probably feeling rather
grownup, and doing what he wanted more or less. As
fate would have it, the worst happened. Barr listened
to the ideas of these two guys, and got into a lot of big
trouble.

These two guys persuaded Barr to help them rob the
market where Barr worked. I can't imagine to this day
why he would do such a thing. We really knew the
difference between right and wrong in our family.
But, he served as the lookout at the market. During the
night the two older guys came and got in somehow
with Barr's help. They were in the process of robbing
the market when the police found them. Well, you can
imagine the shock of my parents when the police

came to our house and asked them to come down to the station. They did what they always did with Beverly and me. They didn't say much at all. We had to try to guess what really happened. Barr came home very shame-faced. I had never seen my mother so disappointed. My father was like a sphinx. What could they say?

In a way I felt sorry for Barr because he looked so defeated. I am sure he must have been in a state of shock over the pickle he had gotten himself into. Well, the upshot of this sad tale is that Barr went before the Juvenile Judge in Los Angeles. Evidently it was decided that he was not the real instigator of the crime so he was sent to the youth camp up in the mountains for about six months. We went up to visit him a couple of times. He looked good and healthy. But, he was hoping to come home at the earliest possible date. We never talked about this episode with Barr. I just took for granted that he had learned his lesson about choosing whom to listen to.

In the meantime I was growing up. There was so much to do. I was now in high school. I started at Jordan High School on Atlantic Avenue in September of 1938. I was in the tenth grade at fourteen years of age. I was becoming a young lady very conscious of my appearance. I would do all I could to make my old clothes look ok, but it was a losing proposition. Anyway, I went to Jordan High with excitement in my heart. Now I was with young adults. It was an exhilarating feeling. I was beginning to think about my own future. It was sad at that time for girls because there were so few options, but the ones I was considering were all doable. I took my tenth grade classes, and did a so-so job. I loved art and music. The other classes were sometimes boring to me. But I always worked hard and did my homework thinking that this would do me some good some day. In the long run, it did.

It gradually dawned on me that religion was holding a spell over me. I was not a fanatic in any way, but I found that when I participated in any of the services at St. Athanasius I was in a special state of mind. I found great comfort in praying. When my mother would go down to Church to practice the organ I would often go with her. I would spend the time listening and dreaming. Then I would be praying for some help in deciding my life. Yes, even though I was only about fifteen I knew that my future was up to me. Up to this point in our family no one had ever mentioned any kind of future for us kids. We were so busy trying to keep our heads above water that we couldn't harbor any dreams. But, I did. I gradually began to feel that maybe I was called to serve in religion some way.

After all, we had spent our childhood participating in so many sacred things. We always recited the rosary, we made quick visits to the Blessed Sacrament, and we always went with Mama and Pop to devotions and Sunday Mass. Our family kept all the rules such as not eating meat on Fridays, fasting from all food and water before receiving Holy Communion, making parish retreats and missions. Why, we even had a son who was studying for the priesthood. In a word, we were what could be termed a 'good Catholic family.' So, it really isn't surprising that I would think about religious things.

I had continued to think about the options open to me that I had talked about with my Junior High School friends. I had no money to take lesson as an opera singer, so that wouldn't happen. I could be a teacher or a nurse and get married. These were all possibilities. But I was really beginning to think about devoting my life to the service of God. I knew that everyone could serve God in some way, but I had always been fascinated by any nuns that I happened to see. They were really mysterious to me. I had heard that they lived very simple lives and gave God their whole life. What a concept. I didn't even know any of them. My only experience with them had been for two months when I was in the third grade at St. Anthony's.

Now that I look back on those days I can see how I was being drawn to the service of God just very gradually. Not one of my girlfriends even mentioned this as a possibility for themselves. I began to think so seriously about it that I finally took my destiny into my own hands.

Up to this point in my life I had always asked Mama to come with me to take care of things, especially things regarding the first day of school. She was my rock. I depended upon her for good advice and help in everything. Well, I gradually came to the conclusion that if I was going to explore the call I just somehow had to be around nuns. I had to find out if this was what I wanted to do. I didn't have anyone to talk to about it so I just kept my thoughts to myself for the time being. Here I was at Jordan High School in the tenth grade. The school year was about three-fourths finished when I made my move.

I decided that I wanted to attend St. Anthony's High School no matter what. It was really providential that the mother of a close friend of ours was the cook for the Sisters at St. Anthony's. This friend told her mother about me. Would she put in a good word for me? She sure did. After a few days this lady told me that the Sister Superior at St. Anthony's would be happy to see me about coming to the school. I was ecstatic.

I had suddenly grown up. I had this sense of independence that I had not felt before. One day very soon I asked my mother if I could change schools and go to St. Anthony's. We were in the shop. I can still see her working on a blue dress for a customer. She looked at me with those wonderful brown eyes and said, "We can't pay any tuition, Honey." I said, "Maybe they will let me work it off, or something." She said it was all right if I could work it out. Just imagine – if I could work it out. How grown-up can you get? So the next day I dressed up as neatly as I could and went downtown on the bus after school to meet Sister Gabriel Marie. She changed my life forever.

Here is what happened. As I was riding downtown on the bus I was thinking of what I would say to the Sister. My mind was a blank because I had no idea what she would be like. I walked up to the old convent on Sixth Street, rang the bell and waited. Soon a nun answered the door. I told her that Sister Gabriel Marie was expecting me. The nun showed me in to the parlor. Well, here I was. I wondered how on earth I had gotten myself to this point. Pretty soon in walked Sister Gabriel Marie. She had a nice smile on her face, and had an unusually soft voice. She started talking to me with interest and kindness. She asked me about my present school classes at Jordan. I told her that I liked school a lot, but that I just couldn't work up steam there. She laughed and said that the classes at St. Anthony would all be demanding. Did I think I could do it? I said I really didn't know, but that I'd like to try. She asked if I could afford the $2 tuition fee. I quietly said that I couldn't afford anything. Then she said the magic words. "Well, that is all right. You just come anyway. We will figure out something."

I was sitting astonished. I am certain, knowing my circumstances, that if she had said that I needed to provide any money at all that I would have thanked her and returned home with regret. But, she didn't do that. She said to come the following Monday with the transfer from Jordan High School together with my grades. She said not to worry about books. She just happened to have an extra set for a sophomore. To me it is as clear as glass. That was the real turning point in my life. I could have gone one way or the other that afternoon. It turned out that I couldn't resist the very kind invitation to attend St. Anthony's. My whole world instantly changed that day.

I was on cloud nine. I hurried home on the bus and ran into the shop to tell my mother that I was accepted at St. Anthony's. She asked me all about it. When I told her about the break about tuition she smiled and said that it must be that I was meant to go there. She said she would help me as much as she could. I don't remember my father saying anything at all. The next day at Jordan I went to the Counselor's office and checked out. They were curious about the move, but I did not elaborate. That was the day I launched off into life a little more mature, more aware of myself as a young adult, and really looking forward to the next adventure. The grand triumph of it all was that I did the whole thing myself. It was a wonderful feeling.

I loved St. Anthony's. For the first time in my life I blossomed into a really good student. I thought the nuns were wonderful. The high school was so small that there were only four teachers for all the subjects. All four teachers were IHM Sisters. They taught all the required college prep courses to all four classes - freshmen to seniors.

When I look back at that time I marvel at how very capable they were. Sister Charles taught math and science. She was busy with Algebra I and II, Geometry, Physics and Chemistry. Sister Reginald was an old 'war horse' she taught Latin I, II, III, and IV. Spanish I and II were her responsibility. She also took care of the four years of history needed at each level. Sister Eymard took care of all the English classes for all four levels. Sister Gabriel Marie was responsible for running the whole school, but she did take over some of the classes for Sister Reginald. Of course, all the nuns taught religion to their homerooms. There was one class at each level, so the atmosphere was intimate.

Before long I knew the names of everyone in the high school. I had never been in such a small school. For the first time I had teachers who spoke to me, who knew my name, who showed an interest in how I was doing. They were always kind, and helpful. No one alluded to the fact that I was not paying. That would have been pretty cruel. These nuns won my heart right off the bat. The school itself enjoyed a fine reputation for its academics. I didn't know it then, but have since learned that it was fully accredited by the University of California because of the rigor of its curriculum.

It wasn't long before I had made some good friends with other girls. Mary Ann Ready and I became chums. I had known her before because two of her brothers were going to the Seminary with Bernie. As fate would have it, they both returned home soon after Bernie did. Mary Ann proved to be true blue. We were pals for the next two years of my high school days. I enjoyed every day because I was doing so well, and because I was thinking more and more about entering the convent when I graduated. I hadn't done anything about it though. I was just waiting to see what to do next.

By the next September, my Junior Year, the nuns helped me again. I still didn't have any money, so Sister Charles asked me if I would like to work for the NYA. What is that? Well, it seems that the US government had set aside funds to be used in any high school in the country for needy students. It was named National Youth Administration. The school could assign some task to be done regularly, and when the paper work was sent in each month the student would receive a check for $7.

I was in seventh heaven. Now I could pay the $2

tuition each month, pay $1 for the student bus ticket, and still have $4 left for things. I couldn't believe it. Here I was paying my own way for the last two years of high school. Needless to say I had more and more admiration for the IHM Sisters. Their kindness seemed unending.

So, here I was getting pretty settled into my studies while the rest of the family was going along in the best manner possible. However, all was not well. I could see that something was going to happen because I noticed that the cleaners was not thriving. It didn't take too much acumen to realize that Mama was doing most of the work. I would see her laboring on into the night sometimes. When I would look around for my father he would be out in the car sleeping. By now I realized that he had stopped doing any extra tasks needed to keep the business healthy. It was Mama who took the load of dirty clothes down to the jobber each day, and bring back those that were cleaned and ready for pressing. It didn't seem to matter to him that my mother also had a lot to do. When it came time to pick up or deliver it was either Mama or Barr who did the job.

It was soon apparent that my father was doing less and less each day. He would sometimes go out to the car in back in the middle of the day and have a nap. Mama would be in the shop working. We kids would come and go, but we couldn't help but observe all of this.

We gradually were more and more short of money. In a word, the business was failing after only about three years. My mother just couldn't carry the whole load herself. She was busy at her beautiful little sewing machine each day working on the ladies' things. My father didn't seem to have a clue about what was going down the drain. He had continued to run up bills at the local service station for gas and oil. He would talk the talk, but after awhile this was not going to be enough. He never seemed to work up a sweat even though he was using a steam press. I think he thought this would all go on forever, and we kids would then take over so he wouldn't have to work. Now I am making that up, but what else could have been his motivation.

The night I knew that we had really hit bottom was when we all went out to the car to drive home to 72nd Street. On this night I just could not believe my eyes. Every tire on our old Essex was flat. My father had not fixed any of them. I suppose he tried to talk the service station man into giving him some tires. But, his power of persuasion had finally run dry. There we were. What were we going to do? My mother was absolutely silent. Bev and I giggled a little bit out of embarrassment. Barr wasn't there.

My father put the key in the ignition, started the car, and we drove up Atlantic Avenue to our house, about two miles, on the flat tires. Of course, by the time we reached home the tires were in shreds. Pa parked the car, and we all went inside. Things were very quiet. I wondered what we would do the next day. Well, in the morning my folks drove down to the shop on the flat shreds. I went off to school. When I stopped at the shop after school I fully expected to see everything in good order, all repaired and ready to go. What a shock it was when I realized that my father had not done one thing to fix the flats. At the end of the day we all climbed into the car and drove up Atlantic Avenue on THE RIMS. I couldn't imagine how this could go on for a few more days.

Out of the blue my mother sold the business, press and all to someone who realized it was up for grabs and came in and made an offer. She got $400 for the whole kit and caboodle. My mother just made the decision then and there that she wasn't going to struggle with making the business a success. I don't think she even consulted with Pa. I think that she had reached the fed up stage with his lack of ambition. She took the $400, and that was that.

Pa didn't seem to care that his dream of owning his own business was over. I forget what he did with the old car. We never had one again. We must have taken the bus home. Common sense would tell one that my father would go out the very next day and start looking for a job. After all, I pointed out earlier in the story that all the men we knew had work somewhere. So there were jobs to be had. There was even the WPA which was available for out-of-work men. Maybe they weren't high paying, but at least it would bring in enough to support the family. My mother finally had had enough of my father's lack of attention to creditors. After all, one of his easiest outs was to say to anyone who stopped by for payment, "You'll have to talk to the Mrs." He never took responsibility for facing them. My mother told me later that she was just not going to continue that kind of behavior. She said that she wanted to be able to look everyone in the eye whenever she met them, and not be ashamed. So she took the whole $400 and paid every creditor a little bit on the bill. She told each one that someday she would repay them in full. A later part of this story will show that she did exactly that.

After a few days it looked as if my father was not going out to hit the pavement. She asked him when he was going to do it. She told me that he said we would live on the $400 until it ran out. When she told him that the money had gone to each and every creditor, and there was none left, he got very angry with her. But, Mama had had it by now. She told him that it was up to him to take care of the family like he should. He didn't say anything. I know for sure that he did not go out and get a job. In fact, I don't have one single memory of my father ever coming home with a check for work he had done, or a bag of groceries for us to eat, or putting any money on the table that he had earned. In a word, the cleaning business was his only stab at making a living. He didn't put enough energy into it to make it a success. So, that was that. He was around 44 years old at this time, the prime of life for most men.

These days were pretty traumatic for us all. There never was any violence in word or deed in our household, but there was a lot of tension now. I went off to school with Bev each day, but I was always worried about what was going to happen to us. Also, we didn't have very much to eat. Barr helped, and so did Bernie. But they were trying to establish themselves in the work world. We still went to church services as a family. My mother played the organ so beautifully. I noticed that she would go down to church oftener than before. I think she must have been praying about the whole situation. So was I.

I was doing ok at school because I had that little job that gave me enough money to get down there and back, plus a few cents a day for a candy bar for lunch.

We went along like this for several weeks or months. It is kind of hazy for me right now. But on a fateful Saturday the sky fell in. It was Bernie who stood up and took over the leadership of the family. He was about 20.

It all happened quite suddenly. We were all at home that morning getting ready for the day. Mama was in the kitchen.

I forget what was said by anyone, but my father went outside to the little garden he was nurturing. It was so meager that it would never have been enough to sustain us in any way. He was out there raking. Well, for some reason Bernie just blew up. I was mesmerized. Bernie ran out the front door and confronted my father in a loud and very angry voice. He was literally hollering at him. I didn't look out because I was so shocked. I could hear him tell my father to "get out". He kept yelling at him to leave right now, and not to show his face around the family again. I am sure my father was petrified because of this terrible ultimatum. I could hear him faintly begging Bernie not to do this to him. But Bernie was so enraged that he made Pa put down the rake, and go right out to the street and not turn back. I can still see my father's back as he trudged down to Atlantic Avenue. Bernie came inside and sat at the table without saying a word. My mother sat across from him and touched his hand. Barr, Bev, and I just stared at Bernie. After all, Bernie had given up his dream of becoming a priest so that he could help out the family. I believe he finally realized that our plight was because of the inability of my father to do a day's work. That must be what sent him over the edge. What a tragic thing for a son to have to do. I always felt so sorry that Bernie felt he had to take such a drastic step toward his father. It was one of the saddest days of my life and, quite possibly, of his. We all sat around the table and talked in low tones. We had never had such a violent scene take place before. I am sure my mother felt terrible about this happening to George, but it seemed that the circumstances of the last several months were pointing to something having to give.

George had shown no interest in saving the cleaners, no interest in building up trade, no interest in paying any bills at all, no interest in the welfare of his lovely wife and four children. I think that just about describes him. He seemed to have no ambition to do anything to better our situation. Even as I write this I am so sad for everyone involved. Bernie was the apple of my father's eye. My father was always so proud of him, but this pride did not make him want to show Bernie that he could provide for us all just as well as the next man. I am sure he did not dream that Bernie would, in the end, send him away. He probably was in a daze for hours. I can honestly say that my father was not a bad man. He was very personable and friendly to everyone. He was a wonderful talker. But none of these qualities would put food on the table unless he used them to obtain a job somewhere.

After we recovered our composure, things began to happen. In a way, it was kind of a relief to have everything come to a head like that, but it was still traumatizing. Even as I write about it I cry a little because it was such a sad end to my father having anything more to do with his family. I never saw him again. We talked about what we would do now. The two boys had small jobs that would carry us over the hump. I said I would try to work somewhere, but I didn't know where or when. Bev was only 14 or 15. She was hit very hard by this tragedy because she was Dad's favorite. He always said so, sometimes right in front of Barr and me. She was very quiet. But we all clung together.

The next morning we dressed up and went down to Mass at St. Athanasius. My father wasn't there. We wondered what happened to him that day. It seems that he went over to the O'Connell's who were friends from church and asked to stay there. I am sure the O'Connells wondered what on earth happened. On Sunday morning they must have driven my father back to our house while we were at Church because when we got home after Mass we noticed right away that the closet was cleared of all of his clothes.

I think one of the saddest aspects of all of this is that my father just didn't get it. I am sure that if he had started pounding the pavement right away and finding something to do my brother might have relented. But he never did that. He never ever got a job anywhere. When I think about that aspect of my father I realize that every single job that he had was gotten for him by somebody. He never ever found his own job. So I think that he was always waiting for someone to come up with the right job. My mother told me that sometimes over the years our good friends who worked in the oil fields or the shipyard would come over and talk to George about an opening at the plant. The opening was usually an unskilled job like sweeper or pipe cleaner. It didn't matter to him that this was a job for pay and could become an entry to higher opportunities. He would just turn down the kind offer, and continue to do nothing.

Soon we were all going about our lives as normally as possible. Sometimes we would get very low in food, but Mama would cook up some bullet soup for us. This was a concoction of flour and water that she spooned into boiling water in small pieces. She would call them bullets. Of course we would be laughing about it even though the meal was not very nourishing. You see, the water had no fat or meat in it. It was simply laced with salt and pepper, and maybe a little bit of lard. She still had a way of making even the sorriest time into something to laugh about. We were close as a family, and would try to take each day as it came with light hearts. We gradually began to live normal lives.

The boys were out working somewhere each day. Mama even got a job working with the WPA as a seamstress. So things were looking up. I got a job as a maid working for one of the Parish families. I was really supposed to be the baby sitter, but it turned into maid. I earned a dollar a day.

This job didn't last very long. I was a willing worker, but the lady acted like I was there to do all of her housework, laundry, ironing, babysitting, and cooking. I was just 16 and had no experience. I would arrive at seven thirty in the morning, and the husband would drive me home about six p.m. That was a long day. On top of everything else the lady would have me standing at the ironing board for hours at a time. Soon my feet began to give out on me. She looked at my old tennis shoes when I told her I had to sit down for awhile. She said the same words that teacher had said to me when I complained that my feet were freezing. She said, "Well, why don't you wear better shoes?" I just looked away and didn't answer. What did she think I was trying to do working for her? Soon after that I told my mother that I would have to do something else, but I couldn't be a maid all day. My feet wouldn't hold up. She was so kind and understanding as usual, and said I didn't have to do that anymore. She and the boys would bring in enough for us. And she was right. Besides I was earning a little with my job at school and paying my own way.

I was now a junior at St. Anthony's High School. I just loved it. I had made some good friends. I was doing very well in my classes. I thought the nuns were the kindest women I had ever met. And I had the NYA job at school. I was maturing. And I was still thinking about the possibility of entering the convent after graduation. I did not say much to anyone about it because I was still thinking and praying about it. It seemed like such a dream. I also thought of other things I could do and be, but being a nun and serving God in such a life seemed to always come out on top of my thoughts.

I hadn't said anything to the Sisters until one day. It

was near the end of my junior year. I was helping one of the Sisters after school. We were correcting papers. Right in the middle of our conversation about the papers I suddenly asked her, "What does someone have to do to be a Sister?" She looked at me and said, "Are you interested?" I said I was, but that I didn't know how to even get started, or if I really wanted to be one. Well, she was very kind, and said she would give me a brochure about it. She said that I was still too young to think about going, but to pray over it. She said she would talk to me about it later on. So I just went about my business, but I had the kernel of resolve in my heart.

Somehow I felt that I was going to end up giving my life to the service of God in some way. It didn't surprise me at all. It just felt right for me. What is strange about it all is that no one had ever talked to me about doing this. It was never a point of conversation in my family or even at Church. I consider it a true calling or vocation. Otherwise, how can I explain the strong resolve to pursue this possibility over the other things I could have been drawn to? I had experienced comfort and peace for several years whenever I would participate in religious events at Church or at the seminary when Bernie was there. So I just seemed to find the thought of the convent attracting me more and more. I knew nothing about the life of sacrifice that would be required especially if I lived up to the vows. I just knew that I would pursue the idea more.

My life just kept going on an even keel. At home we were all getting along fine, still struggling, but not in a quandary about it. Sometime during these days

Bernie joined the Civilian Conservation Corps or CCC. It was a government program for unemployed young men. These fellows were under the direction of the army, although they were not in the army. They were assigned to places in the National Parks and forests. They did all kinds of labor improving the place. They were paid $30 a month. So Bernie was gone for six months I believe. We, in the meantime, spent many happy evenings together around the table, playing cards, drinking tea, and often having a midnight snack which my mother would scare up for us.

These evenings were so quiet and peaceful. I could feel great hope rising in all of us. We would spend a lot of time talking and planning and laughing. I still had not said a word to my family about my plans. It was still too soon. After all I still had some great things to think about. The first thing was the prom. Ralph Dixon astonished me one day by asking me if I would go to the Prom with him. I was so surprised that I said these silly words, "I have to ask my mother first." He said "OK." Actually the truth of the matter was that I really did have to ask my mother, not for her permission to go to the Prom, but to see if there was a possibility of getting a long formal for the occasion. I didn't have anything resembling a formal. I didn't know if it was even possible for her to make one. So my dilemma was what was I going to wear?

Mama came through as usual. She knew that I was growing up, and that having a date with a nice young man was an important step for me. So she told me that the next day she would find a formal for me. I do not know whom she asked, but when I got home from school the next day there was a beautiful pink ruffly formal hanging on the bedroom door. I was ecstatic. She said she asked one of the parish ladies who had older daughters if she would lend us the formal for the Prom. Of course, who could say no to Mama? It needed a belt, so she bought some pretty narrow ribbons in pastel shades, braided them, mounted them on a backing, and produced the prettiest belt anyone had. I was more and more in admiration of my mother. She never let us down in any way.

The very next day I told Ralph that I would be happy to go with him to the Prom. He seemed to be pretty happy about it too. When the night came he came to my house with another couple. He had a beautiful corsage for me. Oh how grownup I felt. We had the prom in the Skyroom at the top of the Breakers Hotel which was the Hilton in those days. I have the beautiful ribbon belt in my box of keepsakes along with the dance cards for the Proms. My brothers also went with their dates, so we had a wonderful time from beginning to end.

What was so nice about all of this is that there was no one in our crowd who caused any trouble. We just had a wonderful time.
I spent my senior year in high school doing all kinds of things. First of all, things at home had calmed down quite a bit. The two boys were working somewhere. They had a busy social life. Of course, they had met some of my school chums, so they didn't want for dates. I had a social life that usually included the gang. We often would go over to the Ready's apartment on Alamitos Avenue for quick parties in the afternoon and evening. We would dance to all the

latest records.

Bev and I went to school together each day. She liked some of her teachers, but not others. It turned out that I liked all my teachers except my typing teacher, Sister Kathleen. I really didn't learn a thing from her. I was doing well in everything else. In fact I realized that I was a very good student. It surprised me because so many of my classmates had been attending Catholic School for twelve years. But, somehow or other, I had managed to assimilate most of what I had been taught in public school. It sure came in handy. My biggest surprise was how well I did in Religion class. All those Saturdays at catechism class really paid off. There were so many times that I could just come up with the answer with ease. I even surprised myself most of the time. Anyway, I was rolling along.

By midwinter of my senior year I had definitely decided that I wanted to try the convent. I still didn't talk about it very much, but I began to have a dream of serving God in any way He asked for the rest of my life. Of course, I weighed and measured all the other options. They weren't half as attractive to me. I envisioned myself as a great missionary, a mother and wife, teacher or nurse. I know I was willing to work hard for my dream. I knew it would be humble life, but I didn't care. After all I had managed to roll with the punches for the last ten years, so why couldn't I achieve my dream? I prayed and prayed about it.

When I got home after school Mama was already there. She had returned from her WPA job so she was resting on the couch. I swallowed a couple of times, and then sat down beside her on the couch. She said,

"What is it, dear?" I said that I had been thinking about going to the convent right after graduation. It seemed like something I could really do. We talked about it for awhile. I am sure she wasn't too sure about the life because she didn't know any nuns either. Anyway, she looked at me for a long time with those wonderful brown eyes and said, "Well, dear, if that's what you want to do, then it is fine with me." We then talked about when I would be going, and what would I need to get ready for such a big step in my life. I told her I didn't know these details yet because I needed to have her permission to go. I was walking on cloud nine after our little chat. Mama was always so supportive of each of us, so I felt her approval and love.

The next day I talked to Sister Eymard again and told her that I had my mother's approval to go to the convent. She said she would tell me what the next steps would be. Well, needless to say, I couldn't believe that I was on the verge of making a huge decision in my life. I felt very grown-up and responsible. I knew that there were going to be things that I would need, but what?

This all happened about March in my senior year. I was doing very well in my studies, and I was keeping busy with several interesting activities. The biggest one was that Sister Madonna, my principal, asked me if I would help out Sister Julia, the second grade teacher, by taking her class for one hour every day. I was very flattered but nervous. The only teaching I had done thus far was to teach catechism to little children every Saturday morning in Huntington Beach. That was an ongoing nice experience, but this new one in the second grade was a challenge. I found out right away that the reason they needed me was that Sister Julia was scheduled to teach the high school chorus/glee club/choir for an hour each morning. So she gave me the Teacher's guide for the reading lesson. I studied it all the way home on the bus so that the next day I would have the right words to say to the little ones. I must have done ok because the children were always very easy to be with, and Sister Julia and the other Sisters were impressed. I did this the whole senior year. This task was the job I did to merit the $7 each month. I feel I really did earn my own way. My only regret about the arrangement was that I couldn't take choir. I had been singing in my mother's choir for about eight years, and I was developing a pretty nice voice. I went to all performances, but I didn't always know the songs real well. So I guess I traded off one great experience for another.

I look back on all this and am convinced the good Lord was preparing me for something. My teaching stint must have impressed the nuns because many of them were still commenting on it years later. My other teaching stint, catechism was also very interesting. The parish priest at St. Simon and Jude Parish in Huntington Beach planned it. He recruited me and three of my friends from our senior class to go down there each Saturday to help him with the large group of kids he had for catechism. The catechism was my forte, so I didn't hesitate in volunteering to go. My Friends Mary Ann Ready, Mary A. McEvilly, and Mary Margaret O'Regan all said they would help out. So every Saturday morning, for many months Father would pick us up outside Mary Ann Ready's house on Alamitos Avenue and drive us down to Huntington

Beach.

The first time he took us down there he asked us to separate into two groups. Two of us would teach with him in the church. He would take the other two out to a little farming community called Talbert. Mary Ann Ready and I volunteered to go to Talbert. It was all agricultural. Well, you can imagine our surprise when we arrived the first Saturday and greeted a small group of about ten children. Father showed us the place we would teach and believe it or not it was a chicken house. Yes, it was the real thing. There was a warm brooder over in the corner with all kinds of puffy little yellow chicks peeping away to their heart's content. There were two benches placed inside near the brooder. We all sat down and proceeded to teach/learn our religion. The little kids were the children of the farm workers on the ranch we were on. They were very well behaved. Mary Ann and I were usually laughing at the primitive conditions, but we would say in our youthful enthusiasm, "It's all for God." We did this the whole year. I can still hear the little cheeps of the chicks.

That nice priest rewarded us in an interesting way. It so happened that there was a gigantic Catholic Conference and festival held in L.A. that spring. There were all kinds of meetings going on all over the diocese. Bishops came from all over the world. There were also some very fancy luncheons and dinners attended by all the national hierarchy and prominent Catholics.

Father decided that he would buy us tickets to a fancy luncheon in town. It was at the Coconut Grove in the

Ambassador Hotel on Wilshire Boulevard. We dressed up in our best things, and he took the four of us up there. I had never been to such a posh event in my life. And, of course, we had all heard of the Coconut Grove because it was famous for being the special place of the Hollywood stars, and the big bands - we were agog. After I got home I had to relate every detail to my whole family. They all said that was a special thing to do for us struggling catechists. I find myself smiling at the memory still.

I continued to be very busy during my senior year. Right in the middle of the year our Principal, Sister Madonna, got a blood clot on her leg. That meant she would be out of circulation for a long while. So there were other sisters sent to take her place. Because things were rather tentative with them no one took up the task of organizing for a yearbook or newspaper. I always wished I could have had them as mementos, but it was not meant to be.

Beside my classes, which were pretty taxing, I was a member of the basketball team. We played other Catholic high schools in the area. I was a center. In those days it was thought that girls could not stand the wear and tear of running back and forth on the court, so the court was divided into three segments crosswise. Each end was for the forwards and guards. The middle section was for the centers. I must have been pretty fast on my feet to play this position because I had to run back and forth catching the ball, dribble twice, and then pass the ball to my forwards. It was fun. I don't remember how many games we won or lost, but we looked real sharp in our culottes. Later Beverly would be a star on the team.

I went to the Prom again in my senior year. Joe Ready asked me to be his date. I liked Joe. He was already part of the group that we palled around with. I hurried home to tell my mother, and she didn't let me down. As soon as I mentioned it she said she would borrow the pretty pink dress again. I was elated. She prettied it up as before. When I tried it on, however, she said I had grown about an inch. What to do? She thought for a minute, and then came up with a wonderful solution. She would add a piece to the underskirt to lengthen it, and put pretty lace around the bottom. It would look like a two-layered dress. How can you beat a mother like that? I was ecstatic. So we all went again. Both Bernie and Barr asked someone from our crowd. My mother must have been astounded the night of the prom to see her little brood all grown up. The boys by now had bought very good looking sport coats. They were so handsome. We had a wonderful time at the dance. It was in the Hilton Hotel Sky Room down on Ocean Avenue. It is still there. Even today I marvel that we all got along so well, and no one did anything to get us into trouble. I thoroughly enjoyed it all.

It was during this year that I received the Sacrament of Confirmation at St. Athanasius Church. Bishop Cantwell did the honors. I asked Miss Anna Hartnett to be my sponsor. I took the name Anne. She was pretty thrilled about it. She and her sister, Margaret, were very good friends of ours in the parish.

One day Sister Eymard asked me if I wanted to go with her up to the Motherhouse in Hollywood to meet the Mother General. I said I was ready to go and find out what I needed to know about it all. She took me the following Friday. She was going up for the weekend because she was taking College classes, so she asked a couple of the high school boys if they would drive us up there and bring me home to 72nd Street. I dressed up as best I could and told my mother I would be a little late. She was in favor of my plans because she had earlier made a special trip down to see Sister Eymard to see if this was all for real. Sister said that I showed definite signs of a vocation but that time would tell. My mother was satisfied with that I guess because she encouraged me all along the way.

We arrived at Immaculate Heart Convent at Western and Franklin around four o'clock. I was shown into a lovely parlor in the front of the very large building. I sat there quietly, kind of nervous. Pretty soon I heard walking and the gentle sound of rosary beads which the sisters wore on the side of their habits. Then into the small room came a most dynamic woman with Sister Eymard. Her name was Mother Eucharia. She was the head of the whole order, the boss. She smiled at me and gave me a hug. Then she sat down with me a talked about the life of a sister. Did I think I would really be happy in this kind of life? How long had I been thinking about it? Did I realize that I would be making vows to God? Was I prepared to do anything asked of me, and be humble about it?

What questions. I thought about each one and answered as best I could. I told her that the life did not frighten me at all. I would do my best to be faithful to my promises to God. She must have been satisfied because she told me that the entrance date would be August 23, 1941- only a few months away. There was so much to do.

I had to get my Baptism Certificate and a letter of recommendation from my pastor, Father O'Sullivan. He had seen me grow up so he was pretty excited that I was choosing religious life - and I was from his parish. It didn't even have a Catholic School. He wrote a very nice letter about my character and I sent everything off to Immaculate Heart. In a few days I received a letter confirming that I had been accepted as a Postulant in the Order together with a list of the things I was to bring with me.

I needed two Postulant dresses with a cape that went down to the waist. A swatch of black material was included in the letter together with the number of the pattern. I lucked out entirely because my mother could sew like crazy. We went down to Walker's Department Store on Pine Avenue and bought the material and the pattern. So that would be my outfit for the months I would be a postulant.

The list included a lot of other things. Mama could sew them all – underpants made of white crinkle crepe material, slip made of the same. I needed black shoes – one pair – and black long hose, preferably lisle cotton not silk. The usual items were included in the list – comb, toothbrush, toothpaste, and personal things, nightgowns also made of crinkle crepe, bathrobe and slippers. We also were asked to bring towels, wash cloths and one blanket. All of this seemed reasonable to us, but Mama was going to be busy. So she did what she was so good at – she invited a lot of her parish lady friends to bring their sewing machines up to our house, and join her in a sewing bee for Doris. They were all enthusiastic about it and so was I. In this way I arrived at the convent with everything intact. I swear my dresses were the best made ones there among the fifteen postulants, or at least I liked to think so. A few weeks before I left in August these same ladies had a surprise farewell for me. They presented me with a purse of cash to help with any last minute things. I was very touched by them all, and told them so. Some of them cried.

I graduated from St. Anthony's in June of 1941. I was seventeen years old. I believe I was named fourth in the class in academics. That was a pretty good confidence builder. I bade farewell to my classmates, but not my chums. We continued to enjoy our youthful pursuits all summer.

We went to the beach, to Orange County Park, to the Pike. In fact, they had a farewell party for me at our house. They all gave me handy presents like scissors, mending tape, etc. I helped Mama as much as I could, but I couldn't get a permanent job because I was leaving in August. But we were doing so much better by now. The whole family kind of gathered around me during the last few weeks when we would have our midnight snacks at the dining room table. We would play cards and talk about our dreams. It was a very special time, and I always cherish their love and good wishes. I would miss them always. In a way, I thought I was going away from the world and into a mysterious life behind a wall. I really didn't know if I would see them very often again. Life was beckoning to me. Little did I know that my adventures were just beginning.

Last family photo the day I entered the Convent
L-R: Barr, Doris, Mama, Beverly & Bernie

House No. 10 - 1941

The Convent

Franklin Avenue - Hollywood, California

The big day finally arrived. My mother had made arrangements for Mrs. Burgard to drive us all up there because we had no car. The night before I was so excited that I couldn't sleep. I was going into a world of mystery and wonder. My suitcase was packed with my new clothes that my dear mother had made so lovingly for me. I don't remember our talking around the table that last evening. But, I am sure we talked about the changes that were now happening to us. Bernie had said earlier that he was going into the Navy in a few weeks. Things were happening. It was a Friday. I had the feeling that everyone was kind of mystified by my decision. No one questioned it, though, which made it easier for me.

I was mystified myself. Here I was choosing to live a life of personal sacrifice rather than wait for my prince to come or for my ship to come in. I had gotten to this point in a way that seemed compelling to me. I had made all the arrangements as a young adult. I just wasn't a child anymore.

This was my choice. Of course, I would always love my family, especially my mother, but I was going to try my wings in the rather exotic place called a convent. I didn't know what awaited me because no one seemed to know. The Sisters at St. Anthony's didn't enlighten me either. So I was filled with apprehension which was tempered by curiosity and hope. I was seventeen years and four months old.

On Saturday afternoon, August 23, 1941 Mrs. Burgard arrived and we prepared to leave. I wore my best dress that, in reality, was the only new dress I had owned since I was about seven. It was a beautiful sky blue in color with a pleated skirt. I got it for my high school graduation. I wore it only a few times before this day. Today would be the last time I would wear it. My mother had on her best dress. My brothers and Beverly wore their best things also. Before we got into the car we lined up together in front of our little house and had our picture taken by Mrs. Burgard. It was the last time we would ever be together like that. I treasure that photo so much because it shows us pretty grown up. It is a sign to me that we made it. The trials and setbacks we had been experiencing were fading away. The two boys looked especially handsome in their sports jackets, shirts, and ties. Barr wore fancy shoes. Mama looks very proud of all of us.

When we arrived at the convent my whole family was amazed. The Immaculate Heart Motherhouse was such a large building. We were greeted by some happy looking nun and ushered into the big fancy parlor. There were several families there before us, all for the same reason. They were bringing their daughter or sister to the cloister. My heart was beating a mile a minute. I looked around and couldn't contain my excitement. I was thinking that this is what I wanted to do. My family sat quietly on the scattered couches and chairs. The parlor was really very beautifully furnished. I learned later that some wealthy friends of the Sisters had donated all the furniture including the grand piano in the corner. There was quiet talking going on from all the families that were arriving. It turned out that there were fifteen of us young ladies entering the convent that day. I would not be without companionship. And there were nuns everywhere greeting all the families so warmly. They seemed happy and hospitable.

In a few minutes I was whisked away by two nuns who took me and my little suitcase upstairs to a very large room. There were already several young ladies in the room being assisted with changing clothes. My two new friends helped me change from the beautiful blue dress into the dress of a postulant. I put on my long black stockings, my crinkle crepe slip, my black dress and cape, and lastly, black shoes. The last thing they put on me was a black veil of very light net material. They just laid it over my head, and I secured it with bobby pins. I was transformed.

The two helpers then lead me back downstairs to the parlor. There I approached my family. They all looked at me with a kind of affectionate awe. They had seen the clothes that my mother was working on, but here I was officially wearing them in the convent. We all sat together talking quietly, visiting, and laughing. They were so supportive of me that I will always appreciate it. I could sense that this was probably the biggest and most serious moment of my life. It was like a girl going away to be married. I belonged to God now, but I also belonged to my dear ones.

Soon we noticed that there were quite a few girls all dressed as I now was sitting with family. Everyone was excited. The parlor soon filled with many IHMs who fluttered around greeting each family. The most loquacious and warm of them all was Mother

Eucharia. She was the one who interviewed me. I was impressed with her then, but today I was amazed. She welcomed my family and me in such a gracious manner that we were all smiling and laughing with her. She passed from group to group telling each one that tomorrow was the Feast of the Immaculate Heart, the patroness of our Community. She told my family that they could come back tomorrow, Sunday, in the afternoon for a visit if they wished. I was promptly worried about it because I didn't know if Mrs. Burgard could bring them back. She said she would. I said that tomorrow I would tell them all about my first day in the Convent. As they were preparing to leave I gave a big hug to each one. They hugged me back. I told them that I would miss them, but we would see each other soon. I hugged and kissed my mother the most. She was my model of kindness and strength. I was hoping to be half the woman she was. Thus ended my childhood.

After we all waved goodbye to our families we were introduced to our Novice Mistress, Mother Rita. She escorted us out of the parlor and across the open patio that looked just like a cloister, to the east wing of the building. We were in the front room of the lower floor. This room was to be our meeting room, study room, classroom, etc. for the next year and eight months. I looked around at the other postulants. I couldn't believe it but there were fifteen of us. Almost all had just graduated from high school like I had, but there were a couple who were a year or two older, and one who was in her early thirties. I was so excited. The group gathered around Mother Rita. She assigned us our places in the group. It turned out that some

Sister had been stationed at the front door as we arrived. Her job was to write down our names as we arrived. The first to arrive would be number one, and so on. It turned out that I was number seven, so I got desk number seven. From then on for the remainder of my days in the convent my place on the roster of Community members would always be in the order of entrance, not actual age. It was an interesting concept that we soon got used to. Later we learned that it was called the Order of Precedence.

Since we would henceforth be referred to as a group I will introduce you to them all in order. Number one was Nancy Raphael from Beverly Hills and IHHS. Next came Cassy Shea from Conaty HS. Then Mary Dambach was from Conaty. Mary Davin was next from IHHS. Ethel Weber was number five. She was from Conaty. Then Lucille Keating was also from Conaty.

Then I came in the order of precedence. I was from St. Anthony. Elaine Dunn from Conaty had worked for a year before coming. Jean Petersen was from Randsburg HS. Dolores Quevedo was from Conaty. Jeanne Albert was from St. Anthony, but I didn't know her. She had been a sophomore, so I was very surprised to see her. Next came Irene Haverluck who was a couple of years older. She was from San Pedro. There were two others whose names have faded from my memory because they didn't stay very long. Last came Carmen Ochoa who was the oldest. We soon found that she fit in with the rest of us very well. She was from Azusa.

We soon found that we were not alone in the novitiate.

The group from the year before had already received the habit and their white veil. They were waiting for us. They were called novices. They wore the complete habit with the exception of wearing a white veil instead of a black one. They also had their sister names, and were introduced to us by Mother Rita. I thought they looked so holy. Each one was so dignified and beautiful. I was surprised that there were only six of them. We learned that they would begin wearing the black veil when they made their first vows in April. Mother Rita told us that we were the biggest group so far. The novices later told us that they were petrified at the coming of so many postulants. They and Mother Rita had to give us the good example and training to become Sisters of the Immaculate Heart.

We were all seated at our appointed desk. The first thing we did was to introduce ourselves to the whole group. The second thing that happened was that Mother Rita told us that we would be addressed as "Miss" for the duration of our postulancy, so I immediately became "Miss Murphy" to everyone there. Mother Rita then took us through the area called the Novitiate. It consisted of three rooms on the ground floor of the convent. The front room was our study/meeting room. The middle room was Mother Rita's office. It was here that she would have words with you if need be.

The back room was for work and recreation. This room was lined on one side with cupboards. We were each assigned one big shelf as our spot for any of our things. It was interesting that we did not give the clothes we wore to the convent back to our families that first day. Mother Rita explained kindly that we were to put all of those clothes in the suitcase we had brought. Later the suitcases were all stored in a nearby boiler room. She said that we should keep those things here for awhile in case we would decide that this wasn't the life for us. In a way it was a wise thing to do, but I determined that I was going to do my very best to be successful in my chosen life. As it turned out, two of the group returned to their homes in a few months.

The next thing we did was go with Mother Rita and the Novices to find the cubicles where we would sleep. They led us upstairs, and upstairs, and upstairs. It turned out that we actually had to go up four flights of stairs to get to the right place. There was no elevator in the whole place. When we arrived there we found that a large room called a dormitory had been partitioned off into fifteen separate cubicles. Mother Rita told us these were called cells. From then on that was how we referred to our room.

Each of the cells was made private by the use of white sheets that were suspended on pipes attached to the ceiling that had been arranged all around the room. Each cell contained a single bed, a chair, and a dresser with three drawers. It was flat on top. There was no mirror. There were two or three coat hangers for our dresses. We could see all the cells at once because the separating sheets were pulled back. This was how the dormitory looked during the day. At night, when we went up to bed, we all pulled the sheets closed so we had privacy. No one was supposed to go into another person's cell except for a good reason. Mother Rita made a point of speaking very quietly while she was showing us around the dormitory and pointing out the nearby bathroom. She said this was because it was a rule that we were not to talk at all in the dormitory or in the bathroom. These were places of silence. We soon learned that there was more to silence than we expected.

After this tour we heard a bell toll. What a sound. To me it was beautiful. The chapel bell was ringing to let the Sisters know that they had five minutes to get to Chapel for prayers. Mother Rita escorted us down to the chapel. After showing each of us our special spot we joined with all the Sisters who were stationed there in prayers. I was overwhelmed with happiness that I was actually there. I couldn't believe it. How had I come from being a schoolgirl, who seemed ordinary in every way, to this point where I was certain God wanted me to be? All I could do was pray thankfully for my vocation, and ask for the graces to be strong enough to carry out everything required to make me a worthy nun.

The chapel itself was beautiful. It had rows of pews in the usual configuration of that time. Up and down both sides of the chapel there were individual kneelers called a prie- dieu. These kneelers had a little door on the front that opened out. The sister could put her prayer books inside. We sat in the pews near the rear of the chapel. Of course, we sat in order of precedence. We never had to put a hat on because we always wore our flimsy black veils. We kept our prayer books in a rack right in front of our space. It was attached to the pew in front of us. It was thrilling to me to hear the sisters' respond to all the prayers together. We postulants immediately became part of the Community.

At the end of prayers a sister went out on the porch bordering the chapel to ring the bell. It was customary to ring the bell for the Angelus at six o'clock.

This is a prayer that is said in three parts, the bell rang three times for each part of the Angelus. We had learned to say the prayer in school, so I knew the responses right off. At the end of the Angelus all the nuns proceeded to the refectory for supper. We walked along the porch and a short corridor before reaching it. When we entered the refectory Mother Rita showed us to our places. Of course, we were in precedence so we always sat next to the same person. I noticed that all the nuns who came in turned and bowed slightly toward the crucifix hanging on the wall. No one said a word. It became apparent very soon that the youngest always came in first followed by all the rest, in order, the last being the Mother General who was Mother Eucharia.

Everyone stood behind her chair with hands under capes or scapulars. As soon as everyone was in and standing still the Mother began the Grace before Meals. It was rather long and was included in our Community Prayer Book, We didn't know any of it yet, but we would soon be chirping away with the best of them. As soon as Mother was finished she said in a clear voice, Benedicamus Domino. All the nuns answered, Deo Gratias. At that moment everyone pulled out their chairs and sat down. The biggest surprise was that everyone began talking and laughing and generally showing a very happy spirit. Mother Rita explained to us later that usually there was no talking at meals. Someone would read from a spiritual book loud enough for everyone to hear. Eating was done quietly and quickly. But, on special occasions the Superior of the house could say Benedicamus Domino and the sisters could enjoy camaraderie during the meal. This was the custom in every convent in the order. Today was, indeed, a special day for the Community.

I have to tell you now about the refectory table. When we arrived at our places that first night there were no dishes on the table, just sugar bowls and salt and pepper. I wondered what was going to happen. Well, as soon as we sat down every nun opened a small drawer right in front of her place. Inside, to my amazement, was a complete set of dishes plus a cloth napkin. We pulled them out, and placed them on the table. The tables were very long and had no tablecloths on them, so the dishes made quite a clatter. There must have been about seventy-five Sisters plus all of us in the refectory. For a few moments, until everyone could get their service on the table, it was very noisy. The novices served our table. The professed nuns served all the others. Professe means those who have made their vows, and were considered real members of the community. They were the ones who wore the black veil all the time. At the end of the meal I was looking to see who would clear the tables. What a surprise it was when the novices came in and placed two large enamel bowls in front of every three people. We were looking at Mother Rita to see what this was about. It turned out that the top bowl was filled with warm soapy water. The bottom bowl was empty. There was a small cloth kitchen towel at the side of the set of bowls. Mother

Rita placed the bowls side by side and proceeded to hold her plate over the empty bowl, and with a small scrub mop she directed the warm soapy water over her plate until it was clean. She then dried it with the towel.

We all followed suit being more or less successful. The idea was to keep the soapy water clean so the next person could use it. We called this arrangement silver bowls. No one seems to know how that term came about, but we think maybe only the silverware was washed this way in the beginning. When the community became larger they must have included the dishes in the process. Each of the sets was meant to be used by three or four people. Mother Rita was careful about anyone who had a cold. They were to take their dishes out to the sink and wash them there.

So ended my first supper in the convent. By now I am agog with all the new and strange things I had learned. We all knew the meal was ended when the Mother rose from her chair. Everyone followed suit. Grace after meals was long, and some of it was said on our knees. All the nuns knelt as one except very infirm ones. We finished the prayer, and proceeded directly to the chapel for a short prayer.

Then we went downstairs to the third room in back. Of course it was called the back room. We were told we would now have recreation. This meant simply that we sat around and talked with the novices and with Mother Rita. She always spent some time telling us what was expected of us, and explaining that there was much to be learned about religious life. It was her job to see that we were well informed and formed by the time we made our vows in a year and eight months. I became aware that she had a wonderful sense of humor that put us all at ease. I liked my companions also because they were light-hearted and earnest just as I was.

At the end of recreation the chapel bell rang again. It was time for evening prayers. All the sisters converged on the chapel and said the rosary. After this prayer the sisters began to chant the Office of the Blessed Virgin. This was a collection of Psalms arranged in such a way that every holy season of the year was honored. The sisters chanted in a single tone taking turns from one side of the aisle to the other – back and forth until the evening prayer was done. It took about fifteen minutes. It was pretty inspiring to hear the voices praising God in such a solemn manner. I had never heard it before. All of these prayers were said in Latin.

By now it is getting close to eight-thirty p.m. Mother Rita said that the sisters rising bell would ring at five-thirty a.m. Therefore it was customary to retire by nine p.m. so as to have enough rest for the work of the following day. So she took us up to the dormitory. Before saying goodnight to us she told us that we were being given a special dispensation to sleep late in the morning. We were all making approval sounds quietly. Someone asked her what time we were to rise. She said, "You are to get up at six a.m." We all started to titter a little bit because that seemed very early. She pointed out that all the rest of the nuns would rise at 5:30 a.m. when the bell would be rung. We all went into the dormitory smiling, but not talking.

I went immediately to my assigned cell. We all did. I closed the curtains surrounding the bed, chair and chest of drawers. I stood there looking around at the pure white walls surrounding me. How quiet we all were. I'm sure all the other postulants were taking note as I was. I pulled the suitcase out from under the bed and took out all the clothes and things. I hung up on the curtain rod my beautiful Postulant dresses that my mother had made. I put everything else into the chest. This piece of furniture was only waist high. It had three drawers. On top of the chest was an enamel bowl that resembled a wash bowl. Mother Rita had told us earlier that we were to fill that bowl with water from the tap when we finished our evening bath. The basin was to be used in the morning to wash our faces when we got up in the morning. It always was an eye-opener then because the water was usually quite cold. I just chalked it up to the kind of things a Sister must do. I had my washcloth at the ready for the morning. My bed was narrow, but ample for me. It had a plain white bedspread on it, and one pillow with a white case. Everything was unadorned, just plain as could be.

My bed had one blanket on it. This was of special comfort to me because it was the one I had brought from home. Included on the list of things we were to bring to the convent was a request for one blanket. I asked my mother if I could take our best blanket because most of what we had were pretty worn. We called it 'the Indian blanket.' This was a beautiful Hudson's Bay weave blanket that my parents had bought sometime along the way. It was cream colored all over, but had the distinctive bright stripes of color on both ends. It was worn somewhat, but I thought it was perfect. I had put it on the bed earlier so I was all ready for the night.

After a warm bath in the bathroom directly across the hall from the dorm and taking care of my evening personal ablutions, I returned to my cell. Before I got into bed I knelt down beside it and said earnest prayers. I thanked God for bringing me this far. I really did consider it miraculous in a way because there seemed to be so many obstacles that just melted away as time passed. I prayed especially for my mother and my brothers and sister. I knew in my heart that God would take care of them, but I remembered them in prayer every day from then on. I prayed to God for the grace to do the right thing and to be strong in my resolve to serve Him all the rest of my life.

With that all said, I jumped into bed and lay there staring at the ceiling. Everyone around me was very quiet. Someone turned out the lights at nine o'clock. A little later Mother Rita came around to each cell. She opened the curtain slightly and I felt a sprinkle of water. She was giving us a blessing with holy water. That was certainly comforting. I was very cozy under the precious Indian blanket. I fell asleep smiling. My first day in the convent was over.

The next day was Sunday, August 24th. It was the Feast of the Immaculate Heart. I was excited because my family was coming back to see me in the afternoon. I would have so much to tell them. We arose at 6 a.m. This was supposed to be our late sleep. That was my first inkling that not everything in the convent was going to be easy to do. We went down three flights of stairs to the chapel.

Everyone was already there. We took our places, prayed, had Mass and Communion, more prayers, and then breakfast. Because this was our biggest feast day the refectory was decorated with flowers. It looked beautiful to me. We had 'Benedicamus' at breakfast so we all got a little more acquainted with one another. The other postulants were very cheery and comfortable to be with. Mother Rita seemed quite happy with us all. The six novices up at the head of our table were beautiful and seemed very holy.

Mother Rita told us that after breakfast we were to go up to the dormitory to make our beds and freshen up. That was fine with me until she said that each and every day we were to completely strip our beds, and make them over from scratch. She showed us how she expected the corners to look, and how there should be no 'just throwing the covers up' technique. So I started learning the very first day that there was a right and a wrong way to do things. She explained that there would be many times during our novitiate when we would be tested for our attitude toward communal living, for our desire to keep the vows that we would make to God a year and a half hence. I said to myself that I would pass every test. There were some slip ups on the way. But, today was the first big day for us.

Mother Rita explained that we were part of a large institution on the corner of Western and Franklin in Hollywood. Immaculate Heart ran a four-year college up the hill which we would attend starting in a few weeks.

There was a large high school for girls on the premises together with an elementary school starting with first grade. So we were not alone there in that big place. On top of all this we were informed that there were boarders living there. They attended the college, high school, and elementary school. There were nuns assigned to watch over all the boarders.

We found out that the reputation of the schools was such that girls were sent there from various parts of the world. Many came from Latin America to go to school and learn English at the same time. There were boarders from Europe and various parts of the U. S. I was amazed and impressed when I saw some of the boarders. There were little girls in first grade all the way up to seniors in college. Nowadays, I don't think anything like that exists anywhere around this part of California. In addition to all these young people there were the nuns. The place was just full of them. We learned that all the elderly retired and ill nuns lived there as well as all the nuns who were teachers in the three schools there on the campus. Also, we noticed that there were nuns who didn't teach there at Immaculate Heart but were assigned to some local parochial schools. Sometimes the parish schools were built before the convent, so the nuns had to commute from IHM to their parishes. After breakfast each day the whole place became very busy with nuns going every which way to get to their assignments.

Today was exciting because it was the day our families could come to visit us. I was just so excited and ready to tell them all about things. After lunch we were all down in the front room which was where our desks were. I awaited the call to go to the parlor. I was so thrilled that my whole family came back to see how I had survived the night. I told them all of my adventures, and explained that we would have 'visiting day' only once a month. In a way they were relieved because they had to ask Mrs. Burgard or someone else to bring them, or take the Red Car. I was always aware that it was a hardship for my mother to come, but she was there for most of the visiting days. I told them that we had permission to write a letter once a month. I remember that we had a bittersweet visit.

They told me that Bernie had enlisted in the Navy. He was going to boot camp the coming week. I looked at my mother. What a time in her life to have two of her children leave home for good. And both within a week of one another. As usual she was cheerful, but sad at the same time. We talked about Bernie's dreams awhile, and then we all hugged each other. I kept the tears back as best I could because he seemed so excited about making the decision. A little later I showed my family up to the beautiful chapel. They said it was wonderful. I thought it was just perfect for prayer. Of course, it was especially beautiful this day because it was the Feast of the Immaculate Heart of Mary, our patroness. It was decorated with a million flowers. I told them about all the people who lived here. They were amazed at that. By about 4 o'clock visiting hours ended so they had to leave. Once again I hugged them all, especially my mother, and saw them all to the door. I did not see Bernie again until he was out of boot camp and receiving his assignment.

Starting right away we were on the convent schedule. This was an important part of communal life, and it made it easy for each member to know where she should be at all times. The schedule was as follows:

5:30 - Rise, do ablutions, say private prayers, and get dressed

6:00 - Go to chapel for morning prayers and meditation

6:30 – Holy Mass

7:10 - Chant two parts of the Office (Psalms)

7:30 - Breakfast

8:00 - Community Room for prayers and announcements

11:45 - Chapel for noon prayers. We recited the Trisagion that was a special prayer to the Holy Trinity

12:00 - Lunch in refectory

At this point everyone was supposed to get ready for their work of the day, teaching, nursing, being retired, caring for the boarders, laundry, housework, etc.

Everyone became quite busy with whatever task they had to do. So we postulants did the same thing each day. We made our beds the right way, took care of personal matters, and hurried downstairs to the front room where Mother Rita awaited us. The novices were usually there ahead of us because they were used to not wasting a minute. The fifteen of us soon learned to do things quickly and with dispatch then report to the proper place. I think that from the very beginning I was a morning person simply because we had to do so many things at the early hours of each day. I became accustomed to doing things right away.

It should be noted here that whenever we didn't have 'Benedicamus' at the meal we ate in silence. However, it was not a dead silence because someone would be assigned to read to the whole group in a very loud voice. At the Motherhouse where we were it was the custom to have members of the novitiate do the reading. Mother Rita assigned the novices to do this for a few weeks. The breakfast reading was always "The Imitation of Christ" by Thomas a'Kempis. Because this was the only book ever read at breakfast it didn't take long for us to be able to quote long passages from it. The whole community could do it. The reading at the other two meals was from a spiritual book chosen by Mother Rita or Mother Eucharia. Thus I became aware right away that I was living in an atmosphere that promoted spirituality and love of God. I gradually fit in to the routine, and tried to do my best with new things.

I soon realized how all the tasks were taken care of. We did not have servants. We were instructed on being of service to all around us, no matter what the cost. To train us for this Mother Rita assigned each of us to a job which we always called charges.

Every month or so she would change our charges around so we would have experience in doing all the tasks needed in the convent. She would watch to see that we did the charge correctly. If we had the chapel as our charge we had to dry mop the entire floor, and dust every single pew and prie-dieu top and bottom.

The whole place had to glisten every time one did the job. It wouldn't do to do it well one day, and slough off the next. We were admonished that we were not doing any task for ourselves or even Mother Rita's inspection. We were serving God by doing each task, no matter how humble. So gradually we were getting the idea that work itself is noble. No job was too menial. There were all kinds of tasks to be done – the chapel, the study rooms, the dormitory, the bathrooms, the parlors, even porches. We were taught to accept each assignment with equanimity, and do it to the best of our ability.

Soon we were also very occupied after each meal. The whole group of postulants was assigned to go into the big kitchen and man the dishwasher. All the boarders had china dishes and glasses that had to be handled carefully. The nuns did their dishes at the table as I have described. But there were all the bowls and serving platters, teapots, pitchers, and a mountain of silverware to be washed. After awhile we all became very adept at running the machine and filling the dish tray. It was a hot and hard job. We would trade off filling the trays with dirty dishes to run through the machine, or stand at the end of the contraption and dry everything that came out. We didn't have an automatic dryer.

Every so often there would be a catastrophe. Sometimes one or the other of us would miscalculate the weight of a tray, or slip on something. In which case all would go flying through the air. Then there would be a very loud crash. All the dishes or glasses would be broken. Mother Rita used some of these events to teach a certain amount of humility to the postulant or novice. She also wanted to impress upon us the importance of being careful. She would ask the one who did the dastardly deed to pick up all the pieces and place them in a basket which she was to carry around for the whole day. The first time that happened I was shocked. Then I thought that this must be the way things were done in the convent.

Of course, the poor thing who had to carry the basket did so with a lot of chagrin but no temper tantrum. Mother Rita was testing the postulant to see whether she was able to accept a hard-to-swallow directive. There would be many tests during the next year and eight months for each of us. I never had to carry the basket around, but I commiserated with the ones who did. There were other tests along the way.

The first couple of weeks passed very quickly. We followed a daily routine that included about three hours of prayer, some study, conferences from Mother Rita, exercise in the gym or tennis court, long walks, and, of course, daily charges. I found my fellow postulants a very cheery group. Mother Rita was the same. We followed a schedule that I have included above, but there was more in the afternoon and evening. Here is the rest of it:

5:00 p.m. - Chant the Psalms
5:30 - Meditation
6:00 - Supper
6:45 - Chapel prayers
7:00 - Community room for recreation
7:30 - Evening prayers in Chapel including rosary and chanting of Psalms
8:00 - Study for school and prepare for bed
9:00 - Lights out

I found the routine with its mixture of prayer, work, and recreation very easy to do. I loved being in such a spiritual atmosphere. I prayed hard each day that the Community would find me capable of sustaining the life that would include the vows of poverty, chastity, and obedience for life. What a thought. I just happily took each day as it came, and hoped that I would not be found wanting.

The IHMs were very education minded. We were started on our college careers right away. On the second or third Saturday we were there Mother Rita gave us each a notebook. She said it was for taking notes in the classes we were to begin in the College. So there I was, a college student, before I could blink my eyes. What a thrill it was to actually be attending classes. We spent each Saturday morning in two or three classes taught by the regular college faculty. In fact, we were in class with all kinds of people, not just nuns. We would line up two by two and go up the hill, which wasn't very hard to do in those days, and carry our books and supplies carefully hidden under our capes. The capes we wore fell from our shoulders to our waist. We were supposed to have a quiet demeanor, and keep our eyes cast down. Little by little, we were practicing the customs that most nuns practiced. It was considered unseemly to be swinging our arms and staring around at the passing scene. It was called 'modesty of the eyes.'

Thus began my long college career that didn't finish for decades. There was always something more to learn. In fact, we actually did become part of the group always present in collegiate circles – full-time worker, part time student. Young people have been doing this for years and years so it wasn't too surprising to me. Eventually we completed all the required course work for our degrees, thank God.

The first few weeks just flew by. The group seemed to be happy and in earnest about their vocation. About three weeks after we entered, while we were gathered downstairs in our front room, Mother Rita made the announcement that we were being assigned to TEACH. We were sure surprised. We had already learned that as a Sister you would be asked to do many things not of your choosing. In fact, perhaps never of your choosing. That was the way of the convent. Mother reassured us that we would have a lot of help in this endeavor.

It seemed that there were parochial schools in the area that had need of one or more teachers. There didn't seem to be any teachers available, so the Mother General said she would ask the postulants to do this even though they had no experience at all. I was probably the only one who had taught in a classroom. Remember what I said about teaching the second grade my senior year. That was just a few short months ago, so I wasn't hesitant about this development. Of course, there was not even a thought of objecting. We looked upon this as one more test. The vow of obedience would figure prominently in our lives until death. So we all waited to hear where we would go.

Mother Rita read the assignment for each postulant. When she got to 'Miss Murphy' she said, "You will teach kindergarten at Blessed Sacrament School in the morning, and assist Sister Vincent, the principal, in the afternoon." Well, I immediately began to pray that I would do a good job. I had never ever even been inside a kindergarten before. So I did start to be anxious about it.

Mother Rita announced that we would have a professed Sister as a mentor each evening at seven o'clock. She would help us prepare for the next day. These IHMs were already experienced teachers. I was immediately relieved. Then I waited to hear who would be my helper. I smiled when she said' "Sister Corita will help you to prepare for the kindergarten." I didn't know Sister Corita at all, but I had seen her going about her business. She was young, about twenty-five, and seemed very pleasant. So I was all set. Of course, Sister Corita had not yet become the world-renowned artist that we now know. She was a young Sister teaching in a classroom somewhere nearby. She would be a classroom teacher for the next several years.

You can see that my life wasn't dull or boring in the least. We had a full schedule of prayer and activities that kept us hopping until bedtime. By the time I hit the hay each night I felt that I had experienced a pretty full day. I was storing up things to tell my family when they would come on visiting Sunday. Sometimes I would think of my mother, and hope that she was doing all right with Barr and Beverly, and finding times a little better. I noticed on the subsequent visiting Sundays that she began to look better and better. I kept praying. I fell asleep each night with prayers for my loved ones, and for myself. I was always praying that if this was going to be the life for me that I would be given the strength and faith to carry it off successfully.

It was now September after Labor Day. All the parochial schools were starting their year. On the first day we all gathered downstairs in the front room to prepare for our first journey outside the cloister. Several of us had to take the trolley to get to our mission. Some were driven in an auto driven by one of the postulants. We all put on coats that had been saved for just such an event. We also took off the light veil we had been wearing, and replaced it with a hat. I still had the hat I wore the day I came up to the convent with my family. It was very jaunty with a brim partially turned up and sported a fine feather that stuck straight up into the air. I was ready.

Mother Rita gave each of us enough money for carfare. It turned out that I was not going to have to go alone to Blessed Sacrament. There were two other postulants assigned – both to grade four or five. They were Miss Cassie Shea and Miss Delores Quevedo. We three went down to the corner of Western and Franklin to catch the trolley that ran along Franklin. We had on all of our black clothes except for the veil. It was our first experience out in public with special clothes on. Nobody seemed to pay any attention to us. Of course, we were careful of decorum. We didn't chatter or talk much because we were learning to keep the day silence. This was a custom whereby one was supposed to live undistracted by gossip or idle chatter and focus on doing God's will, which meant doing whatever we were asked to do. It also could turn into a great waste of time. So we demurely sat there and got off at Hollywood and Vine. Here we were right in the middle of Hollywood. I was amazed.

We transferred to the Hollywood Boulevard streetcar and rode down to Cherokee Avenue. There we got off and walked south for about two blocks to Selma Avenue. The school and convent were right across the street. We went to the Convent first to meet Sister Vincent, the superior and principal. She greeted us very warmly and showed us to a room upstairs in the convent where we could come each day. We took off our coat and hat and put on our veil with the bobby pins. There was also a bathroom so we could take care of any necessary matters. Then, off to the school. It was a pretty strict rule that the professed Sisters were not to talk to us while we were postulants or novices. I know this was one of the directives from Rome for all religious communities. So whenever we did speak to one of them it had to be for a good reason, no idle talk. We learned that the idea of all this was so we would begin to practice interior prayer, and try to be undistracted. It certainly did help.

My classroom was right next to the office. I went in and found the room beautifully decorated just right for little kindergartners. I was so pleased. The Sisters at the school had taken care to see that we felt welcome. I was prepared for the first day, and had no trouble when the bell rang and we all went out to the schoolyard to greet our children. I found this little group of five-year-olds all looking at me. I smiled and took the hand of two of them. It was customary in that school for a student to lead the flag salute, and for Sister Vincent to make any announcements for the day. There were nine grades of classes. Large classes were common. I don't know how many children I had, but it was a lot more than a handful. Some classes had forty or fifty pupils. All the children seemed well behaved and respectful.

Holding the hands of the two little ones, I led my group down a side yard to our classroom. Thus, began my adventures as a teaching member of the Immaculate Heart Sisters. I remember that I would go to school on the trolley armed with plans for the day that Sister Corita had helped me devise. I had some rolls of beautiful flowers and sweet-faced animals that she so deftly painted free hand the night before, and with a few new little songs to teach the children. I taught them some of the shorter prayers. We began each day with a prayer, and ended with one, so they became pretty good in their recital of these prayers. I was also busy teaching them to count, to recognize the alphabet, to learn the colors, etc. These were all included in my curriculum of the day. We also had recesses and a little rest time. All in all I thoroughly enjoyed myself. The little ones seemed happy also.

At noon I dismissed my class, and went over to the convent for lunch. We three postulants sat at the end of the table and ate quietly. The meals were always very simple. We talked quietly among ourselves. After lunch I would go directly to the office to help. Sister Vincent gave me the job of typing all the permanent record cards of all the new students in the school. That is where I really learned my hunt and peck method. I had never learned how to type without looking at the keyboard, so I got pretty adept at typing the way I do to this day. At three o'clock we three postulants would go over to the convent, put on our coats and hats, and take the trolleys back to the convent on

Western and Franklin. My two companions seemed to enjoy their partnership in the fourth (or fifth) grade because they were walking with a light step just as I was. I was ecstatic because I was, at last, working for God. That was what I had meant to do when I entered the convent. So here I was, doing it. And I had been in the convent only three weeks.

When we arrived back at the novitiate each day all the postulants would relate their experiences. Mother Rita then gave us time for a light snack in the refectory. Then we would have a conference from her about some point in our life that we should know more about. Day by day we were learning all about the customs that made nuns act the way they did. Of course, I have learned later that most of the customs, such as always having a companion when going out into the world, were relics of many centuries of convent living. Little by little, we were becoming used to the ways of the nuns, and always remembering the goal, which was to become more holy and closer to God in order to serve Him well. That was the basic reason for it all. After awhile we developed a clear idea of what our vocation was asking of us. For anyone who couldn't see her way clear in accepting all that was asked her days in the novitiate were numbered.

Mother Rita was a very energetic Novice Mistress. She would take us for long walks up hill and down dale. I was so amazed one day when she led all of us, novices and postulants alike, up Western Avenue to walk in the nearby park. When we got up there we found this beautiful green glen with a nice creek running right through it. It is still named 'Fern Dell.'

How cool it was.

I realized that I had been there before. I tried to think of when. It turned out that our whole family visited there when we first came to Southern California. It was one of the nice Sunday trips we took when we still had the big car. My parents had photographs of all of us posing in Fern Dell. One of those pictures is displayed on the cabinet in my living room right now – seventy years later.

After about six weeks we were taken on a lovely walk up in the hills behind the college. We were laughing and singing all the way. Mother Rita was gracious and fun. These walks were very good for strengthening us, and giving us something more than just study, teaching, etc. After all, most of us were still teenagers, and had been very active in sports and other things in high school. It was pretty wise I think.

We found out, though, that on one of these walks one of our fellow postulants did not come on the with us. When we got back downstairs Mother Rita told us that one of the postulants had decided this wasn't the life for her, and her family had come to take her home. That was an eye-opener if ever there was one for all of us. Just like that your life could change. I thought a lot about it that night before going to sleep, and decided that I really liked the prospect of making vows and living my life in the service of God. Before we completed our eight months as postulants, one more postulant decided to go home to another life.

Now the number in our group was thirteen, but it soon became fourteen with the arrival of Miss

Crawford. She was a welcome addition. Two more girls came much later before we received the habit, but only one stayed. So there were actually fifteen of us by the following April.

Our adventures as postulants continued. Mother Rita was always testing one or the other of us to see if we had a willingness to follow directions, to work hard, to pray, to be a congenial as possible, and strive for holiness. One of the hardest things I had to give up was my beautiful Indian blanket.
We usually put clean sheets on our bed once a week. We were used to doing this after a few weeks. One morning Mother Rita announced to us that today we would be assigned to a different cell in the dormitory. She told us to go upstairs and remove all of our things from the dresser and place them in our new place. I was changed to a bed by the far wall. It looked exactly the same as the old bed, but I knew it wasn't the same. We were told not to remove the blanket and take it with us. My heart dropped. The blanket made me feel close to family and home. Oh well, I immediately caught on that Mother Rita was testing us again. Her job was to prepare us for a life where we renounced ownership of anything – and that means ANYTHING.

I thought about that blanket for a long time. In fact, here I am talking about it. That was an important lesson I learned in the convent. And it had to do with renunciation. Do not become too attached to anything because there might be someone who needs it more than you do. I don't believe I ever saw that blanket again because when we made our beds we opened the

curtains only after we were finished, so all the beds

looked alike.

During my short time as a postulant several important things happened. In November of 1941 my mother called me one evening. I was so surprised when Mother Rita called me to the phone. This was never done. It was my mother. She said, "Your father has just died." I was really shocked because I had not heard that he was even sick.

I think my father died of cancer, but I'm not sure. He was 48 years old. It seemed that he did not have a long period of illness before passing away. My mother went to see Pa in the hospital. She said she was shocked at his condition. He was so thin and dying. She took Beverly with her. They were the only family he saw during his last days. I suppose my mother expected him to get well because he was so young. After a few short weeks he worsened, and passed away.

My mother did not have the wherewithal to pay for any kind of funeral, so the county took on this obligation. My father did not leave one cent to my mother. So in essence he died a pauper. The county assigned his grave in a catholic cemetery in Culver City. It is named Holy Cross. They also provided the coffin for his burial. It was a plain wooden box with no adornments. A few friends and the family attended the Mass at St. Athanasius. My father was interred in the pauper's grave at Holy Cross. It was in a section of the cemetery that had not been improved with landscaping. When I saw it my heart sank. There was no grave marker. The place was full of weeds. None of this happened because the family didn't care. It was simply a time when there was no extra money as yet. I still have the statements sent to my mother to cover the modest costs she was charged. His burial costs were less that $20. The county still owns his burial plot. Thus ended the saga of a man who could have had all the love and admiration a grateful family could give, but he squandered the good will by neglect on a huge scale for our family.

I will insert here the postscript of this sad event even though it comes quite a bit later in my life. Today, if one wishes to visit my father's grave they will find it still in the same place, but the cemetery crews have planted it all with grass and trees. In fact, it looks as neat and lovely as any other part of the cemetery. In the early 1970s, when I had a job that paid me actual money, I went up to Holy Cross and arranged to have a nice grave marker placed at his grave. It acknowledges his name, dates, and the fact that he is not entirely forgotten by me, and I hope by his grandchildren. He was a man with many good qualities, but he never seemed to be able to capitalize on them. That is the sad shame of his story.

As time went on I grew more and more convinced that I was in the right place. There wasn't anything standing in my way so far. We postulants continued to be happy, going to our classrooms each day. We attended College classes on Saturdays, taking some classes down in our front room. We had art from Sister Magdalen Mary, penmanship from Sister Rose. Church history from Sister Margaret Mary, Theology from Monsignor Dignan, and we took English from Sister Humiliata. With our teaching, college classes, and conferences from Mother Rita, plus the 3 hours a day we spent in the chapel with prayers we were pretty busy every minute of every day. In fact, it became clear to us that our lives as nuns would be one of praying, serving, or studying every minute of every day. We certainly had time to think about it. Mother Rita was always grasping opportunities to teach us some aspect of the life. We all seemed determined to make it.

Then something really earthshaking happened. On Sunday morning, December 7, 1941, Mother Rita called us all together in the front room. She announced that the Japanese had just bombed Pearl Harbor in Hawaii. We were all struck silent. She led us up to the chapel where all the nuns were gathered praying. I was especially prayerful because I suddenly remembered Bernie. He had joined the Navy in August, and I didn't know where he was. I was hoping to see him before he would have to go overseas. After the prayers we returned to the novitiate downstairs.

Mother Eucharia came down to talk to us. She said that if any of us felt that we had to return to our homes at this time we could do so. 'If we felt we were needed at home' was what she was talking about. Well, I thought about how Barr was home, and so was Beverly. Mama wasn't alone out there. Besides things were beginning to come together for her. She had landed a job downtown somewhere, and was finally out of the pit. Barr was working somewhere also. Bev was still in school. In the end I decided to stay where I was. In fact, all the postulants did the same thing. On the next visiting Sunday I talked to my mother about my decision. She was most adamant that I continue on with my calling. She said that Bernie was also sending home some money each month so things were going along much better than before.

It was around this time that I had my last visit with Bernie while he was a well man. I was teaching my little ones at Blessed Sacrament. One day Mrs. Burgard drove Mama and Bernie up to see me because Bernie had orders to go to Alameda Field in Oakland. I felt so flattered that they would go to all the trouble to visit me.

We had a good hour or so together. When they left I can still see Bernie in my mind's eye looking so sharp and handsome in his sailor suit. He escorted the two ladies down the street to Mrs. Burgard's car. They drove away amid much waving. It turned out that that was the last time I would see my brother standing and healthy. He was about 20 years old. Today it is a bittersweet memory to me.

The war had started. Barr signed up with the Air Force. He was sent to Willams Field in Arizona where he successfully passed officer's training and became a pilot. This was all later though. Mama snagged a good job with a government agency, the OPA (Office of Price Administration) that was in charge of assigning all the stamps for goods needed by everyone. She was the Secretary to the headman there. She loved it. At this time she busily began to learn how to type, how to improve her writing, and how to organize an office. She must have been very good at the job because she held that position all through the war. I still have some of the textbooks she used to hone her secretarial skills. And there are some newspaper clippings showing her in action at the OPA. She was still the organist at St. Athanasius. It was not long before only Beverly was at home with Mama.

We had one real adventure in February of 1942. It is still a rather mysterious event in the annals of that time, but I can say I saw it with my own eyes. All the West Coast of the USA had to be in complete darkness at night because of the threat of Japanese planes or subs. So each night we would all draw the curtains over any light we might have on. Everyone did this. There were even wardens on each block in the cities to see to it that this was done. One night about eight o'clock we heard the warning sirens blasting all over the city. Pretty soon we began to hear thumping sounds which turned out to be the noise made by anti-aircraft guns. We postulants didn't know anything about war preparations, but it seems that all of Southern California was prepared for an invasion of some kind or of an attack. Mother Rita asked if we would like to go up to the tower to view what was going on. Enthusiastically we all traipsed up to the very top of our convent. The tower was an open area with a roof. It was big enough to hold us all, novices and postulants. Imagine my surprise when I realized the night was so clear that I could detect Signal Hill in Long Beach. That meant that I could see the general area of my home that was in North Long Beach.

There before our eyes we could see searchlights raking the skies above Long Beach. The lights eventually found something because several lights converged on a single object. We could see what we thought was a plane flying south over the harbor area. The scariest part of it all was that the guns were shooting at this object over and over. We definitely heard the dull sound of the explosions, and we could clearly see the flash of the guns. We stood there transfixed for about 40 minutes, and then everything faded from our sight.

We definitely saw some object in the sky being shot at from the ground. After the war this whole episode was poo-pooed by the authorities. Later I asked my mother about it. She was very animated in telling me that it did indeed occur. In fact she, Barr, and Bev were very frightened because there were anti-aircraft gun emplacements very near to the house. Some of the shots were going right over them. They didn't know if this was the start of an invasion or not. After that no one mentioned the event for many years. Even today it is called a false alarm. But I know what I saw.

Now it is getting closer to the time for me to become a novice in the Order. It was a time of great excitement for me. I still couldn't believe that I had survived this long. Every so often Mother Rita would remind us that the Community leaders had to vote on whether or not we would be accepted as members. Our postulancy was supposed to be a testing ground for our resolve. So far, all of us had hung in there and followed the rules and lessons as best we could. In March we were told that the Mother General, Mother Eucharia and her Council would vote on our fitness for living the religious life. We postulants were hoping and praying, but there wasn't anything we could do that we hadn't already done just be ourselves and PRAY. Later, Mother Rita gathered us all together in the front room and announced that each of us was approved for membership in the Community, and that we could proceed with preparations to become novices. I was ecstatic. At last my dream would come true. I would become a 'Sister'.

I wrote a letter to Mama telling her the good news. She always was very supportive of my decision. Then preparations began. First of all we had to be measured for habits. This was done by Sister Rosario who happened to be a teacher in a local parochial school, but who was also an expert seamstress. She was very fast. She made two complete habits for all fourteen of us. What a big job it turned out to be. Mother Rita told me to come home early each day from Blessed Sacrament so I could assist with the cutting of the material. We were not going to sew, but we could help in some way. I was happy to do this. The habit consisted of the following.

A long gown pleated in front and back. It hung from the shoulders and reached the ground. There were neat holes placed on the sides for pockets. The color was deep blue. The sleeves were very wide and long enough to be turned up at the wrist. A tiny pocket was sewn on up near the shoulder to hold a watch, if one happened to have one. The habit was very roomy. A leather belt was worn at the waist to hold everything together.

The coif was the white head covering worn by all nuns at the time. It covered the entire head and shoulders. No hair was to be showing. When it was laundered the front piece of it was heavily starched.

The starch made them neat, but I found that I frequently had a headache if everything was pinned too tightly. Yes, pinned. When we got everything on in the morning we just put pins on the veil and scapular to hold them in place.

The veil was made of very light material. It was not heavy to wear at all. The Professed Sisters wore black. These were the nuns who had made their vows. We future novices would wear the whole habit, but would wear a white veil for the year of our noviceship. When we would make our vows a year from now we would be given the black veil to wear for the rest of our lives. The one thing we would be asked to do with the veil was to hem it by hand using a very small roll stitch. We labored over this several nights during recreation.

The scapular was worn over the shoulders front and back. It was black. It was not gathered by the belt or anything else. It hung straight down in front and back. The sole decoration we had on the scapular was a small silver heart that had to be pinned just right 2 inches down and 2 inches in on the left top of the front panel of the scapular.

There were several other small parts of the habit included. We wore fitted inner sleeves because the sleeves of the blue habit were so large and open. The inner sleeves were black. We could make those alright. We made a large pocket which would hang down from the waist under the habit. It would be placed by tying it around the waist. It would hang in just the right position so that when we would reach into the open pocket in the habit we would find all that we needed in the hanging pocket. We kept everything but the kitchen sink in there because you never knew when you would need keys, handkerchief, rosary, pen, etc.

We wore long black cotton hose and very sensible black leather shoes with laces. So there you have it. We wore this habit every day of our lives – winter and summer. In the winter we added a little black shawl which we wore over our shoulders. That was the only concession we made to the elements. I still have my black shawl. It is a treasure because Mama crocheted it for me.

One other piece of clothing was worn whenever we went out into the world. It was an all-enveloping cape that we called the mantle. It covered us from shoulder to toe. It was not meant to be for warmth only but also modesty.

Of course, this might be the place to answer the age-old question of curious children, friends, and other adults, "What on earth do you wear underneath all of that?" Well, finally I will let the secret out. We wore just exactly what all women wore as undergarments. We had many of our things purchased from a Nun's clothing store in the East. Other garments were homemade – usually made of crinkle crepe cotton. Always white. We made our long underskirts, both white and black, ourselves. All in all, it was very simple attire. Our Rule stated that we were to wear undergarments that were plain and untrimmed, so that's what we wore. We had a clean sct to wear every day.

Consequently, we were never out in the department stores shopping around for things. One thing we did wear that was not common was a white cotton undershirt with long sleeves. Everything else was what I wear today. So there you have it. On the outside we had this outfit that was worn by nuns for a thousand years, but underneath it was not especially spectacular.

So now our preparations are nearly complete. The date was set. April 6, 1942 the invitations were sent out, but a big question for most of us became, "What shall I wear?" It had been customary for postulants to appear in the chapel to receive the habit dressed in a real wedding gown. We were to be brides of Christ. Mother Rita was wonderful in letting us all know that if we did not have a wedding gown available from our mother or from someone, not to worry. It seemed that over the years many of the new novices had donated their wedding gowns to the novitiate to be used by postulants who didn't have access to one from family. Several of us were fitted with beautiful long white dresses, and a filmy veil. I knew that there was not a wedding gown anywhere at home, so I told my mother not to worry because we had one for me. It was comforting to know that I wasn't the only one who took advantage of this gift.

A couple of things remained to do. The biggest task was to decide on a new name. Yes, it was the custom to choose the name of a saint by which you would be addressed for the rest of your life. I knew this beforehand. All of us did. We would talk about choices. Finally one day Mother Rita asked each of us to put down the names of three saints. I had thought long and hard. I had even mentioned some to Mother Rita, but she would say, "That is already taken." So I thought and thought. Strange as it may seem, it didn't matter if you chose the name of a male saint. That was perfectly acceptable in the religious world. After awhile I came up with Peter, Vincent de Paul, and Ann. I would have been content with any of the three names. We wouldn't know which one it would be until the Archbishop announced it at the Reception Ceremony, so we had to wait. To this day I can't tell you why I chose these names. They just sounded like pretty good saints, and I was determined to follow in their footsteps if possible. I could have kept my own name of Doris but I wasn't ever too fond of it.

Sometime in March 1942 we finished our teaching at Blessed Sacrament School. All the postulants were finishing wherever they were teaching. I had grown accustomed to the routine and energy needed so I was sad to say goodbye to the little kindergartners. But I had to keep myself focused on the reason I had come to the convent in the first place – to become a Sister. So we all began a week-long retreat right there at the motherhouse in preparation for the reception of the habit. This was the first big step to becoming an actual member of the IHM Community. I was in a state of wonder. Even though I was still seventeen I realized that I was quite different than I was back in August. I had been surrounded with such spiritual events, spiritual people, and spiritual thoughts that I could feel myself appreciating the realm of the holy. I guess this would be a test for someone who did not have a vocation. They would probably be bored, or find it too difficult, or wish that they could just live a normal life out with family and friends. But I reveled in it all. I loved the prayers, the music, the very friendly postulants, the holy novices, and all the activities we engaged in to stay focused and healthy. I liked the idea of striving. I was ready.

Retreat started. I had never been in a situation where one would spend eight days praying, chanting, reading, listening to the meditations presented by the priest who was the retreat master, meditating, quietly doing all the charges, and not speaking a word to anyone. If Mother Rita wanted to speak to us, or Mother Eucharia wished to exhort us in any way, that was all right, but we did not speak to each other at all. This was an age-old tradition that was meant to keep one's mind on the prize – becoming more spiritual and prayerful so as to become closer to God.

Each of us was responsible for determining if receiving the habit and being known as Sister was the right thing for us. This was the time we were given enough guidance and encouragement to take the step. All fourteen of us came through. It became clear to me that this life was one in which my personal preferences were not necessarily to be considered. Everything I did should be done well because I was serving God with every action of the day. I was learning that there was transcendence to the person that made it possible to sustain the requirements for life. In a word – I welcomed whatever was to come. I was truly grateful that I had been given this wonderful opportunity to devote my life to something higher than myself. Believe it or not, sixty years later I still feel that way- an immense gratitude for the gift of my life as an IHM. Still I find it very mysterious.

I don't know where all these thoughts came from in a person just seventeen, but I guess I was like the field ready for sowing. I reveled in the deeper thoughts. I looked forward with great anticipation to my future as a Sister.

Retreat came to a close during Holy Week. Because there were so many nuns in the Motherhouse the religious ceremonies were filled with prayer and song. I had never heard such beautiful singing in my life. When Easter Sunday arrived it was a day filled with celebration, music, and the chapel just filled with flowers, and extra delicious meals. It was the day before our Reception of the Habit. Yes, tomorrow I would change my whole appearance and become a Sister. I have never, to this day, been as excited. I just couldn't believe it. My family was there the day of the Mass and Reception, except for Bernie. He was somewhere in the Pacific serving in the Navy. I did miss him terribly.

The big day arrived. We had rehearsed the whole ceremony several times. Our complete habits were ready, tied in a neat package easy for us to carry, the bridal dresses were all pressed and hanging in our cells, the veils too. It was Easter Monday, April 6, 1942. When the bell rang at 5:30 we all got up as usual, went down to prayers and Mass, and to breakfast. But, after breakfast we were in a whirlwind of action. We all returned to our cell where the beautiful wedding gown was hanging. We were ready at about ten a.m. The chapel was filled with flowers. The choir had been practicing a lot. We could hear them in the previous evenings. The chapel was filling up with our families, friends, Priests, Sisters, even flower girls. Yes, a little girl who was carrying a basket of flowers accompanied each of us down the aisle.

We all were escorted down to the chapel entrance. We each carried a lighted candle that was to be the symbol of our dedication. This was a big day for the Novices because they were going to make their first vows. Then they would be 'Professed' Sisters. That means they are real members of the Community, not on trial as we were.

The procession into the chapel must have been lovely to all who came. My family had good seats so they could view all the proceedings. I was in a state of euphoria because I had my dream come true. I couldn't believe that it was really happening. Archbishop John Cantwell was presiding together with many priests. Father O'Sullivan came from St. Athanasius. I was very happy to see him, but was astonished to see him in a wheelchair. My mother had never mentioned that he had become crippled with arthritis. There were fourteen postulants and five Novices in the ceremony. It was so solemn. The music was glorious because no one could sing like the nuns. Their voices floated out over everything. There were lighted candles everywhere on the altar. It was resplendent. In my mind, even to this day, I regard this as MY wedding day.

At a special time in the ceremony we postulants approached the altar rail and knelt down. We were still holding our lighted candles. Our Community Prayer Book had the words for the Reception Ceremony. We postulants were being received into the Community. At the end of the prayers said by the Archbishop and the Mother General we were all presented with our new habits all wrapped together in a neat package. At the appropriate time we stood and walked back down the aisle with the bundle on one arm and the candle in the other hand. There was lots of music. While we were gone, the Novices approached the altar to pronounce their dedication by making vows of Poverty, Chastity, and Obedience for one year. I have to confess that at that moment I truly felt like a bride of Christ. My mother said I was smiling the whole time. Why not? My dreams were coming true.

We were whisked across the patio to the large community room where a couple of our IHM friends were waiting. Each Postulant had two Sisters to help her get dressed in the habit properly. Sister Eymard and Sister Charles were my helpers. We took off our wedding gown, and put on the habit piece by piece. In about five minutes we were all standing there dressed as Sisters except that we had on white veils. We relit our candles and returned to the chapel for the remainder of the ceremony. I am sure that everyone was agog because we came in completely different than we had been before. All heads were turned toward the rear of the chapel to watch our entrance. I could see Mama looking. She was smiling so big. Barr and Bev were too. We approached the altar railing, knelt down, and recited the remaining prayers of the ceremony from our prayer book. At this point the Archbishop picked up the list of Novices and proceeded to say what we would be called. When he got to me he said, "Miss Doris Murphy will be known in religion as Sister Mary Peter." I liked the sound of it right away. After he finished reading the new names for all fourteen of us he finished the ceremony. There was more glorious music, we walked back down the aisle and waited for our family and friends to come out of the chapel. Here I was – Sister Peter. I just couldn't believe that my dream had come true.

What a grand visit we had. After we all had something to eat we could visit with our families and friends until the bell rang. This was going to happen at four o'clock. So I had the whole afternoon to enjoy their company. I was so happy that I really can't describe myself sufficiently. My sense of accomplishment was profound. After all, there had been no one of my acquaintances or friends who even mentioned the least interest in following a religious life. I had pursued my vocation in spite of so many obstacles that might seem small now, but were huge to me as a seventeen year old. Yes, I was still seventeen. It was April 6th. My eighteenth birthday would be April 27th.

When it was time to say "Goodbye" to my family I gave them all a big hug, and said I hoped they would pray for me, and would come visit the fourth Sunday of each month while I was a Novice. They said they would, and they did. Mama reminded me to write to Bernie – wherever he was – which I did very soon. They came up to Immaculate Heart to see Doris, and they left seeing Sister Peter. I would be called by this name for the next 27 years.

Much of the rest of that day is dimly remembered. I do know that the Community seemed very pleased with all of us. We returned downstairs to the Novitiate as Novices. Now our Novices were gone.

They were part of the larger Community now. There was one Novice left from that group who entered later than they. She was Sister Ambrose. She was our head Novice for the next few months until she had the ceremony of Professing her vows. Then it would be the fourteen of us until August when the next group of postulants would come.

So there we were. Mother Rita started calling us by our new names at once. We had to remember each others' name as well. It didn't take long. Now we were going to learn about becoming a Sister in earnest. The first night was a shock to us because we were taken, one by one, into Mother Rita's room where she explained that we would be asked to make many sacrifices for the rest our life. The first thing was that we didn't need to show our hair anymore. If it was kept long it would be hard to conceal under the coif. So she promptly cut off all our hair. I didn't know quite what to expect. I thought she would just trim it, but she didn't. She had an electric clipper, and 'zip – zip – zip' off the hair came before you could think too much about it. We immediately covered our head with a soft cloth night coif so no one saw us but Mother Rita. She wasn't laughing, but I'm sure she felt like it. Most of us new novices took it in stride, but Sister Perpetua must have been so surprised by it that she said she fainted. We still laugh about it to this day. Actually, this was the wisest thing to do about our hair because the coif and veil would always cover our head. We even covered it at night except in the shower or bath. I can't remember any time in the next twenty-seven years when I had my head uncovered in front of anyone. So, I for one was glad not to have to worry about my hair anymore.

After this first haircut we could cut our own hair when we wanted. If we wanted it all off we clipped it all. If we just wanted it short we cut it to our liking. The main thing was that there was to be no hair falling out of the sides of our coif. That was considered messy. So ends our first day as Sisters.

Our year as Novices was to be spent only on spiritual things. I was wondering how this would be accomplished, but the laws of the Church about Novices were very clear. "Novices shall not engage in any secular activities during their year of Novitiate."

Our daily schedule was very full. We still had one and half-hours of prayer in the chapel in the morning, and another hour and a half in the evening. We did our share of serving the meals or reading to all the Sisters during meals. We were very adept at getting all the dishes done for a hundred IHMs and about a hundred and fifty boarders of the elementary, high school and college. I remember working behind the counter stacking the big wash trays and filling the dishwasher. Sometimes I would be a dish dryer. It would take us about a half-hour to get the whole thing done. We never dallied or talked because we were learning to speak only when necessary. We were all young and full of energy. Whenever we did any jobs like this we were careful to pin up our long sleeves, and pin our veil in the back so nothing would trail in the wet.

We had a conference from Mother Rita every day. She would choose a topic on the vows or the Rule. All nuns in the world had a rule book that was compiled and approved by the Vatican. Many of the rules were so long-standing that no one could remember when or why they were included. It just seemed that the men in the Vatican had decided that nuns had to always walk two-by-two since the Middle Ages. There are many more examples, but I will talk about all of this later. The fact of the matter is at that time in 1942 we were a community of very nunny nuns. Our superiors were very strict about our keeping "The Rule." So each day Mother Rita would take one or other of the items and explain what it was and how we would be expected to comply with it. If we had questions this was a good time to ask.

We continued to take College courses, but all our studies had to be related to spiritual things. Consequently we had priests come in to give us courses in Church History and Scripture. Church music that turned out to be Gregorian Chant, spiritual life and how to live it, the virtues, and so on. So we were not bored with inactivity at all. I was impressed when some of the IHMs who were professors in the College also came down to give us lessons. We were earning college credit because all of our courses were part of the approved curriculum of the College.

The novitiate year passed very quickly. There were a couple of things I remember vividly. One was that I was given the opportunity to take piano lessons from Mother Lourdes. She was a retired Sister who was also a big-wig in the Community.

It seems that by now it was recognized that I had a very nice singing voice. I am sure the thought was that I could learn piano and then be a music teacher. No one asked me, of course, but I am sure that was the idea. I found it very hard to get started. One of the biggest reasons was that Mother Rita never gave a thought to my need for practice time. For some reason she never assigned me time. I kept waiting for her to do so, but since we were not supposed to be demanding I just assumed she would tell me soon to take the time from one of my other tasks. I didn't make much progress on the piano, but I have to say that one of the biggest obstacles in my way was that I was intensely fascinated with Mother Lourdes' piano playing. When I was sitting there watching her show me the fingering I just couldn't concentrate at all. My eyes just kept looking at the middle finger on her right hand. It was only half there. She must have had an accident of some kind that resulted in her losing the top two joints of that finger. Well, I just couldn't get over it. She played beautifully, but my concentration was all shot. After a few weeks I am sure she told Mother Rita that I was a lost cause with the piano because the lessons stopped. I was relieved. Even so, it happened that my talent in music was not neglected because I did receive a degree from the College in which my minor was music. I took many music courses, but no more piano.

Another thing I remember about my novice year was that I became very ill. Up until now I had always enjoyed good health. One day, I began to feel very hot and woozy. I kept going for awhile, but then realized that I was near to passing out. Mother Rita was nowhere to be found. The Novices helped my lie down in Mother's office. I felt hotter and hotter. Finally she came in. Her first reaction was to scold me for lying down there. She told me to get up and go up to the dormitory on the third floor to get something.

When I came back down she must have seen how I was so flushed and faint. She told me to go back up and go right to bed. After a while she came in and took my temperature. She didn't say anything, but I knew it was high. By now my throat had become very sore. I could barely swallow. A little later she came in with Sister Aurelia who was a nurse to pack me up and move me down to the infirmary on the second floor. The doctor was called. I heard later that all the Sisters were praying for me in the Chapel for the next four days. I felt very weak and sick. Now, I think I must have had strep throat and maybe some other infection. In about a week after that I was up and around, and feeling better. Mother Rita never told me what it was.

We were all happily going about our business of being good novices and learning the ropes. We enjoyed long walks in Fern Dell. Volleyball and baseball games up on the court during which we pinned up our long skirts so we could really run. Our daily schedule became routine. We were beginning to see if we really wanted to continue in the life of a nun. The more I learned, the more I was determined that I would be able to make the sacrifices entailed. Of course, there would be a whole lot of inner strength needed to be successful in keeping the three vows, and in living the 'life' with others.

The vows were presented to us in detail. **Poverty** was understood to mean that we would no longer own anything. We were not to treat anything as our own. It was not seemly to hoard things. The whole idea was that we would live at a very simple level in every way. Our clothing was not fancy or, necessarily comfortable. The meals were not special. We were to eat whatever was provided. Our own tastes were to be put in the background. We never had money of our own to spend as we liked. Any money earned by the meager salaries of the Sisters was pooled so that all would benefit when there was a need. One of the Sisters was the procurator. Her job was to do the buying for everyone in the local convent. Whenever I needed something, no matter how small, I would have to ask the Superior for permission to ask the procurator for it. This understanding of poverty was so universal that it was not really too hard to go and ask the Superior for something. If the Superior thought you didn't need a new pair of shoes yet, she could say no. It was very rare for a Sister to have fancy or extra things.

The vow of **Chastity** was presented as a sacrifice we would give to God. It was understood that in any and all occasions where the desires of the flesh would be enhanced we were to do all in our power to avoid these occasions. It meant that throughout life I would have to be alert to these desires. We were not taught that these desires were bad. On the contrary, we were taught that it is in God's plan for the propagation of the earth that men and women were meant to be together. The big thing for us was that we were freely giving up the pleasures of married life in order to devote ourselves completely to the service of God in whatever way we were asked.

These were big thoughts for all of us. Could we do it, or not? That was the question we had to grapple with during this novitiate year. We had to really face the question of whether we wanted a husband

and children more than the religious life we seemed to be called to. It took many hours on our knees praying for guidance. In the end my companions and I chose to remain in the celibate life. We felt it was for reasons that we, alone, could give. To me it is still a mystery how I have been able to remain faithful to this special calling. I guess I was just determined to give my life to God. I felt entirely blest that I would have God's help throughout my life to be a faithful to this special calling. I guess I was just determined to give my life to God. I felt entirely blest that I would have God's help throughout my life to be a faithful sister.

The vow of **Obedience** was presented as a cornerstone of our vocation. After all, hadn't we already answered the summons to the convent in some mysterious way? We showed by our willingness to embrace the religious life that we were ready to give God our whole being. Don't ask me how someone so young can decide this, but it seemed to me to be the right thing to do. I would not be happy in any other life. We learned that the Superior had the say in everything. We would be asked to do things not necessarily to our liking. When this happened we would say, "Yes, Sister Superior", and go do it without complaint. That was the ideal. Of course, there would be times when one would have to speak up about something. This was permitted within reason. There could never be any sign of defiance. Otherwise, the question would be whether or not one was sincere about her vocation, or even fitted to live under obedience. In this way all the activities and work of the convent rolled along very smoothly. So the vow of Obedience was the gift to God of our own wishes, our own choices. We could not choose where we would live or what job we would be doing. It was all "the Will of God".

So we spent the year of Novitiate pondering some very deep and important things. Sometimes I would find myself wondering if I could do it. Then I would wear out my knees praying for strength and guidance. Somehow, I always reached a serenity that made me more certain than ever that this was my calling.

In July of our Novice year we were surprised to hear that Mother Rita was going to be changed and that we would have a new Novice Mistress. Well, that was a shock. We loved Mother Rita. She was named Superior of the Motherhouse there. Sister Regina was named Novice Mistress. She had been Superior of the Motherhouse. So they exchanged places. There we saw 'obedience in action' because I am sure neither one asked to be changed. Oh well, life in the convent. Mother Regina turned out to be wonderful and she carried on with our training. The biggest thing we had to prepare for was the influx of the new group of postulants. They were due in late August. The novitiate dormitories had to be enlarged because there were fourteen of them coming. We, of course, felt very advanced because we had already gone through the year as postulants, and now as Novices.

From August on we were very busy with a full house of young people down in the Novitiate all aspiring to make it. My family came to visit regularly on visiting Sunday. Mama was doing better, but she looked sad sometimes. Bernie was in the South Pacific somewhere. She would get letters from him that didn't tell much because of the war. Barr joined the Air Force and was sent to Arizona for training, so he was gone. That just left Beverly at home with Mama. I am not sure of the timing of events but I know that Mama and Bev went to Portland for a few months.

Sometime during these days Bev met a sailor, Roy White, and fell in love. She was sixteen or so. I am sure Mama didn't know what to make of it, so she hauled Bev with her up to Portland. I can only guess at the course of events. I think Bev went to school up in Portland for awhile, but she never finished. I believe it was during this time that Mama succeeded in selling our little house on the two lots. I don't know how much she got for this property, but whatever it was it gave her a boost. She told me later that she took the money and went straight to all the creditors who were owed money from the cleaning shop days. She paid each and every one in full. She had kept a record of what was owed them. She said they were all so kind to her and most didn't want to take any of her money. She said she wanted to be able to hold her head up whenever she would meet any of them. So Mama was started on her own new life. My admiration and love of my mother was always great, but now it became larger than my heart could hold. She had such integrity, such honesty, and such kindness. What a model she was for me all my life.

The Novice year was passing quickly. We were very busy each day with the regular things we had to do as nuns in training, but we were looking toward the goal which was the day we would pronounce our vows. The many feast days and holy days were always celebrated with beautiful Masses, lots of flowers, and singing. I reveled in the Christmas celebration with all the beauty of the season. Later in the Spring we participated in all the special liturgies related to Lent and the coming Easter.

Easter was the target day for our Profession of Vows. As the time got closer we were schooled more thoroughly in the Vows and the Holy Rule. The date was set. It was to be April 26, 1943. That just happened to be the day before my nineteenth birthday. I was so excited. I am sure the Mother General and her Counsel were asking Mother Regina about each one of us. It was important to be sure that the Novice was ready to become a full member of the Community. It was important from several viewpoints. Did the Novice have an understanding of what was required by making the vows? Did the Novice realize what she was giving up by doing so? Was the Novice entirely willing to take the step and remain faithful to her calling? Was the Novice a woman who was not hard to live with? This last item was very important to the peace and harmony of the Convent where the Novice might be sent.

I am sure there were all kinds of other things discussed about us, but the upshot of it all was that we were told that the Council had voted to approve of us all for Profession. I was greatly relieved to hear this. The thought had crossed my mind during the last few months that I would not know what to do if I wasn't approved. This was the only thing I had been dreaming of for several years, so it was inconceivable to me that I would have to live another kind of life. I was praying about this all the time, my knees actually had calluses.

The big day arrived. I had invited my mother, Bev, Barr, and Bernie, and several friends. They all came except Bernie. He was serving in the Navy on Palmyra Island in the South Pacific. The war was heating up. The Mass was presided over by Archbishop Cantwell of L.A. The postulants who had joined us in August were now all excited because they would receive the habit and the white veil, and be given their new names as Sisters. They would then stay on in the novitiate that was being moved from Hollywood to Montecito near Santa Barbara. Because our group numbered fourteen and the Postulant group numbered twelve or thirteen it was decided to have the ceremony up in the College auditorium where there was plenty of room for all the families and guests. The altar on the stage was decorated beautifully. The Sisters in the choir had practiced their most beautiful hymns. I can still hear them in my mind to this day almost sixty years later. I was ecstatic. I couldn't believe that I was really getting to be a Sister of the Immaculate Heart. It was such a happy day.

We processed down the aisle wearing our white veils, carrying a lighted candle. At the appropriate time during the Mass we ascended the steps to the stage where the altar was fronted by a long row of kneelers called prie-dieus. We were prayed over, presented with the prayer books and our Rule, and a crucifix to be worn at the neck on the habit under the scapular. We knelt down. Then Mother Eucharia and Mother Regina stood behind us and removed our white veil, and replaced it with the black veil that we would wear henceforth. It denoted that we were vowed Religious, and members of our religious order. When that was done they stood behind each one of us. Mother Eucharia placed her hand on my shoulder when she came to me. That was my signal to begin the recitation of my vows. I recited them in a clear and loud voice. I wasn't too nervous. All of my companions did the same thing, one by one. I prayed so hard for the strength to keep my vows faithfully all of my life.

It should be noted, however, that the first vows were not made for life. We pronounced them for one year. We could renew them again for one year. The third time around we would be permitted to make them forever. We were all aware that no one was required to remain in the convent if she became aware that it was not really the life she had thought. At no time were we told we had to stay. On the contrary, we were told that the door swung both ways. Sometimes the young woman would decide to go, or the Mother General and Council would decide the woman was not suited to the life. These decisions were made for the good of the woman and of the Community. Even to this day a member of the Community can decide to call it quits. Consequently, it becomes a case of saying "yes" every single day of our lives. That is pretty heady. It then becomes apparent that I have said "yes" thousands of times My family and friends had a wonderful visit in the afternoon in the parlor. They were all so interested in what would happen to me now. I explained that now I would get a mission to some convent to start my work as a Sister. I told my loved ones that I would let them know what my next move would be. They were very supportive and happy. Of course, no one was

happier than I was because my dream had come true.
I started my new life as a real IHM. I had met my Sir
Galahad, and his name was JESUS. Even now I feel
humble and grateful. This ends the part of my life that
included childhood and aspirations. From now on I
was an adult young woman setting out on my life's
adventure as Sister Peter.

It turned out that I stayed on at the Franklin Avenue
Convent for a few more months. It happened this way.
After our families were gone we were each presented
with a small white envelope. Inside was a short typed
letter from the Mother General. It was what we called
a mission. In this letter she said that for the honor and
glory of God I was assigned to teach fourth grade at
Our Lady of Angels School in Los Angeles, and
reside at the Motherhouse. Now this was the end of
April so how come? At that time some of the local
parochial schools were short of one teacher because
the postulants had been teaching there since
September.

Remember my adventure as a kindergarten teacher at
Blessed Sacrament School in Hollywood? Well
someone had to take my place when I left to become a
Novice last April. So now we were taking the places
of the postulants who were now Novices. So I got the
fourth grade at Plaza school. As fate would have it the
priests in charge of the Plaza parish were Claretians.
It is a small world. Even though I had not taught
fourth grade before there was no question in my mind
that I could do it. Wasn't it the 'Will of God'? And
after all I had taught second grade all year as a Senior
in high school, and a bit of Kindergarten. So I didn't
feel completely in the dark.

I lived at the Motherhouse. Each day was filled with at least three hours of prayer, charges to be done, personal things taken care of, and classes to prepare. How busy we were. In addition to this we also continued to attend college classes on Saturdays working toward our B.A. degree.

Later on we would take some additional classes on Friday evenings. Our teachers were always professors at the College. Most of the time these professors were IHM Sisters. It was difficult, though, to get all the things done that were part of my day. I began to realize that my life was going to be one of continuous labor in the vineyard. Did this distress me? Not in the least. I reveled in the challenge. However, I was pretty tired when it was time to lay my head on the pillow at 9:30 p.m.

There were five of us who lived at the Motherhouse, and commuted to Plaza School each day. We went in a station wagon. One of the Sisters drove it. The first two weeks of May I was troubled because I had a bad case of cold sores on my lips. I think I was just so excited about making my vows that a latent virus in my lips erupted. It was kind of embarrassing because both lips were affected. The principal at the school, Sister Celestine, must have wondered about it, but she didn't ask me anything. Instead she asked one of my companions about it. Of course my companion didn't know what to say. I always thought that was a strange thing for Sister Celestine to do. After about two weeks it all cleared up. I was never troubled again by such a bad case of cold sores.

Teaching the little ones at Plaza went rather well. I struggled with discipline, but finally charmed the kids into doing what I wanted. I was only there until June when school ended for the year. I was not a skilled teacher yet, but I worked hard to learn the ropes. There was no one assigned to help me, so I pored over the teacher's guides very closely. As each success happened I tried to duplicate what I had done so that I would improve. It was very important to me to do as good a job as possible because I was serving God. It would never do to be lackadaisical in my work or life.

When school ended in June we younger Sisters were assigned to teach catechism at local parishes instead of attending College summer session. So I got a mission to teach at Our Lady of Soledad School in East L.A. I lived in the convent there for the six weeks of the summer, but I'm not counting it as one of my 'houses' because it was temporary. I enjoyed it a lot. We lived a very religious life. Each day we had Mass either in the Convent or in the parish Church. It was very interesting because the parish was largely Mexican. What color, what music. I loved it. The children were public school kids who were Catholic, but who didn't attend the Parish school. They were eager and lively. By now I had had quite a lot of experience teaching catechism so I didn't find it too hard to do.

The Sisters were all older. They had either finished College so they didn't have to attend classes. We all enjoyed one another's company at recreation time each day. I would just listen to their stories. I was learning about life in the convent. I was getting used

to being a Professed Sister. I was more determined
than ever to succeed.

It was interesting to me to see that the Sisters did not
have any luxuries to speak of. Our cells were very
small. Here the cells were individual rooms with a
window. There was a narrow bed, a desk and chair,
and a chest of drawers. All the rooms were the same.
There was no rug on the hardwood floor. The wall had
a crucifix and a picture of the Blessed Mother. We
lived what was called the regular life. This meant that
our schedule was just like that in all the IHM
convents. The ringing of the little bell summoned us to
the Chapel for prayer, meals, recreation, and silence at
night. It also served as the rising bell at 5:30 a.m. I
learned as the years went on that all the convents were
roughly the same as far as accommodations were
concerned. Thus, there was no way to become
attached to one's surroundings. Simplicity of life was
the whole idea.

At the end of the six-week session of catechism
classes we were wondering what our next mission
would be. Because I was so new I didn't know just
what to expect. It was nervous time for Sister Peter. I
was happy to get my mission in August. It said that
'for the honor and glory of God' I was to teach second
grade at Holy Spirit School in L.A. Sister Enda was to
be my superior and principal. So on to the next
HOUSE.

House No. 11 – 1943
Dunsmuir – Los Angeles,
California

This was the real beginning of my life as a professed IHM. From here on my story will be about my membership in this Community, and all the adventures I experienced. First of all, Sister Enda, my new Superior, called me to tell me that someone would pick me up at the Motherhouse and bring me to Holy Spirit Convent. I packed my modest cardboard suitcase, and left for my first official assignment. I was excited but apprehensive at the same time because I didn't know what to expect.

When I arrived at the convent I found a group of IHMs who were all new to me. They ranged in age from seventy something down to me. I was nineteen. All were smiling, and welcomed me. Sister Enda was the Superior. She was probably in her forties. She turned out to be kind on some occasions and strict on others. All in all, she was the leader of the pack. She taught eighth grade. Sister Helene was in her twenties. She taught seventh grade. Then there was Sister Austin. She taught fifth grade. I couldn't believe that she was in her seventies. In fact, I think this may have been the last year she would teach. She subsequently lived to be over one hundred years old. Sister Marian was in her early twenties. She taught sixth grade. Sister Alacoque was in her forties. She was the fourth grade teacher. Sister Clement taught third or first. She was only a couple of years older than I was. Then I was assigned the second grade. Someone may have had to take a double grade. So there you have it.

These IHMs were the ones I would be living with for the year. I hoped for the best. Since they were all experienced I hoped I could catch on to things pretty fast.

The convent itself was rather new. It was laid out like all convents were in those days. All the parishes had to provide a home for the Sisters because they had no money to buy a home or to pay rent. It was customary for the parish to pay the utilities, and upkeep of the convent. But the parish did not provide for our food, clothing, medicine, education, transportation, or anything else. In return we taught full-time in the school, and were paid a small stipend. In those days I think it may have been something like $40.00 dollars a month for each nun. Because we all professed a vow of poverty we did not ever see this money. The pastor would give the check to the Superior who would give it to the procurator and have her bank it. Since there were seven of us that meant that we received $280.00 a month. It was required by the Mother General and her Council that each convent send 20% of their income to the Motherhouse for the care of the elderly who had never been able to accrue retirement funds, and for the running of the Community. This meant that in our convent the Superior had $224.00 to use for all our needs for the month. Since we were used to living a very simple life with no luxuries thrown in the money was spread according to the needs of the seven of us. Of course, when I arrived on the scene in September 1943, I was not aware of any of this. I just knew that I would be a teacher, and I would devote my service to God and the Church. I would never expect to be paid in actual money for anything I did.

The convent was quite compact. It was two stories. The first floor had the two parlors by the front door. The chapel was to the right as you entered the front door. It was just the right size for us. We each had a kneeler. There were a couple of extra ones for guests. The sacristy was located in the rear. I thought it was beautiful. Because we were governed by a rule of cloister we could not permit lay persons to any part of our convent except the parlor and chapel. This was an age-old custom practiced by nuns the world over. Everyone probably wondered what was so mysterious about the rest of the house, but it was very utilitarian for us. The practice of keeping the cloister really protected our privacy.

Now into the cloister. Further inside the house was a hallway leading to a large room. This was what was called the community room. It was very similar to a family room found in modern houses. It had a long table surrounded by straight chairs where we could spread out our schoolwork, or do other things that needed some space. We would all gather here after dinner in the evening for half an hour of recreation. I have mentioned before that we spent this time chatting about the day, or darning the runs in our black stockings, or singing, or doing something that didn't keep us from communicating with one another. I always found recreation time relaxing. Sometimes the younger Sisters were permitted to go outside and exercise on the basketball court, or play a game of baseball. I was a happy camper when this happened.

Just off the recreation room was another large room called the refectory. This was the medieval name for dining room. It had a long table suitable for our numbers. Straight-backed chairs were placed along each side. There was no tablecloth. Of course, I soon realized that the dishes and napkin were kept in the drawer at each place. There was always a chair placed separately in the corner. This was used by the reader at meals when we didn't talk while eating. Everything was very plain.

Next to the refectory was a small pantry room that had cupboards for dishes and food. Then next to this room was the kitchen. It was a good size, very clean and neat. We cooked our own meals by taking turns because I really don't remember having a cook. Sometimes the Pastor would hire someone in the parish to cook our supper. If not, then we took turns. You can imagine my panic because I did not have the slightest idea what to do about cooking for seven people.

We had a stairway in the front of the house and another one in the back. Upstairs was very utilitarian. All the cells were lined up one after the other on each side of a long hall. My cell was near the end next to the Superior's cell. There was a single bed with a white cotton bedspread, a desk with a chair, a chest of drawers, no carpet on the hardwood floor, and a small closet for my two habits, mantle, nightgowns, bathrobe, and slippers. I tucked the suitcase in there somewhere. Also, a crucifix hung over the bed. The biggest luxury I had was a sink right there in my room. A mirror and medicine cabinet were right above it. I thought this was quite wonderful. The bathroom was down the hall a ways. We all shared. I was pretty used to sharing by this time. This whole arrangement was very much to my liking since I had come to the IHMs in order to live a simple life and serve God.

I settled in with my new companions. We lived the same kind of life that I had seen so far in my short experience. When school started I was ready to teach my second-graders. I was assigned to a very small classroom. Even though their desks were small, the children hardly fit into the room. I couldn't walk down any aisles. Oh well – I had the books and materials needed. So school started.

It was customary to assign tasks to different Sisters, so I was given the Choir right off the bat. This meant that once or twice a week around two p.m. the older girls would meet with me in the church. I had never been in charge of music before, so I was very nervous about it all. Luckily, I could carry a tune, and read music somewhat. It turned out, that I didn't have any trouble with getting the kids to do what I wanted them to do. So I would choose the hymns to be sung the following Sunday at the children's mass and we would practice them until the music sounded right. This turned out to be the beginning of many years of choir work for me. I always enjoyed it, but there was a certain amount of stress for me. I think I was always worried that the singing would not turn out well. The worst time of the year was Holy Week. Those were the days when Church services were always said in Latin.

Of course, the music for the long services of Holy Thursday, Good Friday, and Holy Saturday took hours and hours of rehearsal. The real problem with this was that all the music was special for the day, so we were practicing difficult hymns that would be sung only once, and then put aside for another year. I was usually a basket case when Holy Week arrived. I was sure that I had forgotten to teach some obscure response or Psalm that was part of the Service. Believe it or not, this did happen a couple of times. On those occasions I would have to sing the neglected part myself – solo.

So here I was, at my first real mission, doing things that a few years earlier I had never dreamed of. I was excited about teaching second grade so I prepared everything to the best of my ability. The first day of school was the hardest because I wasn't sure how I would do. My fears were unfounded. The little class responded to me at once. I was "Sister Peter" this, and "Sister Peter" that for them all. I did have trouble squeezing all of us into the little room, but we made out fine. Sister Superior did give me a difficult assignment right away. Since I was going to be the choir teacher she told me that I was to stand in front of the whole school each morning when they lined up and direct them in some patriotic song. That was a surprise. I hadn't expected it. So each morning the whole bunch would line up according to grade and sing "The Star Spangled Banner" or "America" or some other familiar tune. I would stand up in front of them all waving my arms and hoping for the best. I had to do this the whole year until June. I never got used to the idea of performing. There was a certain shyness that I had that I just couldn't shake – even to this day.

The year passed quickly. I was very busy with

teaching, doing the planning that went with it, going to college classes every Saturday morning, staying up late to study for those classes, and of course, "living the life" as we used to say. In a word, I was busy, busy, busy. And I loved it. I was learning something new every day.

Some things happened that really were funny. The most shocking for me was the day I was assisting the priest at Benediction. This was a ceremony carried out in the evening or a Sunday afternoon. When I was in the Novitiate in Hollywood we were never called upon to do any tasks in the sacristy there. Sister Raphael was the head honcho there. She had been doing all the honors for years. So we finished up our year and a half of novitiate training without ever being asked to do anything in the sacristy. Sister Superior assigned me to the chapel. This was one of my charges for the month. There was always a lot to do. We had to set up the vestments for the priest to wear at Mass. We were responsible for the cleanliness of the sacristy and chapel. We also had to be ready to assist the priest at the altar at Mass and Benediction because we did not have any altar boys in the convent. I took on the task with enthusiasm. I studied the Ordo. This was the book of directions for what was to be read during every Mass of every day of the year. Some of it was in Latin.

I guess I did all right most of the time. But the first Sunday I was to assist at Benediction I really flubbed up. I was to hold the censor during the ceremony until the priest turned to me to hand it to him so he could place incense in it. The clouds of sweet-smelling incense were symbolic of our prayers ascending to

Heaven. I was ready. But when I went to stand up from the prei-dieu I misjudged the balance I would need to stand. One hand held the censor; the other hand held the incense. As I stood up the prie-dieu tipped over forward, and I went sprawling. The incense container fell from my hands. A million little grains of incense were scattered all over the chapel floor. The priest stood mesmerized. I just stood. Suddenly there were all kinds of "tsk tsks". A couple of the Sisters came up and plucked up as many grains as they could and put them into the censor – still tsk-tsking. I was humiliated. I am sure my face was red as a beet, but there was nothing I could do about it. I expected Sister Enda to scold me for being so careless, but she didn't. In fact, no one chided me. I am sure that they chalked it up to my total inexperience. At least, I wasn't removed from the charge.

About two weeks after I arrived at Holy Spirit I was surprised with a grade change. Sister Enda assigned me to the sixth grade instead of the second. I had already been teaching the second grade for a few days so naturally I was surprised. It seemed that the nun in the sixth grade became ill with something that was going to prevent her from teaching for a long time. So there I was, having to do something I had not prepared for.

I just scoured the sixth-grade teachers' manuals over the weekend, and introduced myself to the sixth graders on Monday. The class received me very well. All year we got along famously.

I soon learned that life in the parochial convents was very busy. Beside teaching all day, there were the usual charges to do every day, lesson planning every single evening, prayers and meditations morning and evening, and interacting with one another in what we termed, 'community life'. I seemed to fit into it very well. I was happy, and prayed that I would measure up. I was in charge of the choir, so every Sunday was a day for me to panic a little bit. I was never quite sure if all the kids would turn up, or if I would respond to all the cues at Mass. I was usually very relieved after Mass was ended because everything went well.

One surprise for me was the task the Pastor gave to the nuns. He would bring over the Sunday collection right after lunch. Our job was to count it all out, and wrap all the coins. We would all sit around the big table in the Community Room and do this job. Sister Enda would tote it up, never telling us what the sum was, and put it all in a canvas moneybag. She then took it next door to the Pastor. This was so routine that I just got used to it. After we were finished we then had the afternoon to work on our lesson plans for the following week. These were written in a stylized plan book that had an outlined box for each day of the week. There was enough room to write in what I planned to do in each subject. I found this task rather enjoyable because I felt that I went into the classroom on Monday morning as prepared as I could be. I discovered, as the years went by, that our Sisters all prepared their lessons in this manner. It didn't matter what convent you were missioned to. The routine was always the same. However, I did find that the collection counting was not done by the Sisters in every parish.

My first year was rolling along very well. My mother came up to see me about once a month. I wasn't permitted to make a home visit yet. I didn't expect it for awhile. I thought my family was doing well after the hardships of those depression years. Bernie had joined the Navy, and was stationed on Palmyra Island in the South Pacific. He was an aviation machinist mate. He wrote Mama lots of letters. The war was on, but for some reason he could not identify where he was. I have since learned that this island was a very small coral atoll nine hundred miles south of Hawaii. It was used by the Navy to build an airstrip. His letters, of course, could never describe military business, but he found it interesting. I have a long roll-photo of him together with his group posing there on the white coral. Barr had joined the Air Force. He was in training at Williams Field in Arizona. He was tapped for officer's training right away. After a time Mama told me he made Second Lieutenant. That was a feather in his cap. Bev got married to Roy White, a sailor. I do not believe I saw her very often during this time.

Mama was doing real well. She was finally working in a real job at the OPA. She was still the organist at St. Athanasius Parish, and she was active in a number of parish groups. I was so happy to see everyone doing so well. It seemed that my prayers were being answered. Of course, I worried about my brothers in the armed forces. We were at war.

One Visiting Sunday I had a real surprise. Mama came accompanied by Barr and his new wife, Beth. What a shock. I guess I wasn't expecting this to happen without some kind of notice. We all sat in the parlor for a visit. I tried to be my congenial self. I realize now that Beth probably hadn't been around nuns in her life. During our visit Beth would address Barr as "Mike." After awhile I just had to ask her why she called him Mike. She replied, "Well, that's what he told me his name was." We all laughed, but I still think it was odd. He didn't go by the name of Barr in the Service. His birth certificate name was George Barr. Our family always called him Barr. Where Mike came from I will never know.

It was in this period of time that I heard from my mother that she had been notified about Bernie. It seems that he had contracted tuberculosis. It was a shock to all of us. Mama said the Navy was sending him home on a hospital ship. It overwhelmed me that he was that sick. I know now that my mother was stricken. How sad. He left us as a hale and hearty young man, full of energy and promise. We didn't know what was going to happen to him. When he arrived at the Naval Hospital out in Corona I visited him once. I was shocked. He was absolutely bald. I don't know whether the medicine did this to him, or whether it was shaved off for comfort. He never said why. His spirits were semi-good, but I could see that he was very sick. Later he was discharged from the Navy, and was sent to the Veterans' hospital in San Fernando Valley.

So a lot had happened to our family in just a few years. Barr was married, and so was Beverly. Bernie was flat on his back. I was in the convent. Mama was trying to keep up with it all.

When the school year ended, we all attended College

classes for the summer session. I also spent a few hours a day doing some summer school tutoring for students from the surrounding parochial schools. At the end of the six weeks we had our annual Retreat. I went up to the Motherhouse in Hollywood with about a hundred other IHMs for eight days of prayers, silence, conferences, and soul-searching. It was quite peaceful. Always at the close of retreat we knew that if any mission changes were to be made we would be notified, in writing, of the change.

Everyone was watching Sister Felicia walk into the big refectory as we were eating breakfast. She was carrying a large stack of envelopes. She went from one to the other giving them the news. I wasn't expecting a mission, so I was shocked when she gave me an envelope. When I opened it I was told that 'for the greater honor and glory of God' I was to teach second grade at Immaculate Heart of Mary School, and reside at the Motherhouse. What a surprise that was. After a few days back at Holy Spirit I packed my suitcase, said goodbye to all, and reported to Sister Scholastica, my new Superior, at the Motherhouse. My adventures continue on to the next house. I am now twenty years old.

House No. 12 – 1944

Immaculate Heart Motherhouse – Hollywood, California

I arrived at the Motherhouse wondering what was going to happen. I already knew that I would be teaching at Immaculate Heart of Mary Parish School. It was located down on Santa Monica Boulevard. I was familiar with all the facets of living in a convent by now. So after getting settled in a little cell on the third floor I reported to my new Superior. Her name was Sister Scholastica. She was a formidable woman to me – tall, stern looking, all business. She welcomed me and said she was assigning me to several charges. At first I was ok with this message, but I soon found that I would have my hands full.

For this, my second year of Profession, I would teach each day at Immaculate Heart of Mary School. I was given the second grade pupils.

They were all about seven years old. I prepared myself for teaching them as best I could, but when I arrived at the school a few days before it opened for class I was told my class would have 86 pupils in it. This number was overwhelming to me. I walked down the long hall of the school to the classroom to see if the room itself was double size. When I opened the door I gazed upon a regular sized classroom that was literally crammed with desks. There wasn't room for me to walk down aisles. I inwardly groaned. After all I had just finished my first year of teaching where I had 26 pupils in sixth grade. Now here I was confronted with a giant class. I should explain here that the class size was par for the course in the early forties.

The war had started, people were back at work, the Depression was over, and Catholic families were sending their children to Catholic Schools. They could now pay some tuition. All of my fellow teachers, who were all IHMs, also had very large classes. In fact, in almost every school we had in urban parts of cities the classes were just jammed. This lasted for several years. In later years there was a limit put on class size – finally. It was fifty pupils.

I plunged into my tasks with energy and good spirit. I was very busy at school all day long. Then I would come back to the Motherhouse by about four p.m. and start my charges. It turned out that the things I was assigned to do sometimes conflicted in time. Consequently, I was trying to take a tray of supper to an elderly bed-ridden nun, serve dinner in the priest's dining room, and prepare the towels for the silver bowls. Earlier I had spent about forty minutes sweeping and dusting the Chapel. One can see that I was a very busy young nun. Remember that on top of all this activity we still adhered to our prayer schedule – three hours each day – and even had a half-hour of recreation in the evening. I used this time to repair my clothes, darn stockings, etc, while chatting with everyone nearby. After the last evening chant of the psalms I had a quiet hour to prepare my classes for the next day and to study for College.

I had some good companions through all of my life. Here I was teamed up with Sister Edward. She and I entered the same day, so we were friends. We would leave the Convent to go to school around seven-thirty a.m. We would take a bus, and a trolley. But, if it happened that we missed this transportation we would walk all the way to school. It was down Western Avenue, and east on Santa Monica Boulevard. We were young. The walk felt good. But we were pretty tired when we arrived. I taught my 86 youngsters, and Sister Edward taught hers. She had a class as large as mine. Our rooms were adjacent with a door opening between us.

Sometimes we would both be trying to cope, and one or the other would open the door to the next room and just smile, roll our eyes, and wave. Whenever she did this I would just start laughing because our situation was so unbelievable.

The consequence of this for me was that I became exhausted. I say now that my second year of teaching was my hardest because I was so very tired the whole year. Somehow or other, I just chalked up the demands of my life to be what I had pledged myself to do. So I didn't spend too much time lamenting. I was blessed with a good sense of humor. I seemed to be able to see that I wouldn't always be so busy.

Some of my IHM companions were real characters. The one I remember the most is Sister Stanislaus. She was a scary looking nun.

Somewhere in the past she had cancer of the nose. In those days they didn't do much skin grafting, so she had a misshapen nose. She wore her coif and veil at a high angle. She was a sturdy woman. And she scared the kids. They always behaved real well for her. I was asked on occasion to be her companion for the ride home on the trolley and bus. That was fine with me because I knew her as a kind, but gruff, person. We got along fine. I was always praying that she wouldn't do one of the things we would just cringe at. I couldn't believe it, but if she thought the trolley took too long to come she would just stand on the curb and stop the next automobile that stopped for the light. The startled driver would politely open the window to find out what she wanted. She would ask him if he would kindly take the two of us up to the Motherhouse. I was trying to crawl into a crack in the sidewalk, but she motioned me to come, and we got into this stranger's car. She would spend the ten minutes of our ride chatting amiably with the driver who still seemed to be in a daze. I am sure they didn't know what to make of this nun standing on the corner asking for a lift. That happened to me several times. The whole Community knew of this idiosyncrasy of Sister Stanislaus. We still talk about it when her name comes up.

Several things were happening in my family this year. Bernie was in the Veterans Hospital. I would go up for a visit infrequently. The problem was that the War was going on and there were ration stamps for gasoline. I would ask Sister Superior for permission to have someone drive me up to San Fernando, but sometimes she turned me down because there we no ration stamps. I worried about Bernie a lot. I was so certain that he would get better. How could it be that he was so ill that he wouldn't recover? He had always been so hale and hearty.

Then, Beverly had been married awhile, and had a little daughter, Carol Marie. Her husband , Roy White, was a sailor in the Navy so she was traveling around trying to be near him. Little Carol was just adorable. She had such bright eyes, and those little rosebud lips. Barr was in the Air Force, and married to Beth. I believe he also had a child by now, Danny. I didn't see much of him and Beth.

Mama was still working in the Office of Price Administration, and seemed to be doing all right. She would make the trip up to see me several times this year. They each seemed to have found their way to better times. Of course, with the War going on it was hard to know what would happen.

As for me, I happily renewed my vows in April for another year. The next time around I would be making perpetual vows. That was the dream of us all. I finished off the year at Immaculate Heart of Mary School exhausted, but content that I had done my best in the service of God. I loved my class and they loved me back so I felt it was a good year.

For the summer I was assigned to take a full load of College classes. My charges were changed to serving meals in the Sisters Dining room and cleaning the Community Room. That meant sweeping, and dusting every piece of furniture every day. I was busy as could be. The change of pace from classroom teaching was welcome. But this summer brought its sadness to our family.

I knew that Bernie was not doing well. I had gone out to visit him a couple of times. He seemed to be getting thinner and thinner. Mama was so worried. She would make the trek up there by bus, streetcar, and friends whenever she could. Finally, the doctors told her that Bernie wouldn't live much longer, so would she like to come up and stay in a guest cottage. She did just that. She was with him on July 18, 1945 when he died. Our hearts were broken. Bernie was only 24 years of age.

That morning I was at Mass in our chapel. In fact, I was up in the choir loft singing the hymns with several Sisters. I heard Sister Scholastica coming up the choir steps. She called me out, and told me she had just received a call from my mother telling me that my brother had died. Even though I had been expecting it I broke down in tears. The nuns said some special prayers for him during Mass. I just couldn't believe it. He was always so strong and vibrant. Later that day my whole remaining family came up to the convent to see me. We just clung to one another. My father's death in 1941 came as a surprise, but Bernie's was a blow. I don't think my dear mother ever recovered from the shock of saying goodbye to her firstborn so early in his life. For the next forty years she mentioned his name every day.

The rosary was held at the Sheeler Mortuary on Long Beach Boulevard. It was crowded with friends and nuns. The funeral was at St. Athanasius Church. Everyone was crying. Bernie was laid to rest in Calvary Cemetery. Mama purchased two plots so there would be room for her later. That is what happened when she died at age 90. I have saved the scrapbook Mama made of all the cards and condolences for Bernie's memory.

So my summer was sad. Barr and Bev were busy with their new lives. They had spouses and children to think about. Mama carried on with her work. I was attending summer session at the College, and waiting for Retreat. It was always a time of tension for all of us because at the end of Retreat the missions were given out. I quietly prayed for whatever God would have in store for me.

Would I go back to Immaculate Heart of Mary School with its giant classes, or what? It turned out that I got THE letter. I was assigned to Cathedral Chapel School in the Wilshire District to teach second grade. Sister Vincent would be my Superior. So in August I packed my suitcase with my few things, and started a new adventure.

Both pictures taken in 1944. Top: Mama & Barr.
Bottom: Beverly holding Carol Marie & Mama

House No. 13 - 1945
Dunismur, Los Angeles

Now it is the end of summer of 1945. I have had quite
a few adventures by now. I am still convinced that I
made the right choice of life for me. Now I was going
to a new assignment. I was told I would teach the
Second Grade, and have the choir. Sister Vincent
would be my Superior. It turned out that I would stay
at Cathedral Chapel School for four years. So I arrived
in August ready for whatever the Lord had in mind for
me.

I really had experiences. First of all, the Sisters I was
to be living with were mostly older and experienced. I
did not find them difficult. They were kind and
dedicated. Sister Superior told me right off that I was
to learn to drive. I was surprised. It seemed that the
Sister who had the second grade before me was still
there at Cathedral Chapel. She was a friend of mine
from my group – Sister Christopher. We had the use
of an old Essex or Buick. It was painted blue. For
some reason we named the car, Mariah. Every day for
the next two weeks Sister Christopher took me for
lessons right there out in the schoolyard. The most
important thing she taught me to do was to park
parallel. In fact, she showed me so well that when I
was out for my test drive to get my license I did a
perfect parallel for the man who was testing me. From
then on I drove almost every day.

When I met my new class I was ecstatic because I no
longer had 86 children. I had only 60. That was more
manageable for me. I met them all with a big smile on
my face. They turned out to be just a delight to teach.

I had thought that maybe the children of the wealthy and famous might be a handful, they weren't at all. I should explain that Cathedral Chapel School is located in the heart of the Wilshire District of Los Angeles. At that time there were many movie stars living in the area. They sent their children to parochial school. My experience with them was very good. The children I had couldn't have had better manners. Some of the names come to mind.

There were John Wayne's four children Michael in sixth grade, Toni in fifth, Patrick in second (my class) and Melinda in kindergarten. By the end of my fourth year I had taught both Patrick and Melinda. I also had the two older ones with chorus and choir. Leilani Owens was in the sixth grade. She was the daughter of Harry Owens, the bandleader. He wrote the song "Sweet Leilani" at the time of his daughter's birth. She was a cute freckled-face girl with dark curly hair. There were others who were in bit parts in movies. Anyway, it was an eye-opener for me to see that these children were very nice to work with.

Sometimes Mrs. Wayne would invite all of us Sisters over to her house for dinner. We would enjoy the visit because she was so hospitable, but also because she would run a movie of John's. Since we didn't go out to movies at all, and there was no TV at that time we thought it was very entertaining. One of the movies I remember seeing in her house was "The Wake of the Red Witch." By this time Mrs. Wayne (Josephine) and John were divorced. Mrs. Wayne was very active in the school parents' club, and spearheaded fund-raisers for the school.

One of the fund-raisers we had each year was a paper drive. This was just after the war ended, so it was something the children could do to help the school. My, how we did work. All the bundles had to be tied just right, and placed in the auditorium under the number of our classroom. Of course, there was a prize of some kind for the class that brought the most papers. My class never won because the sixth grade, with Sister Leonella as teacher, always was stupendous. We did our best though. Sometimes the piles would be high enough to be over our heads. I never said anything, but there were times when I wondered if the floor of the auditorium could hold the weight. The school cafeteria was right below it. I envisioned a collapse of tons of paper. Well, it never happened. I never knew how much money we made. The Superior never told us things like that.

So I was very busy here for four years. Each year I felt more and more confident in my teaching. After the second year or so I was just sailing through. I realized that I enjoyed it very much. I made some lifelong friends within the Community. It was interesting how this happened.

There was always a certain amount of bonding that took place. Of course, though, we were always being warned against particular friendships. I used to wonder what that meant, but now I realize it was a way to keep us ever vigilant against unwanted ardor that could lead to much more serious behavior. We lived in such close proximity with one another that it was important to protect your personal space. Somehow or other I managed to do this successfully my whole life. The friends that I did have for many years were really 'good friends' and not needy emotional souls that depended on me to rescue them from their need. Thank God in Heaven for that.

Our daily life went along very smoothly. We all had our charges to do each day, school to teach, prayers to say, and college homework to do. I was always very busy. I had a problem with time because Sister Vincent, the Superior, was always ready to go out to do something right after school. Since I was the only driver I was the one who took her. The consequence of this was that I was always spending evening hours in the chapel making up my prayers that I missed by taking Sr. Vincent wherever she wanted. After awhile I grew pretty tired of this routine, but there was nothing I could do about it because one never complained. Sister Vincent was always planning plays and pageants for the school. We would train the children in their parts. In so many ways I discovered talents that I didn't know I had at all. My artistic talent was used to design and paint scenery for the staged events. My musical talent was used to produce the choral singing needed. I was even put in charge of girls' sports. I could do this last task after school whenever I wasn't taking Sister Superior out somewhere.

The Sisters in the convent changed a little each year. There were always older, experienced ones who knew everything. Then there were those of us just coming along. By now I had renewed my vows three times so it was time to make final vows. This event was an important milestone for each of us because one had to decide if this was truly the life for her. We always made an eight-day retreat ahead of time. These were days spent in prayer and silence. The idea was to commune with God about our future. Usually by the end of the retreat one would have made up her mind about it all. I had come to the conclusion that for me this was the kind of life I could live. The vows we made were called perpetual. That meant that we said we would be faithful to them for the rest of our lives. So it was a great moment for me in April of 1946 to recite my vows, and say 'forever' during the prayer. From here on I was a full-fledged member of the Immaculate Heart Sisters.

During these four years I had visits from my dear family. Things had moved along for all of them. Mama was busy with a job in the Gold Star Mothers. She qualified for membership because of Bernie's death in the Service. Barr was out of the service for awhile, but he rejoined later. I am not sure what his status was at this time in my life. I would see all of them periodically. One Sunday I was shocked by a visit from Mama and Beverly. It was Bev who surprised me. She was her usual beautiful self except that she had dyed her hair blonde, and she was very thin. I tried to carry on a visit in a cheery way, but I was wondering what was the matter with her. I asked her, but she said there was nothing the matter. It wasn't long after that visit that Mama called me to say that Bev was in General Hospital in L.A. with Tuberculosis. I was shocked with the news. I said, "What about little Carol?" Mama said she was caring for her. I don't know where Roy was. That was a real bombshell in our family. First Bernie, and now Bev. My mother must have been reeling from the turn of events.

Here I was carrying out my duties as a teaching nun,

living a rather stylized life separate from the world, and yet I was very concerned and worried about my loved ones. Mama and I went up to see Bev at General very soon. Because it took us quite a while to get together we arrived there at the last minute for visitors. They almost didn't let us in. Mama prevailed while I stood beside her arrayed in all my nunny splendor. When we came to Bev's room she took one look at us and then began to cry. I felt so sad for her. She looked so sick. After a bit she stopped crying. She said she was so scared being there. It seems that on the day before the girl in the room right next to hers had climbed out the window and committed suicide. She was shocked and so were we. I was praying that she wouldn't get very depressed and do the same thing. After all, I really didn't know very much about the hard life Bev had lived since she married Roy.

Mama said that because Bev was only in her late teens she was left out of a lot of things. When Roy wanted to go out to a bar for a drink he would go all right, but he I remember being very nervous about whether or not Bev would recover. It was not so long before this that Bernie had died of the TB he contracted in the Navy.

My four years at Cathedral Chapel School were years when I had a lot to think about. I was worried about Bev and Carol Marie. I was worried about Mama who rose to the occasion as she always had. I didn't know much about Barr and Beth. I am not sure where they were. I remember that they came to visit me at Cathedral Chapel when Danny was a toddler. I did enjoy those visits a lot.

I was busy each year with a class of about 60 children. By now I had learned techniques that worked like magic. My children thrived and so did I. I also was very busy studying at night and on weekends for my college units. I had gradually amassed enough credits to finally graduate with a Bachelor of Arts Degree in the summer of 1947. That was a triumph for me because I was teaching full-time, living my religious life industriously, and going to classes all the time. What a busy life.

I remember the graduation ceremony so well. It was held in the IHM Chapel at the Motherhouse on a Sunday afternoon. Archbishop Cantwell presided. Mama came bringing little Carol Marie with her. They sat in the front row.

When the fourth summer came around I attended classes as usual, taught some catechism classes, and began thinking of starting my fifth year at Cathedral Chapel. At the end of retreat I was astonished to receive a mission. What a mission it turned out to be. I was to teach third grade, and conduct the choirs, and serve as second Councilor in the Convent of All Souls Parish in South San Francisco. This was September of 1949. I was 25 years old, and had tried out religious life for eight years. Little did I know that my adventures would continue.

Martha Murphy, 1949

House No. 14 – 1949
South San Francisco, California

What a flurry of activity took place in August. We had to get all packed and ready for our new school in South San Francisco. There were five of us chosen to go. I was ecstatic. First of all the new Superior was Sister Mary Victoria who was well known for her great good humor and kindness.

I was part of the pioneer group at a new school. I had always wanted to go to San Francisco just to see the great city. We were slated to get there by train. That was another plus. My companion Sisters were all friends of mine – Sister Rosalie, Sister Ethel, Sister Bernard Ann and Sister Dorothea. It looked like the whole group would have a lot of life. This was quite a contrast to the very sedate household I had been living in at Cathedral Chapel with Sister Vincent as Superior, and several elderly nuns. In a lot of ways I was breathing a sigh of relief.

Before we left I had a strange thing happen to me. I had always enjoyed very good health except for that one time when I was a Novice. I can't explain exactly what happened, but the night before we were to leave I was assigned to a cell on the third floor of the Service Building. I had never slept there before so I didn't realize that the rising bell was different from the usual hand bell sound. I must have been turned over toward the wall when the bell went off. It was a screeching fire bell right outside my door. I was so startled that I must have turned my head in shock before turning my body. I soon realized what it was, but I noticed at once that I had a piercing pain in the back of my neck. I tried to massage it, but it wouldn't go away. It was intense. Later I asked the Superior for some aspirin, which she gave to me. But the truth of the matter is that I must have injured the muscles at the back of my neck.

I was in a miserable quandary. Here I was with the wonderful mission. We were scheduled to leave that very day. I couldn't pull out at the last minute, so I just gritted my teeth and tried to ignore the ache. The train trip was beautiful; the arrival in San Francisco was exciting. Mother Eucharia went with us. The Pastor and the people greeted us with open arms. We soon discovered that we were not in San Francisco itself, but in South San Francisco.

This turned out to be a small town near the airport. Almost every living soul in the place was Italian. I mean everyone. They were thrilled to have us come to their new school. I taught third grade, the first year, and second grade the second year. The first night we couldn't sleep in the convent because it wasn't finished. The local physician offered his home to us. After a few days we did move into the convent, but had to sleep in the chapel because the cells were not ready yet. So it was all very exciting for me.

The parish church was right next door, in fact, a door opened right into the church from our parlor. We all plunged into our work with gusto.

Everyone seemed to have so many talents that could be used. We taught all day, then taught catechism on Saturdays. I had the children's choir ready to sing at the 9 o'clock Mass each Sunday. Sometimes Sister

Mary Victoria would pile us into the car and we would take a basket of food down to the beach or some other nice relaxing place. We never returned to Hollywood at all the entire year. We had a lot of company though. Everyone was curious about this new mission in San Francisco. I also had visits from my loved ones. Barr and Beth came to see me, and so did Mama. I kept in touch with all by mail mostly.

Even though we were busy from morning until night every day, there were so many things that happened that kept us in good humor. Sometimes the things that happened have kept us laughing to this day. Here is one event. One of the activities we always did in our schools was have paper drives. I already mentioned this in other pages. Well, Sister Mary Victoria decided that we would have our first paper drive in our new school. This was our first year, so we had only grades K-4. She got the whole school worked up to save papers at home, and then to bring them on the date that she decided. Well, it was her first year of being a principal so she didn't always remember to address the details. It just happened that when the day arrived for the kids to bring their loads they were all instructed to leave the papers by the schoolyard fence under the number of their grade. So far, so good.

The kids and their parents streamed in with piles of wonderful newspaper that we were going to sell, and then purchase play equipment. Later in the morning Sister Mary Victoria informed us that she had forgotten that we were going to a teachers' meeting after school in San Francisco. Well, all looked fine. The schoolyard gates would be locked. The paper piles would be fine. The custodian would keep an eye on it.

So off we went to the meeting. Afterwards, when we were driving back to South City we came to the crest of the hill leading into our little town. All of a sudden we all exclaimed in wonder, "What is that strange gray cloud that seems to be spiraling up over our school?" We could see it a mile away. In an instant we all screamed out, "It's the papers." We had forgotten to tell the kids to tie up their bundles securely. So when the usual wind came up at 2:30 p.m. it swept down over the yard and caught the papers in a wild funnel-like wind, carrying them up and the distributing them all over the neighborhood. We were horrified because our neighborhood included the City Hall, the Police Station and several other civic buildings. As we got closer we could see that the papers were plastered on the sides of houses, on people's cars, all over yards and hedges, hanging from telephone lines, and piled against any fence that got in the way. What a mess. When we arrived at the convent and ran out to the schoolyard to see what we could do, it was too late. ALL the papers were gone. The whole sky above us was fluttering with our precious papers.

You can imagine how we all felt. Sister Mary Victoria took it the hardest. It was her job to try to make amends to the whole town for the faux pas. I am not sure what she did, but we ended up still friends with everyone. The kids later helped us clean up any mess reported.

Sister Mary Victoria had a way of bringing out the

best in each of us with her good humor, and sense of fun. The five of us blossomed. She knew that we could use the Christmas play that would include all 5 grades. We really warmed up to the idea. When we told the children, they were excited and willing. So we put our heads together, and decided to write our own play. Sister Dorothea was creative, so she worked out the scenes of the Nativity story. I was to teach all the carols to the singers. Each Sister was to train her class to recite some part of the Christmas story. In the end I also had to design all the scenery, which I did. In a word, we were going to please the parents with their children's moment in the sun.

When the day arrived we were all busy with practice, costumes, lines rehearsals, singing, and putting up the scenery on a little stage we had in the cafeteria. My depiction of the scene included a horizon showing a village, and several very large palm trees. I had help from everyone in painting them. They were about eight feet high. When I got them down to the stage I realized that they would not stay in place by themselves. Since the only thing we had then was scotch tape I, and my crew, quickly taped all of them to the back wall. The stage was set.

Our program started very well. All the little dancers danced, the singers sang, the readers read. I was down in front with the singers. I was facing the stage. To my very great chagrin I noticed a catastrophe unfolding right before my eyes. There was not one thing I could do about it now. It turned out that we forgot that the cafeteria would be solidly packed with parents, priests, and friends, not to mention all the children and Sisters. Everyone was breathing of course. Well, it soon became very warm. There was moisture in the air. As I looked on, my trees were falling right off the wall one by one. What a sight. There they were plopping down over the manger, the kings, the shepherds, even Mary and Joseph. The scotch tape couldn't stick with so much moisture.

I just went right on with the singing. Everyone else did the same thing. When it was all over we all received a standing ovation from the Pastor and the parents. They didn't care that the trees fell down. They were just ecstatic that their little ones were in a Catholic School doing what Catholic School children do – perform a Christmas Story. When we finally went into the Convent that night we couldn't stop laughing. Believe it or not, we were happy with it all.

My first year at All Souls School was a very happy and rewarding one. By now I felt I was a good teacher. Thus far I was quite happy with my life decision. I was 26 years old.

When the summer arrived we all returned to the Motherhouse for the College summer session. By now I had my degree, but I was working toward my Master's. My headaches continued unabated. When I told Mother Eucharia about it that summer she sent me to a brain specialist whose daughter attended Immaculate Heart High School.

His name was Dr. Rainey. I went to see him. It was a disappointment. Because I looked hale and hearty, and could carry on with my activities with a lot of energy I suppose they thought I was either making it all up, or I was a head case. In this instance Dr. Rainey had xrays taken of my head. He then told me that he couldn't see anything wrong, and sent me on my way. Oh, he did prescribe three weeks of physical therapy on my neck and shoulders. But he never asked me to return to see him. At no point did he ask me about the beginning of these headaches, or did he show any interest. I realized much later on that these doctors were treating the nuns for free, and that they sometimes had nuns come in who were really not sick, but who needed some attention. They kind of took us with a grain of salt. I am sure that if he talked to Mother Eucharia he told her he couldn't see anything wrong. She never again asked me about my headaches. By this time I was in the mode of acceptance of this small physical inconvenience. So I just went on with my life, all the while having an ache. I realized it was not life threatening because I was able to do everything I was called upon to do.

I spent the summer taking classes toward my Master's Degree. We also made our usual eight-day retreat at Montecito. I always looked forward to those days of quiet and prayer. At the end of retreat, when the missions were usually given out, I was excited that I did not receive one. I would be returning to South San Francisco to All Souls. Sister Mary Victoria was to continue on as Superior and Principal. The only change for me was that I was assigned to Second Grade instead of Third. That didn't matter to me. I would still do everything as I had before. I was again assigned to be the choir directress. By now I was so used to all these tasks that nothing daunted me.

When we drove back to South City in August we had one more Sister because the fifth grade was going to be added. Once again we were a very congenial group. Everyone was energetic, all were serious about our way of life, and all were talented and fun. Sister Mary Victoria was her usual self. The parents and children were very welcoming.

We tried to learn from the mistakes we made the first year. The pastor, Monsignor Tozzi, was straight from Italy. He had been here in San Francisco for fifty years, but he still had a heavy accent. He loved us. He would come over to the Convent to visit us in our Community Room. This room was in all the convents. It always had a long table lined with straight-backed chairs. We would gather there each day for recreation, or lesson plans, or meetings. It would be like our living room, only without the overstuffed furniture. He would come over and regale us with stories of his past. We enjoyed him no end, partly because he was so entertaining, but partly because we couldn't always understand his accent, so we would get a different spin on his stories. Sister Mary Victoria was always warning us to be polite.

One time the funniest thing happened. He was sitting at the head of the table in the community room telling us about his favorite dog, DeeDee, that he had in another parish. As he was telling the story he became more animated. It so happened that DeeDee was running down the driveway to greet Monsignor when she was hit lightly by his car. He said he got out and ran over to his pet crying out "DeeDee oh DeeDee." At that very moment in his very animated narration he lifted himself slightly from the chair. When he went to sit down the chair moved a little. The next thing we knew he disappeared. Then we were looking at the top of his little white head. He got on his knees with just his head over the table, and continued the story. We absolutely could not contain ourselves. Here was a talking head. The scene was so funny. He started laughing too. Even to this day when one of us mentions the name "DeeDee" we start laughing.

The second year turned out to be very different from the first. We did all the same things, enjoyed the children and parents, and carried on our lives as usual. The thing that happened that threw us all for a loop was that our Superior, Sister Mary Victoria seemed to be having a nervous breakdown. All five of us were doing ok, but she went into a real funk.

We were all unnerved by the change that came about in Sister Superior's behavior. It was a revelation to me that this could happen. She became quite withdrawn and quiet. We could hardly get a word out of her. We were all wracking our brains to figure out if we had done something terrible to cause her to be this way, but not one of us came up with anything. She went from being very outgoing and cheery person to a distant stranger.

Now in my later years I can piece it together somewhat. Sister Mary Victoria must have been a manic-depressive. We didn't know about this problem then, but we surely do now. When I think back I can see that the pressures and cares of being Superior and Principal of the school were gradually robbing her of the cheerful and happy disposition she had and replacing it with a morose and withdrawn behavior.

Well, there we were. Of course we still did all the things we regularly did in our life, but we didn't know how to handle the Superior. Finally, we all decided that we would have to tell the Mother General about the situation. A phone call was made. Very soon thereafter Sister Nepomucen was sent up to check out the situation. She was a very close personal friend of Sister Mary Victoria. Since it was now after Easter, Sister Nepomucen stayed on with us, and took care of Sister Mary Victoria. After some time we began to notice an improvement in her, but there was still some problem. Thank God we were all able to finish the year in pretty good spirits, but the experience was one we never got over.

I was very happy with my work and life. Mama came up to visit a couple of times. So did Barr, Beth, and Danny. I began to notice that Barr and Beth were not as cheery as they had been.

So I completed my second year at All Souls. By now I have been in the convent 10 years. I am 27 years old. I have made perpetual vows, I am a good teacher, and I look forward to what comes next. Well, guess what? After attending summer school and making the usual 8-day retreat I received a new assignment. Mother Regina appointed me as Superior and Principal of Our Lady of Mercy School in Merced, California. More adventure!

House No. 15 – 1951
Merced, California

Our Lady of Mercy Parish in Merced, California was located in a small town of about 25,000 residents. It is the center of the San Joaquin Valley. Everything for miles around is lush farmland and bountiful orchards of every kind of delicious fruit. The people there were hardworking and friendly. They supported our small parish school whole-heartedly. The pastor of the parish was Father Batt. His two assistants were Irish priests, Father McKenna and Father Byrne. Both had heavy accents straight from the 'old sod.' The parish church was located about five blocks away from the school, so we always had a moderate walk whenever we went to church with the children. Our convent was a wonderful old house on the corner right next to the school. It was a two-story Victorian home that had been rearranged into a nice convent for the Sisters. It included a lovely little chapel. All of our convents had chapels.

There were seven other IHMs assigned to be on my faculty. They were all younger than I was. Which was something because I was 27 at the time. I seemed to take on my new duties with aplomb. When we arrived we all pitched in to open up the convent, air it out after a hot summer when it was closed, and get ourselves ready for the new school year. I went down to the rectory to meet the pastor and assistants, and then we were surprised by the arrival of Sister Mary Victoria and the Sisters from All Souls. They brought us dinner and supplies for the next day. We were very grateful for their thoughtfulness.

My new adventures began. This was August 1951. It would turn out that I would be stationed here for the next six years. Once school began we just rolled along with all the duties I have described before. The children who attended our school were just wonderful. They were all small-town kids who seemed to have a lot of parental supervision. I didn't have any trouble with them at all. I had a big job to do because I was a full-time eighth grade teacher, and principal of the school. We had around 300 students in Kindergarten through eighth grades. One of the best things about it was that we Sisters were all very well used to the life in the convent and aware of our duties in the classrooms. Consequently, I didn't have to do too much mentoring. I did help the newcomers as much as I could.

The people were so generous with us. One farmer delivered two gallons of milk to our backdoor every other day or so. Another farmer donated crates of vegetables when they were in season. Even the Coca-Cola distributor would bring over a crate of cokes every so often. You can't imagine what a big help this was for us because we had to provide our own food from a meager salary of $60.00 a month for each of us. Of course, we pooled our money because we never took it for our own use. Our vow of poverty clearly stated that we were not to possess personal funds.

Some people have said that they thought the parish provided for our total support in return for our services in the school. That was not so. Whenever a parish wanted to build a school the priest and all the parishioners had to figure out a way to finance it. It was considered a source of great pride when a parish could build a school, and secure the services of a teaching order of nuns. What people didn't realize was that the nuns agreed to work full time for a very small salary. I don't know when it was agreed to, but the fact of the matter was that the nuns were one of the least expenses of a normal parish. This was a fact of life in every convent in the country if not the world.

It is apparent that the bishops had access to a large pool of capable teachers who would work very hard in their parishes. These women were not fly-by-night individuals. We all had pledged our whole life to the work of the Church. We did so willingly and with good heart. It will be told later in my story how the women slowly realized that the men of the Church were taking great advantage of them. They were taking the women for granted when these men should have paid more attention to what the women were saying. I will discuss this later in the story.

My years at Our Lady of Mercy were happy ones. Because we were so far away from the Motherhouse in Hollywood we were not expected to return there until the following June. Sometimes I would go south for a Superiors' meeting, but usually we just stayed where we were. This meant that we did not attend college classes. I missed this part of my life, but I was able to continue on later when I was stationed at the Motherhouse.

There were so many interesting things for us to do. We especially enjoyed the whole countryside in Central California. Sometimes on a Saturday we would pack a lunch and go driving in the foothills of the Sierra Nevadas. Sometimes we would go into Yosemite National Park for the day. Seeing all the beauty and enjoying the sounds and smells of these places was a real picker-upper for all of us. Most of the time, however, we would spend Saturday doing laundry, checking papers, preparing lessons, shopping at the grocer's, and just getting things done. Of course, we still carried on with all of our religious duties each day. There was never a vacation from our prayers.

Every Sunday we attended two Masses. The early Mass at 6:30 am was our regular Mass. At 9:30 we all went back to church for the parish Mass. This was the one when most of the children and their parents attended. I was especially busy because I always directed the choir. For several years this was a task I took on. In some ways I loved it because I had developed a good singing voice myself. But no one ever knew that I would often be very nervous about how the children's choir would sound. I also was nervous about their pronunciation of Latin. It took a lot of work for me to get them into shape. My reward was the comments of the Pastor and the parents after services. They were usually complementary, and sometimes ecstatic. So I accepted it all as graciously as I could.

During my six years in Merced I tried to plan as many adventures as I could for the children of the school. We always had a couple of school-wide picnics out at the nearby lake. The parents were just wonderful in providing food and transportation. In the winter I took the seventh and eighth graders up to Dodge Ride in the Sierras for the day. They sledded, skied, and had a ball. Every year I took the eighth graders on a day trip up to Sacramento. We visited the legislature in action, met our representative, visited Sutter's Fort and picnicked on the Capitol lawn. The last few years I was in Merced I even took the seventh and eighth graders to the opera in San Francisco. This was GRAND OPERA.

The stars were all world-class singers. The first one we saw was "Carmen". I prepared the kids for weeks with the story and the whole idea of opera. They seemed to like it a lot. Of course, it was a wonderful outing for them because they lived in such a small rural town in the middle of San Joaquin Valley. It wasn't as if they never went to San Francisco, but they would never think of putting an opera on their itinerary. I told them all many years later how much I enjoyed "Carmen" because I had never attended a live performance of Grand Opera before myself. We liked it so much that the next year we went to hear "Madame Butterfly" with Dorothy Kirsten. The parents seemed to like all of these outings as much as I did. They were always very generous in offering to take a carload of kids wherever "Sister Peter wanted."

So the years went by. I loved it there, and so did all the different IHMs who were sent up there to teach in the school. I could tell that we were well respected in the city. Everywhere I went I was greeted in a very friendly manner.

But one fine day a bombshell landed on our heads. I got a call around 4 p.m. on a Friday evening from the Pastor, Monsignor McKenna, telling me that I had been arrested. I kind of laughed because I thought he was joking. He told me the local District Attorney, Don C. Mayes had decided to arrest me for breaking the lottery laws of the State of California, and also contributing to the delinquency of minors. What a shock. He said that Mr. Mayes tried to get his deputies to come to the convent to serve me the arrest warrant, but not one of them would do it because they didn't want to hurt Sister Peter. This is how this whole thing came about.

It was very common for people to sell chances for all kinds of things. Those of us in the Catholic Church were used to doing this in order to raise money for all the causes we were working on. The people were receptive, and were usually generous. When Mother Regina called all the Superiors to the Motherhouse for a meeting I wasn't surprised with the message. I went south for the weekend. She talked to us and explained that the effort to raise money for the new Retreat House in Montecito was necessary this year. She asked all of us to take the books of chances back to our schools, and explain that the worthy cause this year would be the Retreat House. None of this was surprising to me.

When I returned on Sunday afternoon I talked to the Sisters, and distributed an allotted amount of chance books to each one. They were to distribute the books to their children on Monday. We had all done this each year so it was not anything to think twice about. Also, all the parishioners were well aware that we had no other way of raising money for our works. I could never complain about their generosity.

On Monday afternoon all the children of Our Lady of

Mercy School fanned out around the whole town and got busy with our fundraiser. It just happened that one little boy in the fifth grade had always gone down to City Hall to sell his books. He had done it for several years. He sold several books to the employees there, and then must have asked Mr. Mayes if he would like to purchase some chances. Mr. Mayes took the chance books away from the boy, and then must have started proceedings against me. Because I was the Superior he addressed his accusations at me.

I want to make it clear that we were probably breaking some kind of statute or law in the State of California, but this was the kind of law that no one seemed to take seriously. After all, one of the biggest fundraisers in the State was the Milk Fund Raffle put on by the San Francisco Police Department every year as long as anyone could remember. All kinds of groups besides churches used raffles all the time to raise funds.

You can imagine my surprise to be called by Father McKenna to tell me the D.A. told him I was under arrest. So there I was, in a quandary.

By the time I got my wits together I called the Mother General, Mother Regina, to tell her what I had been told. She said to wait until she could contact our lawyers and the Cardinal. The charges against me were very serious: (1) breaking the lottery laws of the State of California, and (2) Contributing to the delinquency of a minor. There was prison time connected to the second charge.

The next day the news of Sister Peter's arrest was on

national news. All the nuns saw it. My mother found out about it by reading the paper the next morning. I did not think there would be such a hullabaloo about it so I didn't even think of calling her. From here on for the next couple of months my life was in a whirlwind. The parishioners were aghast that this would happen to "Sister Peter."

They started coming to the door of the convent with platters of food, tears in their eyes, and oh so apologetic. I had to keep carrying on because of the children in school.

Each day brought more notoriety. I began getting phone calls from reporters all over the US asking if I was the "Sister Peter they knew in Chicago, Indianapolis, Omaha, etc." Then I began getting letters from all over the country. Most were very sympathetic with me, and irate at the D.A. But to my surprise I did receive a number of hate letters. These letters are now in the IHM Community Archives together with the other things about this event.

It was hard to believe the vitriolic language used. Many of them condemned me to hell because of my sinfulness. I was in constant contact with Mother Regina. She told me that Cardinal McIntire suggested getting a lawyer who was located in or near Merced. I don't know how they did it but a local attorney came forward and offered to defend me gratis. His name was C. Ray Robinson. He actually lived only a few blocks from the convent in a large mansion by Bear Creek. I did not know him at all. He wasn't even a Catholic. But the skinny was that he and Don C. Mayes had always been at odds with one another in the legal business. So here was C. Ray ready to take on the case for the nun and defend me against this preposterous charge.

Pretty soon Mother Regina came to Merced. She was very supportive of me in every way. Of course, she was the one who sent me back to Merced after our meeting in Hollywood with a large packet of tickets to be sold for the benefit of our Retreat House. None of this seemed out of line because we had been selling tickets forever. Also, who should come to my defense but Mama, and other mothers of IHMs. She came up to see that her "Dodo" was not put in jail. She stayed with us in the Convent, and was very indignant the whole time. So were two other mothers who came with her.

The date of the hearing was established. We had many conferences with Mr. Robinson, who turned out to be charmingly pleasant. He couldn't get over what Don C. Mayes had done. He said later that he heard that Mr. Mayes had gone up to Sacramento to see the Attorney General and ask him to make an example of my case. Who was it? It was Pat Brown, later Governor Brown. The word was that he refused saying, "Don, this is your hot potato, so you handle it."

The judge assigned to the case was Flossie Lobo. I had known her, but not on a personal level. She was a Catholic who attended daily Mass at the parish church. Consequently, I actually saw her every day. But from the day she was assigned until long afterward she and I never passed a glance in the other's direction at church.

In the meantime my attorney was very busy getting the case together, talking to Mother Regina and me, asking the Sisters questions, etc. After a few days he explained his strategy. It seems that Mr. Mayes, in arresting me, had failed to think through the unfolding of events regarding the tickets. When Mr. Robinson realized that I did not give the tickets to the boy, but that my part had been to give the tickets to the teachers I could not be accused of contributing to the delinquency, etc. But he had a question, "Who actually gave the boy the ticket?" It was his fifth-grade teacher, Sister Edward. She was not even named on the subpoena. Mr. Robinson said that with Mayes being the kind of person he was that when he realized his error he would probably press charges against her. His advice to Mother Regina was to send Sister Edward to one of our schools out of the State of California. If Mr. Mayes pressed the case it would be very difficult to extradite a nun. The following day Sister Edward went to San Antonio, Texas, and Sister Corinne Marie came to take her place.

The stage was set. At the hearing before Judge Lobo both lawyers stated their case. My dear Mother was sitting in the crowd of spectators. She even told those around her that she was Sister Peter's mother. I sat there quietly, but I was really shaking in my boots. I really didn't know what the outcome would be. C. Ray was calm, as was Mayes. There were reporters and spectators spilling out into the hallways. All were quietly trying to hear what was said. There I sat, in full religious habit, in a courtroom listening to accusations against me. At the close of the attorney's presentations Judge Lobo said that there was evidence enough to go to trial. What a shock it was for me to find myself in this predicament.

For the next two weeks I taught school every day, the people continued to come to our door and cry as they gave us gifts of vegetables, desserts, even gallons of milk. I was so touched by the overwhelming support I received, sometimes from people I didn't even know.

The day of the trial came. I went to the Courthouse with Mother Regina, all the Sisters, my mother, and Mr. Robinson. Mayes had subpoenaed Mother Regina and two of the Sisters as witnesses. They were all nervous. I was actually petrified. I didn't know how it would all turn out. I sat at the table with Mr. Robinson next to me. I did not testify. The courtroom was packed to the gills with parishioners. There were reporters and flashbulbs out in the hallway as we arrived. Mr. Robinson seemed very self-assured. I noticed that he had opened on the table a very large scrapbook. At first I wondered what it was for, but it seemed he had done his homework. He had collected from lots of people ticket stubs of lotteries that had been held in and around Merced. Total strangers gave him copies of stubs signed by Don C. Mayes. It seemed that Mr. Mayes had been participating in the purchase of Lottery tickets for a long time. I am sure he could see the scrapbook with just a sideways glance.

The trial started with Mayes calling witnesses. The first was an older man who worked in the City Hall. I didn't know him at all. When questioned he surprised us all by refusing to testify under his Fifth

Amendment rights. So Mayes called his second witness, a young lady who worked in the City Hall. When questioned she also refused to testify. Then he called Sister John Michael, our second grade teacher. She also refused to testify, as did Sister Lorraine. By now I am wondering what is going on. To my knowledge this had not been planned beforehand with Mr. Robinson. When Mayes called on Mother Regina she did testify, answering his questions clearly. She was so dignified and gracious sitting there. She told him that she gave the tickets to Sister Peter. Mayes even called on the printer of the tickets to testify. He had been subpoenaed in L.A. This whole procedure went on for about 2 hours or more.

After the testimony of only the two mentioned above Judge Lobo called for a recess. She asked the District Attorney and my lawyer, Mr. Robinson, to come into her chambers. I walked out in the hallway with Mother Regina for about half an hour. Then we were called in. I was filled with trepidation when I took my place next to Mr. Robinson. When I looked at him he seemed very relaxed, so I calmed down a bit. Then Judge Lobo said, " In view of the failure of the District Attorney to establish his case against Sister Peter I dismiss all of the accusations made against her." With that pronouncement the whole courtroom erupted in cheers and applause. I was completely limp.

Needless to say, there was rejoicing everywhere. Mother Regina took all of us back to Hollywood for the weekend so we could recuperate from our stress. For my part, I can say that I have not ever sold another raffle ticket to anyone since that experience. It was so traumatic for me to have such a seemingly innocent thing turn into an almost catastrophic event.

The next couple of years in Merced were much quieter. We went right on with our teaching, praying, and making great plans for our students. In 1954 the Pastor, Monsignor McKenna, decided that the school was growing so well that it was time to build a high school. He and I talked it over a lot. I told Mother Regina of the possibility. She had to know what assignments to make for the higher grades. Plans were made and building started. In September of 1955 Our Lady of Mercy High School opened with the ninth grade. I was principal and part-time teacher. My responsibilities broadened. The next year I continued on with the school. It now was getting quite large. I was now responsible for a school that had grades K – 10. There were so many activities: i.e. teaching, athletics, May processions, field trips, school plays, Christmas Pageants, and our ongoing religious regimen that was always there.

Finally, my six years were coming to an end. I would miss the children and parents so much. But there was a rule in Canon Law that no Superior could remain in one place longer than six years. If this had not been so I imagine I would have stayed in Merced for many years.

When I left Merced I had just turned 33 years of age. My experiences as Superior and Principal had served to bring out all of the talent I had for the jobs I was called upon to do. I felt very confident and ready for whatever the next task would be.

House No. 16 – 1957

Franklin Avenue - Hollywood, California

It is now the summer of 1957. I knew that when I returned to the Motherhouse for the summer I would be assigned to a new position at the end of the summer retreat. We all had to wait for this time to come before we learned of our mission. I spent the summer attending a class in the College and even teaching a class in the Education Department. It was flattering to me to be asked to do this. The course was meant for new teachers and older ones who hadn't yet received their BA degrees. I believe the topic was "How to teach Social Studies." By now I had a lot of successful experience in the classroom so I knew what to teach. All of my students were nuns. They seemed to enjoy the course. In the long run I did this for several summers.

I made my annual retreat up at Montecito with about 80 other IHMs. I spent a lot of time praying that my new mission would be one that I could do with some ease. Well, what a surprise I had when I opened my letter and read that I was appointed Elementary Supervisor of all of our IHM elementary schools. I just took for granted that I would either be appointed as principal of a parochial school or I would be assigned to teach in the classroom again. I was ready for whatever happened, but not for the assignment I got.

When I caught my breath I realized what this meant. At the time our Community ran over 50 elementary schools in California Arizona, Texas, and British Columbia. My job was going to be to visit them each year, and assist them with their curriculum problems, teaching problems, and any other thing they might need during my visit. So in one fell swoop I went from being responsible for one school to having some responsibility for our teaching mission in over 50 schools.

Because I was repeatedly re-appointed to this position for the next twelve years my story during these years will always be in the setting of my job as supervisor. It covers my adventures from 1957 to 1969. What a journey it turned out to be. It was during these years that our lives changed far more than we had envisioned, but nothing happened overnight. I will just go through that narration as things happened.

My first big surprise was to be assigned as supervisor together with another IHM, Sister Corinne. I didn't know her very well, but for the next six years we worked together every day. Sister Elizabeth Ann, Dean of the Education Department, was our boss. After lots of planning we developed our approach as follows:

Every August we sent letters to each school telling them the dates we would be there. Our visit was usually two or three days. Sometimes we could cover two schools in a week.

Each year we developed strategies for one or two areas of the curriculum that we proposed to emphasize that year.

We invited each teacher to send us questions or requests for special assistance ahead of time so we would be prepared to help them individually.

We studied the information we had on hand about the school and faculty before we arrived there. We gave special attention to problems or challenges from the previous years.

When we arrived at the school I was responsible for four of the grades, and Sister Corinne was responsible for the other four. If there was a Kindergarten I looked in on it also.

We visited each class. I was always at ease in the classroom, thank God, because we had a diverse assemblage of schools from very poor families to rather upscale. For the next twelve years I adapted myself to whatever the occasion required. And I did this without losing my serenity. Since those days many IHMs have told me that they loved having me come because I was very positive in my approach to their efforts. That makes me feel that it was worth it. The years passed quickly. I earned my Masters Degree in 1960. I had been stationed out of town for eight years so I was a little late in getting it. But I finally received all the degrees and credentials possible for my work.

I saw my family every so often during these years. Mama was always one who would come to visit. I did have some visits with her in Long Beach. I didn't see too much of Beverly or Barr. Their lives were rolling along on a different track than mine. We always kept in touch by letters or phone. So I was somewhat aware of their activities. Carol and David were growing up, as was Danny. But Mama was the one I saw the most of.

By the early 1960s I was considered quite accomplished and professional in the IHM Community. I turned 40 in 1964. I was very busy doing my supervising during the school year, and teaching a College course during the summer sessions. Our Community was thriving with many new young members. But remember this was the 60s. The whole country became restless with the political scene and the Vietnam War. We all became aware of the turmoil sweeping the nation. As a Community we knew very well what was happening.

The IHMs were considered the most forward-looking nuns in the country. There was even a survey taken of several hundred religious communities in the USA, and we came out on top in regard to educating our members, going on for higher degrees, awareness of the world around us, and creative thought. We all knew this was happening to us, but we didn't dream what the out-come would be down the road.

Several things happened to me that gradually changed me into a woman who could think out of the box. The first thing was that a Dominican priest from Montreal directed one of our regular annual retreats at Montecito. We were all in the habit of course. This was around 1963. I went up there as I always did ready to have eight days of quiet meditation. What a surprise awaited. First of all,

Father Mailloux did not intend to conduct a regular retreat because he said it was time to think about things. His talks were wonderful to my soul because he suggested that we open up to one another in a humble and holy way.

We could then begin to talk about issues that we all wanted to discuss about religious life, but were not ready for. He helped to make us ready. Before long we found ourselves talking about the deepest things in our way of life, and asking one another questions that made us think bigger than we had ever done. I felt that that time was what made me able to make massive changes in my life five or six years later. This was the opening of the door to modernizing.

Of course, none of the changes came about over night. In the first place the meetings of Vatican II were going on. We were made aware of all the proceedings. That was one thing about the IHMs. Our leaders wanted us to be informed about world issues. Instead of hiding behind the wall we were walking right out in front of the wall. Our annual retreats became a source of our growth in knowledge about the Church and the world. We had retreat masters come from all over the world to take on our questions. Many of these men, and they were always men, had actually attended the second Vatican Council. They were most informative about the provisions voted in that were dealing with religious life of both men and women. As we read, discussed, prayed, and questioned we, as a Community, changed little by little.

In the meantime all during the early 60s I was still traveling around visiting schools. I had so many adventures just getting to some of them. The most difficult one was our Indian boarding school in British Columbia. It was called Christie Indian School. It was located on an island on the West Coast of Vancouver Island. It was so remote that there were no roads or bridges available for us. When we planned to go there it took planning galore. First, we flew up to Victoria B.C. Then the IHM sisters there took us by car to Port Alberni. At this point we boarded a small seaplane. I was surprised to find that the passengers were mostly Indians. The plane held about 14 people. Since I had not ever flown out over water in such a small plane I was nervous.

We flew over pristine mountain peaks covered with snow. It seemed as if we were going to have to land right there in the ocean when we got to the school. And that is exactly what happened. The priests and brothers were all dressed in work clothes, lined up on the beach. The Sisters were standing there on the shore waving at us. Sister Corinne and I looked at each other and said, "What now?" The next thing we knew there appeared a small tractor pulling an open wagon like farmers used. To our astonishment the tractor headed right out into the waves, it came straight to us. I then realized that at this point on the beach the water was very shallow. The plane couldn't move in any closer, so our hosts had to come out and get us. If they didn't do this then we would have had to jump right into the water and wade. We stepped out onto the pontoon of the little plane and jumped into the wagon. The pilot tossed our bags into the wagon. And the tractor backed up onto the beach where a hundred children, nine IHMs, several priests and brothers, and the local cook greeted us.

What an eye-opener Christie school turned out to be. It was unlike any of our other schools in that the Sisters not only taught the kids, but also lived with them. The pupils ranged from first grade through senior in high school. The Sisters did all the teaching. The priests and brothers took care of the upkeep of the whole place. This was a boarding school for Indian children. All of the children were baptized Catholics. Each day at the end of schoolwork the Sisters planned all the activities. They were busy with just about every aspect of life there. I noticed that in the morning right after breakfast one of the nuns would act as nurse. Any of the children who had a cold or any cuts, or anything wrong would line up for Sister to check them out, and apply medicine or bandages as needed. I was so impressed with the cheerfulness and loving care the Sisters gave to the children.

I am sure there was a certain transformation that would take place in a Sister who really longed to be a missionary. If one didn't have this calling then it must have been a very trying assignment. But for those who loved it there was no turning back. In fact even today there are three IHMs, Laura Distaso, Anita Lucia Tavera, and Margaret Bauman, who stayed in Tofino. They taught the Indian children for many years in the public school of Tofino after the Canadian government integrated the Indian children into the regular schools. All three of them are now retired, but they have been serving their people up there for forty years or more. What a calling.

I had several wonderful educational opportunities during my twelve years as Supervisor. Just for the record, I was a National Science Foundation recipient for study at Northridge State University for the summer of 1961. I was ecstatic because I wanted to broaden my knowledge of earth sciences. I took Geology, Astronomy, and Modern Math. How I enjoyed it all. I did very well. However, I stayed at our convent in Northridge for the summer. It turned out to be one of the hottest on record. We were in full habit, so I was really sweltering. My biggest thrill was to go on a field trip to Bakersfield to participate in a dig. We drove out to the barren area north of the city where the oil fields are. It seems that the whole San Joaquin Valley was, at one ancient time, an inland sea. It dried up eventually. They think the last low place to evaporate was south near Bakersfield. Consequently thousands of fish, including sharks, migrated there and died. The fun of the dig was that the teeth of the sharks were very close to the surface of the ground because this all happened a relatively short time ago.

Our bus stopped right next to a roadside cliff. It couldn't have been more than ten feet high. We all had trowels to scoop, and box screens to sift our dirt. We dug in right at eye level. It was a thrill for me to uncover about 12 shark teeth. I was the first human being to look at them. I wanted to dig all day, but we had to make the journey back to Northridge. I gave some away as gifts, but I'm not sure others appreciated them as much as I did. After I had worked as supervisor for about seven years I began to feel jaded. Even though it wasn't the usual thing to do I went to Mother Humiliata and talked to her about the job. She said she liked having me in the position because I was so well received by the nuns, but she asked if I would like to go away to study for a year. It would be my sabbatical. I was so thrilled that I accepted. She even gave me the choice of where I would study. It turned out to be Northwestern University in Chicago. I had read about their Geography Department. Since I had had such an enjoyable summer at Northridge studying Geology and Astronomy I felt that study of the earth was my cup of tea. After discussing the plan with Sister Elizabeth Ann and Mother Humiliata I was sent on my way. I actually went for the summer session and the following complete year.

This was my first venture into another world on my own. I wasn't really alone however, because I was told that I would be living in the local convent of Dominican Sisters who taught in Evanston.

It turned out to be a fine friendly group of Sisters. My room was in the attic of the convent. It was no surprise because I found that these nuns lived exactly the same way we did. The room was simply furnished with a bed, desk and chair. I shared a bathroom with another nun who was also studying. I was given some money by our Treasurer to use for my personal needs. I would call the Community Treasurer when I needed more. I never saw my rent and board money. This was taken care of between the local Dominican superior and our IHM superior. I didn't have a car so I walked to the University and back each day, and some weekends. It was about eight blocks. I loved it.

This was a chance for me to become even more

independent. I could choose the classes I would take. I felt that the IHMs could rely on me to do the right thing. They must have felt the same way because I often received letters of encouragement, and some telling me that they missed me.

Believe it or not, I was not homesick. I think I was so entranced with the opportunity to expand my learning that I just ate it up. Most of my classes were pure geography courses. I believe I took around ten or twelve. I also had labs to attend that were part of some of the courses. I had papers to write, oral talks to give, and tests to pass. I just can't tell you how much I enjoyed every single course. It seemed that anything that had to do with the earth or the heavens just stuck in my mind like glue.

In the course of the year I turned 41. There were so many wonderful opportunities to hear world-renowned speakers. I attended as many of these as I could. But one sticks out in my memory more than all the others. I didn't realize it but I became middle-aged overnight. This is what happened.

The University had invited Adlai Stevenson to come and address the student body. He was running for President at the time. He was going to appear outside on top of the one-story science building there on campus. Everyone who wanted to hear him just came and gathered on the lawn below him. Unfortunately I arrived late so there were no more chairs left. So I stayed in the back leaning against the flagpole. I wanted to be able to see him as well as hear his eloquent speech. It turned out that the afternoon was very windy. Soon after he started the wind caught his papers, and blew them all away. There he was up on top of the building; he had no way to retrieve his speech because everything went in a whirlwind. We were all laughing, and so was he. Well, I was very impressed with him that day because he continued on with a wonderful presentation just as if he had the words right there in front of him.

The next morning I hurried to my first class of the day which happened to be held in the auditorium. Each day all the geography students gathered there first for a lecture on all the basic things needed to know in any geography course. There were about 400 students present. One thing we all enjoyed was picking up the campus newspaper each day before we went into class. I was sitting there eagerly reading it, and looking for any remarks about Mr. Stevenson's talk. Imagine my surprise when I read these words, " Yesterday Mr. Adlai Stevenson gave a rousing speech to all who came…It was well attended by students from around the world dressed in their colorful costumes, and one middle-aged nun." I sat there stunned because I had not yet thought of myself as anywhere near middle age.

Because the reference was obviously about me since I was the only nun at the gathering I cautiously looked around at my fellow students. Thank God no one was snickering or pointing. But I spent that whole day feeling different than I had up to then. I am sure no one else on the planet has had his or her middle age announced in the newspaper. People don't throw showers or parties to celebrate this milestone. And they certainly don't print articles in newspapers to announce that someone has become middle-aged. Oh well.

I had many opportunities to enjoy cultural events while in Evanston. We were very close to Chicago so I attended plays, an opera, Philharmonic Orchestras and other such things. It was the first time in my life that I could make decisions about what to do and where to go on a given day. Needless to say I thoroughly enjoyed my whole time at Northwestern. The year was drawing to a close, and I was beginning to feel anxious to return home to Hollywood. It was during my last few weeks of study that I discovered a large lump in my abdomen. It was causing me some discomfort. I was really alarmed. I decided that I could not complete the thesis necessary to receive a Masters Degree in Geography. I had passed all the required classes, and was ready to finish. But the fact that I needed attention soon overrode my plans. I called the Mother General and said I would be returning to the Motherhouse in June. She was very concerned about my condition. So I said a fond "goodbye" to all the Dominican Sisters with whom I had lived for a year, and flew home. Thus ended my wonderful sabbatical year.

I was greeted at the Motherhouse with lots of hugs. Everyone was ready for me to do what I had been doing for so many years – teach and supervise. Well, first I had to have surgery. It turned out that I had a large fibroid tumor, so a hysterectomy was performed. That was my first experience in a hospital. Instead of teaching in the college for summer session I recuperated at Montecito for a few weeks. After that I was ready to resume my work in the schools.

This was the summer that Mama went to Europe with Aunt Hilda. She was gone a long time. There are notes, diaries, and papers in my things that I saved that Mama wrote about her adventures then. She didn't know I had surgery until she returned later that summer. It was during the following year that I had a wonderful opportunity fall right in my lap. It happened like this. I was going around from school to school as usual every week. Sister Corrine and Sister Rosa Mystica were my fellow supervisors.

One day our boss, Sister Elizabeth Ann, came into my office with a little batch of papers. She said, "Sister Peter, maybe you would like to look through these and see if there are any you would care to pursue." I said, "Oh, ok, I will see what's here."

Imagine my surprise to find that the whole collection of papers was the listing of all the offerings of scholarships given by the US Government for study all over the world. I was amazed that Sister Elizabeth Ann had given me carte blanche to pick and choose. I couldn't believe that I was chosen to do this. My self-esteem rose sky high. I set to work reading everything the papers listed Fulbright Scholarships available for study in many countries of the world. I was in a state of excitement hard to describe. Was this a possibility? Each offering included all the information about how to qualify. I read everything over and settled on the offering for study in India. Was it possible that I would become a Fulbright Scholar? What a thought. What an honor. I discussed the India possibility over with Sister Elizabeth Ann. She encouraged me to send in the application, she would write my letter of recommendation.

Soon after this everything seemed to fall into place – just like a miracle. Our Community was in the beginning of our restructuring according to Vatican II. Everyone was excited about the possibilities for the future. We had made some modifications to our habit. We wore shorter skirts, not ground level skirts. Our veil was simplified. We allowed some of our hair to show. In a word – we were trying to gradually look like modern women of the 20th century. None of this came about easily, but we considered all the proposals as a total Community. When votes were taken, the overwhelming number was for reform and renewal. A very small percentage of members never approved of anything, but we didn't worry about them. We were sure that they would come around someday soon.

It was in this electrified atmosphere that I became a recipient of a Fulbright Scholarship. When the letter arrived from Washington I was ecstatic and dumbfounded. I was to be a member of a small group of 19 educators from across the country that would spend the Fall semester in India. All of our expenses were paid. Our air flight was scheduled to leave from Los Angeles, go on to New York, then on to Europe, Asia, finally ending in New Delhi. Because we would be half way around the world when we arrived in India we were told that we could continue on home at the close of the seminar by continuing our travel eastward. All expenses would be paid. But if we backtracked to Europe or other destinations none of the expenses would be paid.

After I read all of the rules I couldn't believe my good fortune. In reality, I was going to travel around the world. Never in my wildest dreams had I ever imagined such a thing. I was being given opportunities as an IHM that I never imagined possible.

When I look back I can see what good fortune it was for me to choose to become a member of the IHMs rather than some other community. Who knows, I may have gone to a very conservative group, and never be heard from much again. I know now that the IHMs were one of the most forward-looking groups in the whole Church.

Once it was decided that I could accept the scholarship there was a flurry of activity. What shall I wear? Should I wear a veil? What about traveling alone? Where will I stay? Are there any Catholic Churches there? How long will I be gone? Is my health good? The questions were endless. All the IHMs were giving me free advice about everything. In the end I traveled dressed in a modified habit. This meant street-length blue dress, my hair was grown out. I wore a short blue veil sometimes, but not every day. I also took along two sets of skirts and blouses of other colors to wear when I wanted to. This was my first experience being out of the habit. I have found out since then that I was one of the first to experiment with regular garb. The Sisters all wanted to lend me whatever I needed, i.e. luggage, coat, scarf, etc. By the time I was scheduled to depart I had everything including a brand new passport. I also purchased a travel diary, which I carefully kept during the entire adventure. All of the Sisters seemed as thrilled as I was to see me off. I, of course, had butterflies galore as we drove to LAX.

Around the World 1964

I left Hollywood in late September, or early October. My stay was to last until the first part of January. I flew to New York to meet with the group. The other eighteen were very friendly and welcoming to me. I found that they were superintendents, professors, supervisors, and specialists from all over the U.S.A. I was impressed. Everyone seemed as excited as I was to be going to India. I was surprised to see that there was another nun. She was a Dominican from Michigan. She was dressed in full habit. Since their habit is white, I began wondering how she was going to manage. I will tell later my impression of that. So the group consisted of seventeen regular people and two nuns.

I stayed overnight with an IHM who lived in New York, Sister Caroline. We never really visited because she was so tied up with her reading project. I arrived at the Hotel a little late because on the way in our taxi stopped for a funeral going down Fifth Avenue. It seems that some firemen had been killed that week while doing their duty. So I was a bit breathless when I finally joined the group.

The Director gave us preliminary instructions, and then we were off. We all hurried to the bus that took us to the PanAm terminal. It was at this point that I realized that I had brought too much stuff. I could hardly carry my two bags and purse. I was tempted to dump some of the things in the trash, but I held back because I really didn't know what things I would need in India. I was in state of exhilaration when it was time for our flight. We all got on and found our places. I was seated next to a nice gentleman who was State Superintendent of Schools in Connecticut. When we took off I sat quietly and started writing in my travel diary. Sometime I plan to transcribe it because I was writing faithfully up to the very end of my journey.

Because this was not a jet plane it was slower than it would be today. We had to stop for fuel at many places along the way. The most interesting thing for me was that we could view all the cities from the air, but because we were in transit we could not venture forth from the area in each airport reserved for those in transit. What a fantastic journey it was for me. I was still pinching myself wondering if it was all a dream. Here I was not only away from the convent, but flying over Europe and Asia. The plane kept heading east hour after hour. I tried to see out the window as much as I could. In the end it took us twenty-four hours to make the flight from New York to New Delhi.

It was dark night all the way to England. When I roused myself in the morning it was light enough for me to see the green, green fields and hills of England. I was thrilled to see the church steeples, the little villages, the rolling hills, and finally, to fly over London. I just couldn't take my eyes away from the window. When we landed we were escorted to the transit lounge while the plane fueled up.

Then we took off and flew across the Channel to Frankfurt. We stopped for awhile. Germany looked so beautiful and green. There were all kinds of small towns, lots of grazing land for cows, and long highways. The next stop was romantic Vienna. In between some of the stops we were served our meals. Because we were always going east we were ahead of ourselves as far as eating was concerned. Sometimes none of us could eat very much at the time the attendants brought our trays. For them it might have said lunch time on the clock, but for us it was just an hour and a half since breakfast.

Now things began to be exotic. We flew high over Hungary, with its high mountains and dense green forests, and proceeded on to Istanbul.

The whole terrain had changed from lush green fields and farms to rather dry and rocky looking desert. The city itself spread out below us. We could clearly see the minarets and domes of the mosques. I was actually flying over the Bosporus. I was wishing that we could have had some time to really visit these cities. But I can't complain because I would have many opportunities to visit equally exotic places before my seminar was over in January. Later in the evening we landed in Beirut, Lebanon. We stayed in the transit lounge, stretched our legs, and generally were pretty tired. The next stop was Teheran, Iran. I couldn't see any of the city because we landed about ten p.m. We saw city lights, but no sights. And wonder of wonders, we knew we were in a barren part of Arabia, and it was raining. It wasn't long before we were off again. I knew that the next stop would be New Delhi.

We landed in New Delhi Airport at about 4 a.m. After we all got off the plane, and were looking for our baggage we realized something strange. There was no one there to meet us. We were all looking around rather bewildered at this. After some talking to the people in the airport someone made a call. It seemed that our hosts had mixed up the arrival time. They thought we were going to arrive the next morning. Soon a bus arrived. We got all our things on board and we started our time in India by driving in the very early morning through this exotic country.

I think one of the first sensations I had while driving to our hotel was how flat the city was. I couldn't see any skyscrapers at all. The next sensation was the pungent odor in the air. I realized later that it was the common result of poor sewers or no sewers. None of this bothered me at all because I was prepared to take everything as it came. That was part of the adventure.

Thus, we arrived at the Lodhi Hotel. It was two stories tall. A few hundred rooms were spread around an inner courtyard. We each had a private room. Mine was on the second floor next to Sister George Agnes, the Dominican. Talk about simplicity. The bed was just wide enough for me. Ropes strung back and forth across the frame supported the thin mattress. When I tried it out I found it quite comfortable, although it was a little bit like a hammock. We had clean sheets and warm blankets. There was a section along the wall to hold my clothes. The door did not have a lock on it except some kind of contraption made of interlocking pieces of wood. There was a small chest of drawers, and a bathroom. It did not have a bathtub. The shower just sprayed down onto the cement floor into a drain. Someone in the group must have complained because in a few days my bathroom had a bathtub made of tin or steel. It was not really big enough to get into so I just stood up in it to take my shower.

The first day we were told that this hotel was chosen for our stay because it was what the average Indian stayed in. It was considered third- class. At least we learned that those who could afford it stayed in a third-class hotel. The very wealthy, and foreigners stayed in the five-star hotel about two blocks away. Well, I just loved it. Can you imagine my surprise when the first day I happened to go out my door onto the balcony and saw – to my amazement – an Indian man was sitting in the driveway playing his flute? There right in front of him was a basket out of which a cobra was emerging. I am sure he made his living by entertaining tourists. I had heard about snake charmers all of my life, but I never expected to actually see one in action. So it was really true and not a myth. That was a wonderful start to my India adventure.

I will tell you how the seminar was organized. Each morning we all went out to the front veranda and waited for the taxis. We piled in three or four at a time and were driven to the headquarters of the education group that hosted us. It was always an adventure even getting there because it seemed that the taxi drivers were really short of cash. They would buy gas a gallon at a time. We often had to stop for a few minutes while the driver bought his gas. Then we would all arrive at our destination. I was especially uneasy because they drive on the left side of the road. Along the way I would feast my eyes on any and all scenes. We met for our seminar classes on the second floor of a good looking building. Our hosts were mostly Indian teachers, writers, and specialists who gave us information for three hours each morning. We would have a break about ten- thirty during which servants would give us hot tea laced with buffalo milk and lots of sugar. Then we would continue until noon. We went back to the hotel Lodhi for lunch, a short break, and then a field trip to some place of interest in New Delhi. Later we would have dinner, and either free time or another field trip for evening enjoyment. I was busy, busy, busy and I loved it. I spent the whole time there pinching myself because I couldn't believe this was happening to me.

One of the most exotic things I had to get used to was the food. I managed all right a good amount of time, but there were meals when I could not eat very much. I know the reason was that I was not used to the unusual flavors present in so many dishes. The herbs and spices used in their cooking were some that I had never tasted. It wasn't so much that the food tasted terrible. It was just that it was unappetizing to me. I tried to eat whatever was presented so that my hosts would not be offended, but sometimes I just couldn't eat very much. We were in India, a country that did not ever serve beef. That didn't mean that we did not have meat. Oh no. It just meant that we had mutton, goat, fish, and chicken in place of beef. I learned later in our stay that some of the men in our group got so hungry for beef that they walked the two blocks to the five-star international hotel for a steak dinner. I am not sure this is true because the people there are so adamant about not harming cows that I can't see them permitting it even in fancy western-style hotels. The consequence of the food situation for me was that I lost about ten pounds during my stay.

I survived on breakfast. It usually consisted of eggs and toast. We also could have ample amounts of corn flakes served with piping hot buffalo milk and unrefined sugar. The corn flakes individually were very tiny due to the fact that corn in India grows very small on the cob. It was explained to us that this is because most of the farmland is entirely depleted of the nutrients needed to produce robust corn like we see here in the U.S. One of our lecturers told us that a very important and large import of India is fertilizer.

I had so many exciting experiences. Our hosts invited the highest authorities in the nation to come present a lecture to our group. I don't know what kind of clout our seminar hosts had, but when we were going to discuss the agriculture of India the next day who would show up to enlighten us but the Minister of Agriculture. If our topic was to be Education in India then the Minister of Education was the speaker. This was true about all of the topics we discussed. It was like having the Secretary of Labor in our U. S. Cabinet come for a lecture on that topic. We were given time to ask questions, and ask for more details. Every one of the speakers was most courteous and eager to share their expertise with us. And so the days went.

Our hosts had planned a very full and interesting schedule for us every day. We even had cultural events to attend in the evening. After awhile I was becoming really steeped in Indian culture. We discovered that the weekends were spectacular for us. We were taken by bus to a new area away from the city for a taste of other sides of India. Once we went to a desert town near Pakistan for two days. Then we had a wonderful trip to the hill country up to the Himalayas. We visited Agra, the city of the Taj Mahal. The arrangements were made so that we could visit this gorgeous building during the day for a few hours, then we returned at 10 p.m. so we could view it by moonlight.

Before I go further I want to say how Sister George Agnes and I did our thing. Every morning we arose early, and took a taxi to a nearby neighborhood to go to Mass. There are not too many Catholic churches in this country, but there are some. While we were in New Delhi we went to daily Mass at a residence that was a seminary for aspiring young men to study for the priesthood. There were three or four in residence.

On the weekends when we were traveling we sought out the nearest Catholic Church. It was not easy. Sister and I did not become close friends. For some reason she seemed distant to me. I don't know what it was. Maybe by that time I was too modern for her. I was not wearing a veil all the time.
Sometimes I wore regular skirts and blouses. All the time she was clad head to toe in a pure white habit with a black scapular and long black veil. I think maybe I was too avant-garde for her. To this day I don't know how she did her laundry, and kept her habit looking so clean. We did not have access to washers and dryers anywhere. We were always assigned as roommates in the hotels. She and I never had a real conversation about religious life.

It was here in New Delhi that I was proposed to for marriage. He was a man from Afghanistan staying there. He was not in our group but I had seen him several times in the lobby. One day he started talking to me in a conversational manner, we were just chatting. Then out of the blue he asked me if I would come to Afghanistan with him and be his wife. I was taken aback to say the least. I could tell by his face that he wasn't joking.

I immediately put him straight that I was not available. I explained that I was devoted to my vocation in the Catholic Church, and it would not be possible for me to accede to his request. He seemed disappointed. I noticed that from then on when we would return from our weekends he would often be in the lobby. Sometimes he would look in my direction. It all made me feel a bit uneasy because I really didn't know if he would do anything. In a way I was flattered because no one had ever approached me like that. I never knew what he was doing there in New Delhi. But from then on I found myself looking around the lobby when we returned so I could make a quick get-away. He never bothered me again.

Eventually we left New Delhi to tour some major parts of the rest of India for two weeks. We flew to Hyderabad to spend a few days viewing the ancient monuments. We spent a few glorious days in Bombay. Visiting the Elephant Caves was especially thrilling. This is a place on an island that was developed by people of long ago. They literally carved a temple to the Elephant God out of the inside of a granite hill. It is very large and ornate. They call this kind of work "carving out the living rock." Another of the interesting places we were taken was to a nuclear facility. I was so surprised to see such a modern place in contrast to the ancient historical spots we had seen. There was a lot of security before we arrived there. They took our cameras from us. But I can say that I actually gazed down into the blue-green water of a nuclear reactor. It didn't seem very big, but I have learned since then that these things don't have to be large to be lethal.

The last major city we visited as a group was Madras in South India. It is located on the east coast down across from Sri Lanka. We called it Ceylon in those days. We spent a few days enjoying the historic places. I was always amazed at how colorful the whole country was. I was also amazed at how poor the people were who were the ordinary folk.

Sister Agnes and I found a catholic church in nearby Pondicheery. This was still an enclave owned by the French. It was run just like any place in France. So there was quite a contrast when one would cross the line into this city. The streets were clean. The people, who looked Indian, were well dressed and very tidy. I didn't see any homeless families anywhere. In a word, the place was a prosperous French enclave. I learned that in later years the Indian government took back all of these places. We found a very European looking church there. By this time Sister Agnes was not really enjoying the trip. I couldn't tell whether she was just exhausted, or just homesick. She took to her bed. I didn't know how to handle her because she never really said much to me. So I just told our hosts about her, and said I would take her something to eat for a day or two. In the end she seemed depleted by all the activity. I have never heard from her since. I still think that she found me a little too modern for her taste.

It was the middle of December, we had reached the end of our official seminar. The weather was getting colder. The whole party was scheduled to fly up to Calcutta, and leave from there. I had made arrangements with my hosts to take a few days to go west to Cochin in the state of Kerala to visit four Indian sisters I knew. They had come to Immaculate Heart College for four years to get their degrees.

Then they went to Marquette to get their Masters degrees. I had visited them in Milwaukee when I attended Northwestern University. So after our farewell dinner in Madras I said goodbye to our seminar group. And for the first time in my life I was all alone in a foreign country. But I was looking forward to seeing my friends in Kerala.

The first thing I had to do was go into the downtown part of Madras to the ticket office to get my ticket to Cochin. A nice Indian gentleman who was wearing the usual turban served me. He signed me up for a round-trip ticket. I was feeling confident about it. The ticket was about $400. It turned out later that my confidence was misplaced, to say the least. I decided to go to a local folk art shopping center. I got in a taxi and started off. I was enjoying the ride when suddenly the taxi driver turned toward me slightly and said, "Would you be so kind as to marry me?" I just about flipped over. I was so startled that I couldn't believe he was serious. Maybe he wasn't, but he sure looked like it. I quickly said I wasn't available, thank you. He didn't say much more, but my anxiety about it continued until we arrived at the shop. I was nervous because I had read recently in one of the Indian newspapers about an English woman who had been kidnapped. I was also nervous because the driver wasn't alone. He had another man in the cab up in the front seat. I was shaking by the time we arrived. It was a great relief to me that he did bring me to the place I had requested. Then he said, "Go on in. I will wait for you." Lordy, by now I was in a tizzy. I said, "Don't wait." I will be a long time." He didn't say anything. So I quickly got out of the cab and hurried into the shop. I went toward the back as fast as I could, and then found a spot where I could turn around and watch the front. I was greatly relieved when I saw the taxi drive away. It took me quite a while to calm down enough to buy a few things, and then call for a taxi to go back to the hotel. It turned out to be a fine ride. All of this happened within the first few hours I was all alone, and on my own in Madras.

The next four days turned out to be pretty hard for me. It wasn't that I didn't want to visit my friends. It was simply a whole set of circumstances that turned my visit into a nightmare. First of all, this was my first day alone in India. After my adventure with the taxi driver I was on edge. When I returned to the hotel I ate some dinner. Then I read a little in my room. Then I called to make arrangements for a taxi to pick me up at 6:30 a.m. to take me to the airport. All was going along until I realized that I was very apprehensive even about the early-morning taxi ride. I didn't know what to expect. This caused me to go to bed feeling uneasy. The consequence of this was that I tossed and turned all night waiting for the alarm to ring at 3 a.m. I didn't sleep a wink. I ate my breakfast of cornflakes, checked out of the hotel, took the taxi without incident, and arrived at the airport on time. I was really bushed. I had literally been awake for 24 hours.

With ticket in hand, I boarded a middle-sized plane for the 3-hour flight to Cochin hoping that I could sleep a little on the way. My peace was disturbed almost immediately. Before we even cleared the runway I was petrified to see smoke filling the entire cabin. I look around with alarm and was very surprised to see no one acting afraid. The attendants, dressed in their beautiful saris, walked up and down the aisle as nonchalant as could be. I soon realized that this was not smoke. It turned out that when they put on the air conditioning a mist developed for a number of minutes. It soon dissipated. But, once again I was on edge. I passed the time looking out the window at the broad expanse of South India below.

Finally I reached Cochin airport. I saw the Sisters immediately. They were waiting for me at the entrance to the waiting room. We were all so happy to see one another again. But before I did anything I went to the window to confirm my return trip. I was told there was no seat available. I was stunned. The man said happily, "But you are first on our waiting list." I was in a quandary about what to do. I thought it would all work out. So I went out to greet the Sisters. Their Mother General accompanied the three of them. I believe her name was Mother Josephine. She was very nice and welcomed me warmly. I was instantly aware of the climate change. I was now in an almost tropical part of India.

Banana trees and Palm trees were everywhere I looked. The area was a busy seaport so there were little boats out on the bay. The Sisters asked me if I wanted lunch. I said, "yes." So we ate at a local café. The food was different, but I managed ok. Then we took a taxi to their town that was a few miles south of Cochin. We were all talking at once. I noticed that there were many Catholic churches scattered around as we drove. The Sisters had explained to me when they lived with us in Hollywood that The State of Kerala is the most Catholic and Christian of all in India. They are not in the majority but there are enough of them to make it very noticeable that the Hindu temples are not the only places of worship we see.

I was alarmed about my return ticket. It was imperative that I make my flight connections from Madras to Calcutta on the day I had arranged. The Indian government required my seminar hosts to accompany each participant to the airport personally in order to ascertain that he or she had truly left the country. So my hosts were waiting for me in Calcutta. I had exclaimed to the ticket man in the airport that I had a paid return ticket in my possession. They didn't seem to be in the mood to honor it. I was furious and very worried. This all added to my exhaustion.

After about twenty-five miles we all arrived at the convent. When I could finally catch my breath I was shown around the convent. There was a large college connected with the convent that was for young women. It was in session. The Sisters asked me if I would like to rest for awhile. I was so glad they asked. So I was shown to my room. The bed was just perfect.

It is now about 3 p.m. My exhaustion was getting to me so I lay down and closed my eyes. In about ten minutes I heard a light knock on my door.

One of my Sister friends entered and apologized, but she had a favor to ask. Would I mind coming with her over to the college to address the entire student body? The Sisters told the girls about my visit, so they were all anxious to see me. So, up I got. I was feeling kind of wobbly, but I got myself together and went with her. There was the auditorium full to the back with all those beautiful smiling faces. I didn't have a speech prepared so I answered questions. They wanted to know about our Community, and the things we were doing to modernize. I appeared before them in a blue dress, knee-length, and no veil. I answered any and all questions. My Sister friends were glowing. I guess I was a celebrity among them.

Then the Sisters decided that I should see something of the area. I wobbled along to a local cashew factory. Here were endless rows of Indian women sitting on the ground. Each had a large pile of cashew nuts in front of her. They all were busily pounding each of the nuts open and retrieving the nuts. The good whole nuts were put in one pile, and the broken ones were in another pile. Some of the women had small children near them. You can't imagine the din. We could not speak. There must have been several hundred women all pounding the nuts like crazy. To this day whenever I eat a cashew I think of those hard-working women. Thankfully we returned to the convent.

I was expecting to go back and try to get on with my much-needed nap, but they informed me that it was time for supper. We were eating a simple meal and chatting when out of the blue Mother Josephine asked me if I would like to see Cape Comorin, the southernmost tip of India. I said, "That would be lovely, I would like to do that". I went on eating my supper, and chatting with my five friends, and dreaming about going to bed and having a really good sleep, when Mother Josephine said, "Alright, let's go." I looked at the others. They told me we were going to Cape Comorin now.

I am in the dark about how far we were going or how long this was going to take. Imagine my shock when we got in a taxi and went to the local train station. We were actually going to go by train. By now it is getting dark and I am more tired than ever. It is about 36 hours since I have had any sleep. We all get on the steam driven train. It had bench-like seats with no cushioning. The car windows were open. So we started.

Now I usually am game for any kind of trip that involves seeing new places. I had just spent many weeks reveling in the beauties of northern India. I love seeing the countryside.

This trip was disappointing to me right then because the sun went down. It was soon pitch dark outside. I could see nothing. I sat by the window and chatted with my five friends. No one told me anything about our journey. I just assumed we would stop soon and find a hotel for the night. Imagine my shock when the Sisters began saying they were going to sleep right there. I looked all around me. There were no beds, no pillows or blankets, no nothing. My shock increased when I saw them, one by one, climb up to the luggage racks and settle down. I had never seen anything like that in my life. Not one of them indicated to me where I could spend the night. There were people around me who settled down on newspapers on the floor. There I was with an open window with black soot coming in on me, all my hostesses were laid out up in the racks. By now I got the point. This was how they traveled. I sat up all night in a state of numbness.

This was my second straight night without any sleep at all. As the long night wore on I was becoming more and more exhausted. On top of that my ankles were beginning to swell. I didn't know what to expect from now on.

We finally arrived at Trivandum in the morning. I now know this was about 200 miles south of the town we started from. The Sisters all roused themselves and asked me how I was. They didn't ask me how I slept. I couldn't tell them very much because I went from one astounding thing to the next. Because there was no rest room on the train we all very quickly got off the train at the station. We rushed into the public restroom. I was happy about that. I came out of my stall to see my five companions all hunched over the sinks brushing their teeth. I couldn't believe my eyes. First of all, this was such a public place for this to occur, but secondly I was stupefied that not one of them had told me we were going to be gone overnight, and maybe I should bring some things. I asked them if we were in Cape Comorin. They all said, "No, not yet." I forget if and when we ate breakfast, but I was ready to hurry up and finish the trip so I could get some rest.

It is now two days – 48 hours – since I have had a wink of sleep. What happened next really was unbelievable to me. We had a taxi take us on a little tour of Trivandum. I asked when we would be seeing the Cape. They said it would be today, but later. My anxiety was becoming profound because I was so in need of some sleep. They didn't seem to be aware of my need at all. I couldn't say anything because I wasn't sure what we were going to do next, so I just soldiered on. We ended up at the State Prison.

Mother Josephine was in charge of all of this so I just figured she wanted to come to Trivandum for some reason. It seemed that there was a priest in prison convicted of murdering a woman. Mother Josephine was convinced of his innocence, so she got us into the prison. She asked to see the Warden, but she was told that wasn't possible today. Instead we were given a tour of the place. Of course, there were convicts all around us. We were in the habit so they were very polite.

In the end Mother Josephine asked the guide if we could see the death chamber where the priest would be hanged. He said, "Yes, of course." This was the last place in the world I wanted to be. We were shown to a small outlying structure. When we entered it raised chills in my body. There was the platform above us, and the rope. We paused for a short time and recited some prayers for the priest, and then left. I was sure we would soon be on our way to Cape Comorin. It was probably not too far. So back to the taxi we went. We drove south through a fertile and tropical tip of India. Finally, we did reach the Cape, but it took us all afternoon. It must have been another hundred miles below Trivandum.

Imagine my chagrin that when we finally did get there it was sunset. We all got out of the taxi and walked across the sandy beach to sit and watch the sunset. I was struck by the unbelievably beautiful sand. It was a light violet color as far as the eye could see. This was caused by eons of erosion of volcanic rocks. I loved the beauty of the sun setting over the Indian Ocean, the turquoise sea, and the purple sand. How idyllic. The only fly in the ointment for me was that it had now been two and a half days since I had slept, so I wanted to just lie back on the sand and nap.

Throughout this field trip the Sisters were very cordial in every way. They just never seemed to think that maybe I was in need of a breather. There was no sense in my saying anything because there was not a hotel or inn anywhere.

Now it was getting dark. We took a last look at the beautiful ocean, and returned to the taxi. I was sure we would go to a local hotel for the night. How mistaken I was. Mother Josephine directed the driver to take us to the train station in Trivandum. The ride north took us a couple of hours. When we arrived at the train we got on and sat in the same kind of car we had come down in. After eating something, and visiting for awhile, everyone began to find a place to sleep. Here I was in the same predicament as last night. For the third night in a row I did not sleep at all. By now my ankles were swelling up like melons. I was beginning to feel giddy. The train chugged along all night. Finally, in the morning we arrived back at Cochin. I was so exhausted that I could hardly respond to my hostesses. But they were so excited having me there that they wanted to show me off some more.

It was Sunday, so they took me to Mass at the local Cathedral. There were no pews, so I stood for the service. After the service they took me over to meet the Bishop. He was cordial, but I could tell he wasn't that interested in meeting me, especially since I was not in full nun's habit. He was busy showing me a gallery of photos on his wall that showed everything he had ever done in his life. Then he wanted me to meet his dog – Tommy. I got through this with some grace, and then we returned to the convent.

The first thing I did was ask Mother Josephine to call the airport to confirm my return flight for that day. She called. Then she told me that they had no seat for me but said, "You are first on our waiting list". I said I simply had to get back to Madras by tomorrow to connect with my flight to Calcutta the next day. So we all talked about the problem and decided that I would take the 3 o'clock train. Mother Josephine said she would arrange for me to have a first-class seat so I would be comfortable on the all-night ride to Madras.

Sisters took me to one of their local convents to meet the nuns. I did as they wished, but I was almost reeling. I tried to be cordial throughout, but it was hard. I even posed with a large group of them for a photo. I visited some more, picked up my bag that was still packed from my arrival, and went down to the station with my four friends and Mother Josephine.

Mother Josephine went up to the window to get my first-class ticket. Of course, she had not made any arrangements ahead of time. She paid for my return trip. But, surprise, surprise. She came back and told me that there were no first-class seats left – just third-class. The train pulled into the station. I kissed them all goodbye, and got in the car. There was only one seat left. It was a bench facing backward. I managed to wave to the Sisters. It seemed to me that they looked a bit stricken that I could get only a third-class seat. This would be my third night on a train and my fourth night without any sleep at all. My body felt like I would fall over at the slightest puff of wind.

I looked around and realized that I was the only woman in the whole car. All the men were getting settled in some fashion. They would look in my direction, but then go ahead with their settling in. In a short time I was approached by one of the young men. He asked if I would like to trade seats with him. His seat was facing forward, and was cushioned. I was so grateful and pleased. I thanked him profusely, and settled in to my more comfortable place. The trip would take the whole night. I truly hoped that I could be comfortable enough to rest, but it was not to be. I nodded some the whole night, but I could never drop off into real slumber. The train made many stops. At each station people were running alongside the train carrying plates of hot food for sale to the passengers. The men would reach out with some money in hand and grab a plate. All I could think of was "What a country."

Of course, I never went to the bathroom, if there was one. I couldn't see a sign of it anywhere. Besides, I probably wouldn't want to use the one that everyone else was using because there was no toilet – just a hole in the floor. By now I am on another planet. When it was evening all the men prepared for bed. You guessed it. They climbed up to the luggage racks. These were quickly filled. Several men came prepared. They had a newspaper that they spread out in the aisle and under the benches. They fell to sleep at once. I just sat there looking at it all while my ankles got bigger and bigger.

In the morning I finally arrived at Madras. By now I had made my plan of action. First I was going to the travel agency to confront the man who sold me a one-way ticket for a round trip ticket price. By now I was so numb from sleep deprivation that my brain was in another realm. I took a taxi to the agency. When I walked in I went directly to the man at his desk. I loudly accused him of cheating me. I demanded my money back. He didn't say much back. His manager came over to hear what I had to say. When he heard my story he was very apologetic. But when I asked for my return-trip refund, he said that he could not do so. Well, I just about gave up. I asked the manager to get me out to the airport on time. So I was taken there in a truck.

The weather in Madras had turned stormy. So when I got to the airport I was worried. Since I had a couple of hours to wait for my flight to Calcutta I decided to take advantage of the nice couch in the waiting room. At least I would make my connections with my hosts as planned. So I lay down for a much-needed nap. My first sleep in four days. After awhile, I felt a slight tap on my shoulder. I awake to see a young dark-eyed Indian Man. He asked me oh so politely, "Madam, would you like cup of tea?" I said, "Yes, thank you so much." So he brought me a tray that had a beautiful china tea set placed on a lace doily. As I sipped I realized that it was getting close for my flight. I could see very dark clouds and a lot of rain outside the big windows. There were not too many people waiting for flights. I soon found out why.

An announcement was made on the loudspeaker. The voice apologized for the bad weather. He said the storm had become a hurricane. It was blowing over Madras as he spoke. I didn't know what to do. All flights were canceled until the same time tomorrow. There was no place to stay in the airport, so I went out front and hailed a taxi.

Even though the wind was blowing furiously I had to get into the city to find a place to stay overnight. So where would I go? Yes, I went straight back to the travel agency. They probably groaned when I walked in but I didn't care. I asked the manager to find me a hotel room, not too expensive, at once. Soon I was ensconced in a little hotel room that seemed beautiful to me. Everything in the room was white – the walls and all the furniture. The manservant asked me if I wanted anything. I said, "Please don't disturb me for dinner. Please wake me by 8 a.m." I sure didn't want to miss my flight to Calcutta. I quickly got out of the clothes I had been wearing for four days, took a quick shower – Oh, it felt so good – and got into bed. The time of day was about 2 in the afternoon. I went straight to sleep, and woke up with the tapping in my door. The manservant said it was 8 o'clock. Oh, did I feel better. As I was dressing I looked down at my ankles. They had returned to normal shape. So I was in fine fettle. My adventure to Cochin had turned out to be just that – an adventure. I felt sorry that I didn't enjoy to the fullest my visit with my friends there, but it just didn't turn out right from beginning to end.

The hurricane has passed on so all schedules were resumed. In the early evening I arrived in Calcutta. Two of my hosts were there waiting for me. They, of course, knew of the delay. They were quite happy to see me, and asked how I enjoyed my visit to Cochin. I said it was fine (I didn't want to go into detail) but that the travel agent in Madras had sold me a round-trip ticket when there was not a seat available for my return. I said they refused to refund my money. My hosts said they would take care of it. But several weeks later I learned from them that the Indian government would not permit them to send any cash out of the country. They said I could order artifacts and other things to the same amount, and they would see that I got everything.

Before I was shown to my hotel room, my hosts decided to take me out to dinner. Where did we go but to a nightclub. It was in this place that I heard a trio of young men sing "The Yellow Submarine" by the Beatles. So Calcutta was even hip. The following morning I bid "Goodbye" to my hosts and India. I loved it all even the last part and I shall be forever grateful to the US Government for giving me that wonderful opportunity to open up my horizons.

It is now late December 1966. My grant gave direct stipulations that if we proceed eastward on our return trip to the USA all our expenses would continue to be paid with the grant money. If someone wanted to backtrack to Europe then those expenses would be his or her own. I planned short stops in five cities on my way home. The first destination was Bangkok, Thailand.

After spending so many weeks in India with its crowded cities, and very poor people all around, I was surprised to see that neighboring Thailand looked so fresh and prosperous. Flying over the city, I was struck by the beauty of the blue tile roofs. All the buildings looked so shiny compared with those in India that showed the mold resulting from so much dampness in the monsoons. I went to my hotel, the Siam International. It was like night and day for me. Everything was very modern and up-to-date.

After freshening up and enjoying a hamburger in the café, a beautiful young lady met me. She was going to be my escort for two days. She was the sister of one of our students at Immaculate Heart High School. Her chauffeur drove us to many temples, gardens, tearooms, and the king's palace. Yes, it is the same palace where Anna taught so long ago.

My next stop was Singapore. How exotic. It is almost on the equator so I experienced the heat and the daily cloudburst. It was wonderful. I stayed in the grand old historic Raffles hotel. They didn't have a single room for me so they assigned me to a suite. I was thrilled. The next day I took a bus trip to see the very modern city, and go across the river into Malaysia. The following day was Christmas day. I attended Mass at the Cathedral. Then I wanted to do something special so I went out in front of the hotel and hired a bicycle rickshaw. The young man said he would show me some of the special areas of Singapore. So we went through Chinatown. It was very crowded and bustling. I loved it. This jaunt helped me not be too lonesome on Christmas day.

The following day I boarded the plane again and flew to Hong Kong. Here was another eye-opener. The airport is in the bay right down by the city. I thought we were going to land on top of a skyscraper. My eyes were darting everywhere. Chinese junks were everywhere as were small sampans. The city itself is very modern. Hundreds of skyscrapers set against very high hills. It reminded me of San Francisco.

I stayed with the Maryknoll Sisters there. They were very hospitable. They showed me all around Kowloon and Hong Kong. Then we took a train out to the border with China. I was surprised that it was about 15 or twenty miles inland. There was the railroad station at the border, and the Chinese soldiers guarding it all. We saw farmers out in the fields across the border. So I can say that I have seen China, but didn't step a foot into it.

My next stop was Tokyo, Japan. I was there over New Years Day. I stayed several days there. My host was a priest who was a professor at the local Catholic University. His niece was a volunteer from Belgium who helped them. She was about 20 years old. She spoke very good English, so we both went all around Tokyo to see the sights. The priest entertained me later in the day after his classes. One night he took us to the Kabuki Theater. What a treat for me, it was the real thing. The plays go on and on for hours, so the patrons just come and go whenever they wish.

We viewed Tokyo by night. I swear that I have never seen so much neon lighting as a saw there. Sometimes a whole tall building would be covered with brilliant colors from top to bottom. It was really quite beautiful. We went on a train down to Kyoto one of the days. We visited a shrine and took a boat ride across a lake to some volcanic areas that are steaming vapor. On the way home our bus took us on a route where we could view Mt. Fuji. It seemed to loom over us. I don't know how people can climb it in a day.

Soon, my Asian saga was drawing to a close. I took the plane for my next stop – Honolulu. The plane took off in Tokyo at 11 p.m. It was a very long flight to Hawaii. We crossed the International dateline. I arrived in Honolulu it was 11 a.m. of the day before. I was getting closer to home. I had a whole day of layover in Honolulu so I took advantage of the time and went on a tour of Oahu. I had never been there before, so this was an eye opener to me.

The pineapple fields, Pearl Harbor, the tropical weather, was so very pleasant. But this too came to an end. I boarded the plane to Los Angeles early the next day. I managed to get the last seat on the plane so I was located in the very back.

By now, I am looking forward to returning to Immaculate Heart. I had successfully fulfilled my scholarship requirements. I had been in touch with IHMs and my family many times in the past few months. I was wearing a modified habit with a short veil. I even had a shampoo and haircut while in Honolulu so I would look halfway decent.

When I landed at LAX I was greeted by about 15 IHMs. What a grand reunion we had. I was so happy to be finally at home.

One funny thing happened at the airport. Unbeknownst to me Cardinal Spellman of New York was on the same plane – in first class I'm sure. I never laid eyes on him. The nuns told me that he was the first off the plane. I'll bet he thought the nuns were there to greet him. Well, I finally showed up last of all, and was greeted by all of them with so much love.

House No. 16 – 1967

Franklin Avenue - Hollywood, California

It is now January 1967. I thought I would return home to continue in the same old way as before. How mistaken I was. Now begins the next saga of my life in the IHM Community. It has certainly not been a dull life.

After getting all settled in I started to plan my usual activities as Supervisor of our IHM schools. By now the Motherhouse was abuzz with the directives coming out of the Vatican regarding the Council pronouncements. We as a Community were always on top of the latest moves and changes that were mentioned. So I found myself listening to many viewpoints offered by those who were keeping abreast of the Vatican news. When I was home from visiting a school I would catch up with what was happening in Rome. By now there were many of us wearing a modest blue dress, scapular and veil. Some were still wearing the long habits that covered everything but the face. I had let my hair grow before I went to India, so I was ready for just a short veil. Others took more time to get used to the idea.

Before long the whole Community was being asked to give very serious thought to the suggested changes coming from Rome. We were reading the latest books on Renewal of Religious Life by eminent scholars who were at the Council. We participated in discussion groups on all topics related to our life and mission. Several world-class theologians were invited to come to Hollywood or Montecito to give a retreat that opened our eyes wide, or to simply share the news from the Vatican Council.

Most of us in the IHM Community were energized and elated by the prospect of moving into the future as a modern group of nuns. By this time we were a group numbering about 600. We had a large percentage of the Community under the age of forty. There were so many in our own group who were very well educated, creative, and undaunted by the unknown. It was during the summer of 1967 and then 1968 that we decided to move ahead and renew our whole way of life.

We elected delegates to go to the meetings that we called "Chapters" to discuss each and every rule that we had. Each member of our Community was given two little books at the time of Profession, that is when we made our vows. These little books contained several hundred rules and regulations we were to follow meticulously as vowed nuns. It was in these books that one will find the rule that nuns were to go out in public in twos or more, never alone.

We were given rules for every aspect of our lives including our prayer life, our spiritual life, our convent life, and our teaching life. There was not one part of our life that was neglected. It was so important for us to follow the rule that any serious infraction could bring about chastisement from the Superior, or even expulsion from the order. We all knew the Rule by heart. It was what we agreed to obey when we made our vows. For those who were truly called to this kind of life it was not a burden at all. To someone who did not belong, it could be a cause of suffering that usually ended in a return to one's home.

I personally did not find it difficult to follow the Rule. We did not set about to modernize our way of life because we did not like the rule. We set out to ,modernize because we were told that the Vatican Council had put out a decree encouraging all religious groups in the world to review their Rule and to update it to the modern day. That seemed like a straightforward direction.

We had discussed, planned, and articulated so many ways we could better serve the Church that it was not jolting to most of us that we would examine our whole way of life. At no time did we ever consider that we would move away from working in Church-sponsored schools and Institutions. We never considered that we would drop out of our teaching and nursing works. We just wanted to explore ways that we could do a much better job than we were now doing. So when the Chapter of delegates met to work on renewal we did not have any fear or trepidation that we would be displeasing to Rome or to our Bishop, Cardinal McIntire.

Most of the Religious Communities of men and women in the world were founded hundreds of years ago. It is true there are some more recent foundations, but so many were founded in long times past. The rules adopted by each one came directly from Rome. Most of the rules arose from the needs of the times, in some cases centuries ago. ALL of the rules were written and approved by men only. No group could claim to be official if the Vatican did not approve its rules. The consequence of this was that the men decided everything we did.

I was elected as a Chapter delegate four times so I was in on the ground floor of all the discussions. We met in Montecito all summer long. Our task was to look at each rule and ask the question, "Is this rule relevant for us today?" After much discussion on the pros and cons we would vote to keep it or change it. If it was agreed to change it then the questions was, "Change it in what way?" A small committee of writers would compose a new wording that would then be voted on for approval or not.

The whole summer progressed this way. We sometimes had long and heated discussions about issues, but there was always the feeling that we were responding to the wishes of the Vatican Council to truly renew ourselves. There were no men in on this revision. This was our own. For a change, we women were deciding what was best for us. We only had consultants who were theologians to tell us if the issues were on the right track according to the thinking of the Council. If not, then we went back and started again. By the end of the summer of 1968 we had developed what we called "the Decrees of the Ninth General Chapter".

I for one was very excited and hopeful that we could proceed with our renewed rules and serve the Church even better than we were doing at present. After all, I had given my whole life to serve the Church since the age of seventeen. Now I was forty-four, well educated, energetic, devoted to my vocation, and eager to begin our renewal.

The 60's was a time of tremendous turmoil in our nation over the war in Vietnam. Also the drug scene had grown to immense proportions all over the country if not the world. Young people were rebelling in huge numbers. They had found their voices, and were using them to protest. I don't think there was any portion of society that wasn't influenced, both pro and con, by these events.

We as a Community were very aware by now of all the questions being asked of our government leaders and of society. After all, we were teaching in 58 elementary schools located all over California, Arizona, and Canada. We had nuns teaching in eleven high schools, and others teaching in our College in Hollywood. Besides this we were running three hospitals and two Retreat Houses. So our sphere of knowledge about what was going on in the world was very wide.

We were a Community that encouraged questions. I believed we were very up-to-date indeed. By now we had already made major changes in our habits from the old stylized "cover the whole body except the face" to " below the knee dress and scapular and veil" that showed that we actually had hair.

So the saga begins. We asked each member to be a part of a Commission of Study to learn about and discuss all aspects of our lives. All IHMs shared the items that were voted upon in the Chapter. Comments and revisions were welcome.

Our Mother General, Mother Humiliata, (Anita Caspary) was our spearhead. She was well up to the challenge since she was one of the best-educated and devout members of the IHMs. She had the confidence that all of us could make the journey into the future if that was our desire. We were looking forward to being modern women in a modern Church. After all Vatican II had directed all nuns to bring their Community life up to modern times.

It just wasn't going to turn out as we expected or hoped. After the whole Community had spent countless hours bringing everything up-to-date, revising where needed, checking with those Theologians who had attended the Vatican Council, much prayer and some trepidation, we decided that everything was worded the way we wanted. By now we were excited about the future service we could give the Church. We planned to give every single IHM the opportunity to finish her college course and earn her credentials in whatever field she happened to be in. This only seemed like good old common sense. We did not plan to leave our service to the parochial schools. Instead we were going to have well qualified teachers in every school. Those who would be engaged in other works would also receive the preparation that was needed to fulfill their duties. So you can see that we were very enthusiastic about our future.

If the reader of this story would like to know all the details about what happened next they should read Anita Caspary's book, "Witness to Integrity".

I will not relate all that happened next. Suffice it to say that we were declared by our Bishop, Cardinal McIntire, to be 'bad women' and we were not to do any of the things we had prepared for so long to do. We became a cause celeb in the whole world, especially the world of the Catholic Church.

Suddenly there were newspapers writing about our clash with our Cardinal, magazine articles were written by the ton, TV stations were coming around to interview our leaders. In a word, our case had become worldwide news.

We IHMs were astounded at the reaction of our Cardinal. He had attended the Vatican Council. He knew what they had voted in. He knew that we were just following the lead of "The Document on Religious Renewal".

We had learned that he did not approve of very many of the changes approved by the Council. He was a man who had spent most of his clerical life in positions of authority. He was not used to having anyone oppose him in any way. He demanded strict obedience to himself and his dictums. So here he was being confronted by a group of nuns that had been working in his Archdiocese for a hundred years, who conducted 28 elementary schools, five high schools a college, a hospital, and a retreat house, and who were trying to upgrade all of their apostolic endeavors. We should have received congratulations from him. We felt confident that the authority in the Church would welcome our new Decrees. Instead our whole world was 'bombed.'

The Cardinal had been having problems with our leadership for a few years over some innovations we wished to start. The College was a source of irritation to him because it was so modern, and at times, avant-garde. Our Community fostered the talents of its members including the renowned artist, Sister Corita Kent, who later became known simply as "Corita." At one point he demanded of our Mother General that Corita be forbidden to pursue her art. Thankfully, our Mother General refused to stand in the way of Corita's talent. It was because of our College that so many in the Community became well educated. We wanted all of our members to enjoy this goal. To us this was a very worthy ambition. Even today we have not changed from this high expectation of our members.

For the next several months the Cardinal and our leaders were locked in an ongoing battle to see who was in charge. The Cardinal was adamant that he and he alone, had the one and only say about what we were to be. We were as equally adamant that the second Vatican Council had given all religious women and men the directive to update their way of life without having to have any approval of the local Bishop. We had followed this directive for at least two years by intense study and meetings. The whole Community had been in on all the new ideas emanating from the General Chapter meetings. We were ready.

A group of IHMs was selected to write up our new way of living. They produced the Decrees of the Ninth General Chapter. These were to be our new Rule instead of the archaic rule books we had. Some of the rules in the old books were so old that they were probably put there in the fourteenth or fifteenth centuries. From here on our lives were in a constant turmoil and anxiety.

The Cardinal used all of his authority to request a papal investigation of our Community. But first, he had his own investigation. We were subjected to interrogation by three local priests as to our agreement or disagreement with the new Decrees. Each IHM was interviewed privately. I personally was insulted that any priest or Monsignor would question me about my loyalty to my Community, or to the Church. We all had been in on so much preparation for our new direction that we all could express ourselves quite clearly. No one was coerced into doing anything she didn't wish to do. I heard later that the priests went away shaking their heads. They were overheard saying we were hung up on Vatican II. Of course we were. That was the basic reason we were revising our lives to bring us up to the 20th Century.

Next on the program was an official visit of Bishops and an Archbishop sent by the Vatican to see what was going on. There were several meetings with these three Churchmen. Once again we were all interrogated separately or in small groups to see what we were thinking. We felt confident that when they could hear us out about our responses to Vatican II that they would recommend that we go forward. After all, this renewal was voted on, and passed by an overwhelming majority of the Bishops and Cardinals at the Vatican. We felt that we would come out of this ok. How wrong we were.

The interrogators were in close contact with Cardinal

McIntire at all times. He was in close contact with the powers that be in Rome. We were not included in any of their meetings so we didn't know what agreements were made between them in our regard. Our Mother General, Mother Humiliata, was not treated with the respect she deserved. I was with her and several of our other leaders at some of the meetings with the Hierarchy. I came away furious at the contempt they showed her and the rest of us.

This must have been the first time in Cardinal McIntire's life that he was confronted with a group that was working out its own way without asking him for permission. And to think it was a group of women. We were all informed of the progress the leaders of the Community were making. It wasn't much. They were in the dark about decisions. Our Mother General, Mother Humiliata said that she was going to Rome to speak to the highest official she could find. It would seem that the Pope would be a loving father and listen to the pleas of his "children" in Hollywood. Not so. She did go to Rome and she did speak to a high-ranking Secretary of Something. He gave her 15 minutes of his precious time. She said she never heard from him again – no pro or con. What a fiasco.

By now we were getting very tired of all the secrecy and insults that were being heaped upon us. The Cardinal was demanding that we backtrack completely and return to the way we were. We were to forget about the whole thing.

Well, not so fast. We all agreed to go ahead. The Cardinal then fired us from all the schools in the L.A. Archdiocese. We had labored in the L.A. Diocese for

99 years. The Cardinal didn't care. He let go of the largest group of nuns in his Archdiocese because he didn't get us to do his wishes instead of following the Vatican Council directives.

The hardest part for us to swallow was that the Vatican upheld him. The old boys network was alive and well. All those men just couldn't let a small group of women make decisions regarding their own lives when for century upon century only the men could make these decisions for the women. The women in the Church had absolutely no say as to what they would do or be.

The whole Community met together to decide what to do. The Cardinal told us that if we did not do what he commanded then we would be asked to renounce our vows, and leave religious life. We were stunned. Our dedication to service in the Church was going to be cut off just like that.

Our Council called the whole Community together to discuss what to do. In the end we had a secret vote. There were 400 IHMs who voted to opt out of the canonical status. There was a small group of 51 who voted to stay the way we were.

All the nuns teaching in the parochial schools of the LA Archdiocese spent the latter part of the school year of 1969 clearing out of those schools. I was still the Supervisor so I had to do a lot to help with the transitions.

The Pastors were dumbfounded. We had been laboring in some school for over 50 years. The parents were equally sad and angry. They had not been informed of any of the Vatican Council changes by Cardinal McIntire. They didn't know what to make of us. Now many years later they understand what the problem was, but at that time they didn't have a clue except what we told them. We were in the unbelievable predicament that we had no jobs, no money, no severance pay, nothing. We were going to have to use all of our ingenuity to survive.

At the summer break of 1969 we had two Communities. A large group of us was ready to move on into the unknown. A small group followed the lead of Sister Eileen MacDonald. All fifty-one of them moved to a large home in the Los Feliz Hills.

Even though we still had about 30 schools spread around six other Dioceses where the Bishops were not giving us any problem, I felt that I had spent enough of my energy on the work of Supervision. This was the end of my twelfth year in that job. So I told Our Mother General that I would be going elsewhere. She was in total agreement.

My own personal feelings about all of this were that we at no time meant to leave the status of vowed Religious. We started out in the whole endeavor to respond to the call of the Vatican Council to review our way of life, and make changes in the spirit of our Founder. Since we had been founded to offer education to all who came to us we wanted to offer the very best. We listened in a very prayerful manner to all that was said about renewal. We read prayerfully all that was written about it. We consulted with the most eminent theologians in the world at the time. Many of them had been in attendance at the Council so they said we were on the right track. I was in total agreement of our moving ahead. I didn't know what the future held, but I had so much trust in the guidance of the Holy Spirit in our group that I was resolute in my approval.

We were heartsick at the thought of giving up our vows. After all, these were what made us the dedicated women that we were. I personally was in my 29th year as an IHM. I was 45 years of age. I had been a faithful nun since the age of 17. Now I realized that my Bishop did not care one whit about all the years of dedication we had given to serve the Church.

There were some members of our group who were in their seventies and eighties, even nineties. They also had to decide if they would proceed into a new life. What an edification they were. So many decided to accompany us on the unknown road ahead. The oldest one was Sister Austin who was in her late nineties at the time. They gave me the example of trust in the Holy Spirit who somehow had seemed to lead us into an unknown and rather scary world. We started out a few years ago heading in one direction, and gradually found ourselves pointing our ship into a sea that we had not navigated before. Ever since this happened I have always looked upon all of these events as blessings from God.

We as a small Community in California had succeeded in breaking the chain of masculine dominance over our lives. We led the way for Religious Women all over the world to seek the same freedom. Somehow we were called to do this. The events of the time showed that we had the strength to carry it out. I have never looked back with any regrets.

My next decision was whether to stay in Parochial school education or what? I thought I would continue working for the Church, but I couldn't do so in the Los Angeles Archdiocese, so I opted to go to a Parochial school in the San Francisco Archdiocese. My choice was St. Gregory in San Mateo. After all, I had to work somewhere to earn a salary. The parochial school salaries were still very small for the nuns, but I felt I could do ok.

We voted to continue on to our modern life, we could choose to wear the habit or not, we could make decisions about our own life rather than have a letter come telling us what we were to do. In a word, we sailed into the future. My future was to be at St. Gregory's School in San Mateo. I was hired as the Principal. The year was 1969.

House No. 17 – 1969

St. Gregory's School,
San Mateo, California

It is now summer of 1969. We as a Community have voted many times on issues vital to us individually and as a group. Our final decision was to follow the winds of fate. We did not set out to leave the canonical religious life that we all had embraced in our youth. But the battle that we had been fighting turned out to be one that led us to decide that we were somehow being called to start something new. It wasn't what we set out to do, but here we were. I had to be instrumental in ensuring that all 28 of our elementary schools in the Archdiocese of Los Angeles were vacated properly and in good condition.

The Sisters worked conscientiously to be sure that all records and supplies were left in such a way that someone coming after us would not find it too difficult to pick up where we had left off.

It was new to me that now I would be expected to make the decision of my work rather than having a letter arrive assigning me to serve in some place. All of us were testing our wings in this regard. After a lot of thought I decided that I would venture into administration of an elementary school again.

By now we were not wearing our traditional habits. I had acquired some dresses that were the style of the time. Now when I look back I see that we probably looked like hippies at times. We didn't have the faintest idea of what to wear. We just wore what we could find. I even made a poncho out of the bedspread on my bed. It was getting old and worn so I just pulled it off the bed and cut a slit in the center, pushed my now curly head through. After a time we got some fashion sense and presented ourselves better. I am sure there were some who had a good laugh at our naiveté.

I had to get a move on and try to find a job in a parochial school somewhere. Of course, we could not teach in any of the parochial schools in L.A. We actually were in dire straits as a Community because there were suddenly several hundred nuns, now former nuns, fired from their jobs. The pay scale for nuns was extremely minimal. We always pooled our incomes so we could manage to buy food and necessities, but there was never any extra for emergencies. And, of course, there was no such thing as severance pay offered to us. In a word, our Bishop left us destitute without so much as a "thank you' for the 100 years of service we had given to the Church in Southern California. So here we were with no jobs and no income. There was no big pot somewhere in the Motherhouse that we could draw from. How would we support ourselves?

I decided I would continue on in parochial school in the San Francisco Archdiocese. I offered my services as Principal at St. Gregory's School to the Pastor, Monsignor Brown. I was accepted by him I am sure with a sigh of relief. The clergy in all the other dioceses were not challenging us at all in our efforts to modernize, but I suppose they must have been holding their collective breath because they weren't sure what we were going to do next.

I want to say at this point that it was so fortunate for all of us that the IHM Community had provided most of us with a fine education. Many of our members went immediately into public school teaching. We heard that all the local Superintendents were vying with one another to obtain as many IHMs as possible for assignments in their districts.

I chose to continue in parochial school because that was what I had known all of my professional life. St. Gregory School was in a nice neighborhood in San Mateo, California. Our Sisters had taught there for almost twenty years. I needed a job. This looked very appealing to me. Before I arrived up there I had to do something brand new in our Community. I interviewed IHMs for the two openings – third grade and eighth grade. I was surprised at how many wanted to come up there with me to teach for the coming year. I chose two good teachers to come do the job. I thanked all the rest and they went on to other interviews. We had just recently changed our ways of doing things. It was thought that we should all approach our work in a mature and professional manner. No more letters assigning us (whether we were fitted for the job or not) to a school. We were urged to make mature decisions on our own. This was one of the new directions we wished to take. We felt we could serve the Church better in so many ways. I for one was happy with it all. There turned out to be some pitfalls and disappointments. We were scheduled to drive up to San Mateo the latter part of August.

A few days before we were to go the IHM I had hired to teach the eighth grade came to my room in the

Motherhouse and said quite calmly that she had changed her mind. She said she decided to stay in the L.A. area in order to be closer to her family. I was dumbfounded. But I shouldn't have been. After all we had said that we could make decisions – and were encouraged to do so. My dilemma was that there were just a few days left before we would be driving north. By this time all the other IHMs I had interviewed were going other places. There was not one available. This left me with the task of phoning the Pastor up there and telling him we would have only four IHMs instead of five. He would have to find a teacher. He graciously said he would do that. So now I felt more settled.

Off we went to the north. It took us all day to drive to San Mateo, but it was a new adventure for me. I was looking forward to being in one place for the whole year for a change since I had just finished twelve years of traveling all over the place at least twice a week in order to visit all of our schools. I was ready.

What a life. The two IHMs who rode with me were young and energetic. They were also good teachers. I was confident that they would be a real asset to the school. The other IHM I had hired at the interview time had chosen to go to San Mateo ahead of us. She was already in the convent when we arrived. I was glad to have my IHM staff together. Another surprise awaited me.

It wasn't long after I got settled in my room in the convent when this other IHM I had hired at the earlier interview came quietly to my door and said, "I need to talk to you." This didn't sound too good to me.

Whenever anyone said that to me in the past it meant that some earth-shaking event had come up in that person's life. So I said, "Oh, of course, what is it?" She said as calmly as she could that she was leaving the Community. She no longer wanted to be an IHM. She had fallen in love with a man in the last place she had worked. She was going to move out of the convent, and wanted to be addressed as "Miss" not "Sister" as we were still being called.

You could have knocked me down with a feather. My mind was in a whirl. Here I was having to tell the Pastor that there were only three nuns at the school. He didn't have to hire a new teacher for this IHM because, thank God, she said she would honor her decision to teach in San Mateo for the whole school year.

After we talked I told her that that was her decision to make, but that I was disappointed. She was apologetic, but I knew that there was nothing I could do about it. So I said to myself, "Welcome to our modern life." It was just my luck that both of the IHMs I chose turned out to be a problem for me in some ways. I knew that they were both experienced and good teachers at that time. They also had reputations as being reliable, etc. I started my first day on the job with an ominous feeling about St. Gregory's.

I suppose that the event that took place the very next day was a portent of my year in St. Gregory's. Since school hadn't started yet, and because it was Saturday, I asked my companions if they would like to go on a picnic down to the beach. We all agreed that it would be a wonderful start for our year together. We all piled into our old red station wagon. We had put together a great lunch of hero sandwiches, some fruit, and cold drinks. I didn't realize that the beach was really quite a way from our school. We weren't going to the Bay. It was close and even in sight. We decided to go to the real beach over the coastal mountains and down into the Half Moon Bay area. There we would have good sand to walk in and big waves to admire.

As it happened I was not the driver that day probably because I really didn't know how to get there. So one of the younger IHMs who had been at the school for a couple of years offered to drive us over. When we arrived I couldn't believe what I saw. A dense cloudbank had descended upon the coast. We were going to have a picnic in cold, dreary weather. I checked with them all to see if they wanted to stay. All agreed it would be a fine idea to just go ahead with our plans.

The driver drove our car right onto the sand. She drove out to the edge of a cutoff of beach sand. The cliff in front of the car was probably about five feet high. Instead of jumping down the shelf of sand we all decided to just walk a ways to the right where we settled in with a beach blanket and all of our food. I just couldn't believe what happened next.

Suddenly we heard loud calls from folks who were on the beach on the other side of our car. We heard them, and turned to see what they wanted. We stood transfixed. Our little red car was moving forward slowly. We watched as it got to the edge of the cliff. Then it just quietly went over headfirst onto the sand below. So there it was sticking straight up in the air. No one said a word for a minute. It was so unbelievable.

When we finally could gasp out a few words we said, "What happened?" We all turned to the driver who was as red as a beet. She said she must have thought we had parked on a level spot so she didn't put on the emergency brake. By now a large crowd had gathered to examine the predicament. There were all kinds of suggestions, but the best one was that someone had an auto club card that we could use. One of the kind onlookers called for us.

Soon the truck came with a winch attached to the front. I was quite chagrined because the local Police also showed up. They all asked how on earth did this happen? We explained that the emergency brake was not on. That satisfied them all. After about fifteen minutes the truck had raised the car up and pulled it away from the edge of the cutoff. I jumped in to see if it would start. It did. Everyone examined the car all over to see if it had any damage. It didn't.

We decided to continue on with our picnic since it was going to be our supper, then we would drive back home. The upshot of the story is that the car served us very well for the rest of the year. Thus ended my first two days in San Mateo.

I am not going to relate very much about the year. In my life it was one of transition from the old style ways of the nuns to our new direction. I felt confident about directing the school, but a big change was that I was not the Superior. Not that I was anxious to be one, but we were experimenting with a more collegial way of living. We all had a say in things that needed to be done. No one was ordered to do anything. I was sure this would work out all right, and it did in most circumstances. There were a couple of occasions when we had some good heated discussions about something. But in the end we were always able to agree on a course of action.

St. Gregory School was a nice school in a middle class area of San Mateo. Our IHMs had taught there for 20 years or so. The people were used to us, and cooperated in every way. However, by the time I came we had made several changes. First of all, I wasn't wearing a habit. I was called 'Sister Doris', which sounded so strange to me after being called 'Sister Peter' for almost 30 years. I gathered early on that the parents were not enamored of our new look. I don't know if they had been advised as to our changes, but they seemed rather distant to me. I turned on my charm every chance I got, but it was an uphill battle. I entered in to as many of the school activities as I could.

As the year went on I began to realize that there was so much work to do in instructing the parish about the changes in religious life that it would take more energy than I had at the time. Remember that this is at the very moment when we had been dismissed from the schools in L.A. and had been told that we were to renounce our vows. Because this effort had been going on for a couple of years I found myself emotionally exhausted.

After thinking about it for a couple of months I went

to the Pastor and told him that I would be staying only until June. In a lot of ways I felt sad about my decision because I went up to St. Gregory's fully intending to continue on in Parochial education for as long as I was teaching. My next thought was "What to do?"

I galvanized into action. By taking the action we had in becoming lay people instead of nuns it meant that I was going to be responsible for my own upkeep. The Community did not have any money. And since I decided not to return to San Mateo, I decided that I would go back to the L.A. area and get a job, hopefully, in the public schools. In this way I would be supporting myself while doing the work of the new Community. I wasn't sure how to contact the Public School people so I went to the local public library and found some catalogs of all the school districts in California.

After some thoughtful searching I decided to write letters to three Districts. My choices were the Los Angeles Unified, Torrance Unified, and Long Beach Unified Districts. I sent them a letter of interest in employment for the following year. I was glad to hear from each one, and was invited for a personal interview. This happened at the Easter Vacation break. Later in May I received an offer of a contract from each one. But, by now, I was thinking how fortuitous it was that I could actually work in Long Beach and be on hand to help my aging mother who lived alone at the time. So I wrote 'thank you' letters to the other two, and an acceptance letter to Long Beach. So that is how I came to be a teacher in the Long Beach Unified School District.

One of the most moving things I have ever had to do happened during this year at St. Gregory's. The IHM Community had finally come to the realization that if we were going to move ahead in any way we would not receive any encouragement or recognition from the Cardinal or from the Vatican. So after many meetings and much discussion it was decided to take a vote of members who wished to move ahead, and those who wished to remain as we were. When the results were published it showed that about 500 IHMs wanted to move ahead, and about 50 IHMs wished to remain as we were.

The consequence of this was that the larger group of 500 was told that they would have to move out of Canonical status, and renounce their vows. The smaller group was told that they were safe. Needless to say, this caused an enormous amount of anxiety in all of us. I chose to go the modern route.

By now Cardinal McIntire had semi-retired. Archbishop Manning consulted with our leaders. He said the directive from Rome was that we were to go back to the way we were or we could not be nuns anymore. We met together many times to decide all the ramifications of such a move. In the end we opted to remain together and form a new Community. So that is how the new Immaculate Heart Community was born.

Sometime later in the year I received the official form to sign in renouncing my vows. I looked at it a long time because my vows represented my dedication to serve God faithfully all of my life. After quiet prayer and meditation I realized that I could serve God just as well without vows as I had with vows. This piece of paper was not going to make me change my character. So I signed it and sent it in to Anita Caspary. It meant for me that I was willing to launch off into the unknown world of being part of a new lay community. I had worked with so many others to develop a Community of modern women, and I believed that we were following the mandate of Vatican II.

The school year at St. Gregory's was coming to a close. I was feeling more and more relieved. I hadn't realized how much stress I was under trying to cope with so many life-changing things. So in the middle of June all of the IHMs living there packed up and went south to the Motherhouse. Each one of us had signed the fateful vows letter. This was a form letter we were sent by Archbishop Manning. He was now heading the Archdiocese of Los Angeles because Cardinal McIntire had finally retired. I remember so well taking the letter up to my room in the convent. I read it over a couple of times. In essence, it was the form used by the Church to relieve one from the three vows. Of course, this meant the end of my formal days as a nun. I thought about it for only a few minutes, and then I signed it. That is how certain I was that we were on the right track for the future. The men in the Church had condemned us heartily, so we said, "Ok, we will have trust in the Holy Spirit guiding us to a new kind of religious life."

Over 350 IHMs signed the paper that day. This was the end of my life as a canonical nun with vows. I had been in the Community serving the Church for 29 years. I don't recall hearing any thanks from the clergy or hierarchy for this dedicated service. I was forty-six years of age and ready for the next adventure. It is now June 1970.

House No. 18 – 1970

Ocean Avenue - Seal Beach, California

Now begins my journey as a member of our new lay community. We were no longer considered nuns but we chose to establish a community of lay persons to serve God in the future. This was a totally new adventure for all of us. I came down to Hollywood to our Motherhouse for the summer. I was in good condition regarding my employment for the coming school year. I had received notice of my employment from the Long Beach School District. I even had my school assignment. It was to be Grade 4 in Carver Elementary School in Long Beach. This was the start of my sixteen-year career in the public schools.

I was settled for the Fall, except that I didn't have a place to live. I knew that I couldn't stay up in Hollywood because it was way too far from school. I happened to mention to my friends at lunch one day that I needed a place to live in the Long Beach area. Sister Loraine overheard me and told me about a priest in Seal Beach who owned some apartments. She knew him personally, so she gave me his phone number. I called him and introduced myself. He was very cordial, and invited me to come down that afternoon to look at an apartment he had in mind. So I took my dear friend, Sister Johanna, now Frances Labonge, to see it.

We drove down there in my newly acquired, used VW hatchback. I bought it from Rose Eileen who had purchased it from Peggy Zeyen, formerly Sister Denis, and her new husband. She told me $2,000 was the price. Since I now had a contract for work. I told her I would make regular payments until it was paid off. I now had wheels. Frannie and I met with Dominic Bebek, the priest, and looked at a charming little studio apartment very close to the ocean. It really was only one house from the beach. He said it was his living quarters at present, but that he planned to move to a larger place. Was I interested? You bet I was. It was ideal for me. The rent was to be $150 per month. I could afford that all right. This was the first time in my life that I had to wheel and deal for anything. Up to now I had lived with a vow of poverty that forbade me to use money in any private way. It always had to be for the good of others.

I couldn't believe my good fortune. I phoned my mother in Long Beach to tell her that I would be seeing her often because I lived close by, and because I now owned a car. She was always happy for me, but I am sure she couldn't quite figure out what I was really up to. I couldn't keep up with it myself. On the first of September I moved into my small apartment at the beach. Everyone helped me move my things from Immaculate Heart in Hollywood to Seal Beach. I was to live here for the next six years.

I settled in to my new abode where I discovered that I could hear the waves breaking at night. My apartment had just one large room that served as living room and bedroom. There was a small kitchen and a shower bathroom. That was all I needed. The living room had a large sliding door that opened out onto a nice, roomy patio. My apartment was the only one in the complex of four that had access to a patio. I filled it with potted flowers and pretty plants.

I was starting a new life. I had certainly not planned on living alone, in an apartment, at the beach, as a lay woman. I was reeling in many ways at the turn of events.

Sometimes I would sit and meditate upon my life, and try to put some sense into the why of my new life. I still wanted to be an IHM with my whole heart. That was what I had pledged myself to be when I was just a teenager. Now that I had reached maturity I still desired to continue my dedication. I grew to realize that it would be in situations that I had not dreamed of. I felt up to the challenge, and began to look upon it all as the next adventure in my life.

I think that this is a good spot to tell about my real feelings about what happened to us IHMs. At that time in 1970 I was astonished at the shabby treatment we had received from the men of the Church. We were supposed to be protected from Bishops like Cardinal McIntire because we were what was called 'a Pontifical Institute'. In Canon Law it was prescribed that Pontifical Institutes were under the direct protection of the Vatican. There was even a high ranking Cardinal in the Vatican who was proclaimed as our Cardinal Protector. We always knew just who this gentleman was. We were supposed to be protected from Bishops or other authorities in the Church who might find us at fault for something, and would want us punished in some way. Our Cardinal Protector was always our hope in case we had to appeal to him for help. We have records of many letters sent to our protector asking for his help in resolving the difficulties we were having with our local Bishop, Cardinal McIntire. In the end it turned out that it was all wasted effort on our part. The men stuck together.

We came to the realization that no matter how well we explained our love and loyalty to the Church in regard to our lives as dedicated religious women the powers that be constantly rejected our pleas for help. Cardinal McIntire was upheld in every instance, even though he was taking a stand that was directly opposed to the directives of Vatican II. The upshot of the whole thing in my view was that we were sacrificed so that this elderly Prince of the Church could have his way and save face. He was not going to be told to step back so that we could follow the directives of Vatican II in renewing, in peace, our own Community. I was sorely disappointed in my Church leaders. And to be honest, I am still shocked that these men would have such a bond that the women did not matter in their scheme of things.

It is with these feelings that I took up my new life in Seal Beach. I determined that a new direction was leading me on to new adventures. Here I was at the beach in a small apartment living alone for the first time in my life. I was forty-six years old.

There were so many first for me to experience. I would soon have a job in the public schools. I could come and go as I liked. Shopping became a challenge. Cooking for one was next. Handling money, paying rent and taking care of insurance. In a word, just living a daily life as a single woman was all new to me.

So, here is what I did while I lived in this little apartment on Ocean Avenue. It is six years of my history. One of the first things I did was call up my mother and tell her I was coming to take her for a ride. She was delighted. I picked her up and we drove over to East Long Beach to look up the school I would be teaching in come September.

She and I were elated at the sight of the beautiful school named George Washington Carver Elementary School. I drove completely around the block, and observed its spacious campus. It was also built of very modern lines. I wondered just which of the classrooms I would be assigned to. To me it didn't matter a whit because I was ready for a very relaxing year. After the travails I had endured for the past four years this was going to be a breeze. I already loved it even before I met anyone there.

I then took my mother to dinner. It turned out that this was a practice I would follow for the future. Every week I would pick up Mama. We would go out to dinner somewhere, and then we would go to the Safeway grocery store and get her supplies for the coming week. I paid for everything from then on. I discovered that she had a very small income from Social Security and Bernie's pension. I do not know how she managed. I knew she could pay the small government subsidized rent for her apartment. But that didn't leave too much for anything else. At least, now she could use it as she wished without buying groceries.

This is not meant to take away anything that my sister, Beverly, was doing for Mama. The fact of the matter is that I didn't really know what she was doing. She never spoke about it. She never asked me what I was doing, so I just left it at that.

In any event, everyone was happy with the way things were turning out. I could finally become better acquainted with my family. I felt lucky to have them so near. I had visits from them all on and off over the years, but now I could go home and see them whenever I wished. They all meant a lot to me, and still do.

It wasn't long before the IHMs found out that I was living at the beach. I began to have a lot of company. Sometimes several would stay overnight. That meant that they had to sleep on the floor. I did too if someone older came along. I did give up my bed to Frannie a number of times.

During these visits we often had a prayer group time. We were new to all of this so we began doing things in new ways. Finally we decided as a Community that those who lived in areas that were near to one another should try to establish a permanent prayer group that would meet regularly. That is just what I did with those who lived south of L.A. For several years I met in this group with Mother Regina, Virginia Reynolds and several others from the beach area.

Sometimes I took my mother with me. All the IHMs were very sweet to her. She loved it all, but I am sure she just didn't understand what happened to the NUNS. Here we all were dressed in street clothes, but acting like we always had. She never asked me any questions about it. Even to this day I don't know whether or not my family understands what really happened to us. For reasons of their own they do not show any interest in religious things. But they are always supportive of me and any needs I may have regarding my own religious desires and yearnings.

What great six years those were. I was always entertaining IHMs. We would laugh and sing for hours. Sometimes we would all don bathing suits and go ride the waves. I would cook, or someone would bring a bag of good food. In this way I kept in close touch with my IHM sisters. I did not feel away and isolated. We also continued having meetings up at Immaculate Heart. We had retreats at Montecito; our prayer group thrived. I was feeling very good about everything. The question about our future as a religious community was always paramount in our discussions. We seemed to be thriving in spite of the neglect and harm that had been done to us by our Churchmen.

The above describes my feelings about my move to Seal Beach. But another part of the picture was my move to an entirely new world. One world that I never thought I would enter - The world of Public School.

The day came for me to report to Carver School. I was hoping I looked right because I had never started school before except in the religious habit. So I looked in my closet and chose a plain blue a-line dress with a plain neckline. I put on a string of fake pearls I had there, hose and high heels. My hair was combed in a kind of bouffant. I sure hoped that I looked ok because this was going to be the first look my new Principal would have of me. My heart should have rested easy. When I arrived I went up to the counter in the school office. There stood a lovely looking blond woman with a short haircut. She took one look at me and said, "You must be Miss Murphy." Secretly I was pretty astounded because there were four other new teachers due at that very time. I laughed to myself later thinking I must have had a sign on me, or I looked rather modest. I was immediately made to feel at ease.

The principal's name was Mildred Hawley. We always addressed her from then on as 'Miss Hawley'. She welcomed all five of us so warmly. Then she gave us a short tour of the school, and showed us which classroom we would be teaching in. My room turned out to be Room 18. I was so surprised to see that the school Office area and classrooms were identical to the Parochial schools I had just left. So I began to relax and feel good about my decision.

Miss Hawley carried on beautifully, all the while wearing high heels for the whole tour. I learned later that she wore them only on that day. In fact, I have not seen her wear heels ever again. After the tour was ended, and we knew where the book room was, and who was Secretary of the school, Miss Hawley surprised us by saying that she was going to take us all out to lunch. So that was a very nice touch. It gave us time to meet one another in a rather informal way. By the end of my visit that day I was very happy with my assignment, my Principal, my classroom, and my school. I was ready to relax, and teach fourth graders to the very best of my ability.

That afternoon I was busy on the phone to my mother,

my sister, and my IHM friends telling all of them what I would be doing. I had already told our IHM President, Anita Caspary, that I had a job in Long Beach so she didn't have to worry about how I was going to support myself. Thanks to the IHM Community I was well educated, and had all the degrees and credentials I would need for the rest of my life.

That afternoon at Carver we had time to spend in our classroom. We looked over the books, curriculum materials available, and all such things that make the opening of school easy. As I was opening the teachers' guides to lesson we were expected to teach I came across one that mystified me. It was entitled "Industrial Arts". I had never seen this subject in any of the curriculum requirements in parochial school. I actually had a moment when I thought that maybe I would be fired if I couldn't follow this manual. Just at that very moment Miss Hawley came into my classroom. She asked me how I liked everything. I told her I was delighted, but I had one big worry. She said, "What is it?" When I showed her the manual for Industrial Arts she started to laugh. She told me to relax. When it came time for me to build a house or something there are experts available in the School District who will come and help me with it all. This turned out to be absolutely true. I discovered that the District had experts in every part of the curriculum. What a help they always were.

My days teaching fourth grade at Carver School were so relaxing and wonderful. Miss Hawley was an excellent principal. One must remember that I had just come from supervising fifty-eight elementary schools located all up and down the West Coast of the US. We were responsible for a few schools in British Columbia also. I had been occupied with this work for the last twelve years. On top of that, I was exhausted because of the momentous decisions we as IHMs had been dealing with for the past four years. I was ready for a break. And this was it. When school started in September a class of about thirty little nine year-olds greeted me.

On the first day I was early so that I could get everything ready. I was doing something at my desk when I happened to overhear a little girl who was sitting with a friend outside the open window say to her, Do you see our new teacher?" The other girl said, "Oh yes, she looks like an old bag." I was shocked because I thought I looked pretty good, dark hair, no wrinkles, and good smile.

That started my first day at Carver Elementary School. I taught there for four lovely years. By the time I got going my children seemed to love me, and I loved them back.

I found that I could do a lot of things that I couldn't do before. One of the things that dawned upon me was that I was being paid quite well for my efforts. No one was telling me what to do with my income, so I learned to save a little, invest a little, spend a little, and do things I enjoyed.

One of the things I started to do right off the bat was to take guitar lessons. It turned out that a guitar method using only the chords was perfect for me because I could sing quite well, and on tune. So I would provide the song, and my guitar would provide the beautiful chords. Did I ever have fun with this? Of course, I used this new found talent in my classroom. My children were always ready for our music class of the day. If I was even a minute late they would call out, "Miss Murphy, it's time for our music." One or other of the pupils would be in charge that day of getting my guitar case opened, and carefully handing the guitar to me. We learned almost every folk song I could find. This was during the seventies so everyone knows about the folk singers so popular at that time.

During these four years I was busy at my semi beach house entertaining numerous IHMs, family members, friends, and anyone else that showed up. Right away it seemed in the cards to become a friend of my Principal, Miss Hawley. She invited me to a football game in Pasadena. This was just after Christmas. I enjoyed the whole day, and became more acquainted with her. I liked her quiet personality, and she seemed to like my way. Soon after this I began to call her Mil instead of Miss Hawley when we were not at school functions. Her name was Mildred.

On this day I also discovered that she had a roommate named June Dehls. She was a retired Principal of some Long Beach Schools. Their home was a wonder to behold. It turned out that June was a true artist. In fact she seemed to have the talent to produce something beautiful in any medium. She painted, carved wood, welded jewelry, and welded large iron garden pieces. She made a gigantic macramé piece hung in the upstairs room with so many other art pieces. There were also many things June purchased over the years. What a treasure trove. That is how I met Mildred. She was my boss at school, but she became a dear friend outside of our professional work.

I was down at Seal Beach living in my nice little apartment, enjoying the ocean and trying to quietly get my life in some kind of order. Of course The IHM Community was formed right away. I said I wanted to continue my membership because I truly believed in our mission. I attended most of the meetings. I even had some meetings at my little place. Most IHMs loved coming down to see me. I always urged them to bring their bathing suits.

One of my biggest pleasures during these years was going home after school. Here I was, driving my hatchback VW down to Ocean Avenue in Seal Beach. I would unload my papers and books and Guitar. Then I would go into my snug little apartment, only one house from the beach.

Many, many times I would put on my floppy shoes and head out to the sand. This was late afternoon. There were not too many people. I would stroll along the beach facing the west. What a sundown. I look back on this time and realize that because I was still in a state of exhaustion from our battle with the Church I needed a lot of time to think, to meditate, and to relax. God had helped me immeasurably by letting me find this little place by the sea.

I lived in Seal Beach for six years. My IHM friends kept a good eye on me. They would even come and stay overnight. We would all go swimming, have dinner, pray, talk and sing then bed down on the floor.

Because I was in my late forties at that time I could always manage the floor. So whoever needed a bed could use mine. When my mother came down of course she had the bed. So I was always busy with IHM meetings and friends. By this time I was inviting my new friends Mildred Hawley and June Dehls. They seemed to take to all of us right away. Our prayers, our singing, our talking, our humor seemed to entrance them. We would often have a mixed group for our get-togethers.

After four years teaching at Carver, Mildred asked me to transfer to her new assignment. It was Starr King School in North Long Beach. I did so. I was happy about it all. Mildred and I were friends so I had to be very careful about showing it to the rest of the faculty. I succeeded somewhat, but I know there were times when it showed.

For the first three years at King I commuted from my little place in Seal Beach. I had made a practice of taking my mother with me on any little or big trips. I was usually driving. On one of these journeys up the coast she became very ill. It was while we were visiting Uncle Gus in Oakland. I had to take her to emergency in Oakland. She was in big trouble with her colon. The doctor warned me about taking her home by plane. He said she could hemorrhage. I just had to trust in the Lord to see us through to Long Beach. I left my car in the parking lot at the airport, and flew down to LAX with Mama. She did ok, thank God. I rented a car and got her to St. Mary's as quickly as possible.

She had colon cancer. The doctor removed the

cancerous growth, but the surgery left her with a colostomy. While recuperating in the hospital the doctor looked at me, and said, "Who is going to look after her now?" I looked right back at him and said, "I am of course." I had to fly back to Oakland to retrieve my car. Different IHMs came to the hospital and stayed with Mama. I was so grateful. So this is the reason I moved to House Number 19.

It was during my stay at Seal Beach that I had two surprises that broke my heart. I am sure my mother's heart was broken too.
Barr and Beverly died. Both of them had very sad adult lives. I saw them and their families on occasion.

Barr was 50 years old. He could have had a successful career in the Air Force but something was always going wrong. He had four sons: Danny, Michael, Peter, and Bernie. Barr divorced Beth and remarried.

I lost track of him. I do have the great pleasure of keeping a close friendship with Barr's eldest son, Danny, and his family. He has a lovely wife, Pat, and two children, Meredith and Collin.

I did go up to see Barr and his family a couple of times. Barr looked so ill to me. He was thin. He said that there was nothing wrong. That was the last I heard from him. Then one day I received a call from Danny saying that his father had died. Barr must have had a heart attack while living in some hotel in Seattle. The year was 1972.

The very next thing I did was go to Mama's apartment

on Artesia Blvd. She was just getting ready for breakfast. She was so surprised to see me so early in the day. I told her about the call from Danny with the news about Barr's death. Mama just looked at me with those beautiful, but sad, brown eyes. Then she said, "Why did he have to go and do that?" Barr is buried in the cemetery in Olympia, Washington.

Mama had lost both of her sons and youngest daughter early in their lives.

House No. 19 - 1977

Linden Avenue - Long Beach, California

I was in a flurry getting all the plans done in order to move my mother from her lovely apartment in Del Amo Gardens to our new apartment. Of course, I had piles of work to do in getting myself moved from Seal Beach. I had found a very nice two-bedroom apartment in Bixby Knolls just off Atlantic. It would prove to be perfect for the two of us. So here I am in the 19th house of my life adventure. It is so strange to me that I am still writing about my houses.

I am now 51 years of age. The Long Beach Unified School District has employed me for the past six years. It is quite peaceful teaching the fourth grade at Starr King School out on Artesia Boulevard. I still have a certain knack in dealing with the children. They seem to like being in my class. I am busy teaching them to play the guitar on the side. Several of them have learned to strum pretty well. We have music every day just before lunch. By the end of the year they could sing every folk song popular at that time. This is 1976 and on. Needless to say I was really relaxed and enjoying myself.

As far as visitors were concerned I noticed a definite drop off. I now know that my place at the beach was very popular. Here I was with more space than I had at Seal Beach, but my mother was living with me. That was a fine arrangement. But it wasn't as spectacular for my IHM friends to go out walking on Atlantic Avenue instead of along the beach. Very few came to stay. I was not too happy with this because I wanted to maintain my closeness with all of them. My feelings about this were not too good.

As time passed I got over it and got on with my life. We did have company now that I am thinking about it. Dan, Pat, Meredith, and Collin stayed with us during a visit. Collin was just a toddler. Mama loved seeing her great-grandchildren. I loved seeing Dan and his family. He certainly grew into a very fine man. His trumpet really did get him a long way in his professional world as a teacher. I am so proud of him.

My cousin LaJean and her teenage son, Mark, came down from Portland for a visit. They stayed a few days taking in all the sights as much as possible.

Mama and I were doing fine. I went to work every day about 8 a.m. leaving her home all day. I thought that maybe she would enjoy seeing other people, so I enrolled her in a senior citizen day-care program held nearby. Someone would come each morning and pick her up. Then I would go and get her about 5 p.m. That was a long day for her, but they did provide accommodations for all the elders to have a nap in the afternoon, so she was in good fettle when I would arrive. By now I was noticing that she sometimes seemed out of it, so to speak. It worried me somewhat, but I couldn't do anything but hope for the best.

Mama was ok in most respects, especially in playing the organ I bought for her. It was right there in the living room. She loved getting out her music books and playing for me, or for anyone who wanted to have a little concert. I realized that Mama's hearing was failing more and more. There were days when I would open the front door of the building. I would be at street level. I realized that I could hear Mama playing some beautiful hymns on her organ. But it was so loud that it could be heard all over the first floor.

It was hard seeing Mama become more and more unable to think clearly. I was always wishing that I could be at home with her. But I was busy at Starr King School. Working with Mildred was easy because she was so gentle. The staff loved her, and so did the kids.

The years when I lived in the apartments with Mama were 1977 to 1980. Then something happened to change my live again. The manager informed all of us that the apartment house had been sold to some group. That was a shock by itself, but to be told that instead of paying rent we would have to buy our apartment from this new group. I thought about it for a few minutes, but I had to turn down the offer because I did not have the money.

There were a couple of other reasons. I noticed something alarming about our little apartment during the third year there. It was a puzzle to me that the reading lamp used by both of us for evening reading, TV, and puzzle-book solving etc. would be full of dead bees.

The big question was. Where were these little things coming from? I noticed that they were always gathered around the lamp. During the day we were never bothered by them, that would have been awful especially for Mama. One day I went out onto our small balcony. I looked down the side of the building. I saw an alarming gathering of bees flying in and out of a hole in the outside of the building. It must have built a hive they were living in. It seems that at night they would be attracted by the light within our apartment and would enter by means of the little space at the lamp connection in the ceiling. The hive was in the ceiling. After entering they would fly right toward the light. Of course the heat would kill them right away. I discovered that the bowl that held the lights was full of dead bees. Thank God they didn't buzz around Mama.

I decided I could afford to buy a mobile home in North Long Beach. Mama was amenable to the idea as long as I was there. So I looked around and found a place right across from my old high school, Jordan, on Atlantic Avenue. Off we go to the next house.

Oh, but I need to digress a bit now. Even though I have concentrated on my adventures in each house, I feel that there are a couple of things I would like to share with you. The most important part of my life after I retired was that I decided to spend some of my days as a volunteer for the Community. My life as a volunteer continued on for the remainder of my days up to now. So it didn't matter what house I lived in. The things that mattered were that I could drive, and stay healthy enough to carry on. I worked 16 years in Long Beach Unified as a teacher, vice-Principal, and Principal. I received a modest pension that helped me retire in 1986.

After relaxing for a few months I began to think

about doing something with my time. Two or three ideas came to mind. The first thought was to see if Sister Stephanie would like to have a volunteer with the Corita collection. I was delighted when she said that she needed help. So I started driving up to the IHM office two mornings a week. In the end I did this for ten years. I was busy counting, sorting, framing, and doing whatever Stephanie asked of me. I enjoyed every visit. She must have been satisfied with my work because she never hinted that I should move along. She herself was retiring from the position because the Community hired a professional curator. Since things were changing I decided that ten years of volunteering there were enough.

I was always aware of Anna Cecilia Hatfield working across the hall. She was the Community Archivist. Every so often I would stop in for a few minutes. My, it looked like such interesting work. I told her that when I finished helping out in the Corita office I would love to help her. She was very amenable to the idea. After helping with the Corita collection for ten years. I retired from that task and moved across the hall to the Archives. On the first morning when I arrived I greeted Anna Cecilia with a cheery, "Well, here I am to help you." She astonished me by replying, "Good, and welcome. Now I can retire."

What a shock. Instead of running away I just dug in my heels, and determined to learn as much as possible about Archives so that my work would be an asset. It took awhile but I was soon at ease doing archive tasks. I loved it. The Board soon appointed me Community Archivist. It turned out that I served for ten years. What Bliss. I drove up to the Community offices two mornings a week to do the needed work. Jeanne Albert assisted me the whole time.

After awhile Anna Maria Prieto came to help. She was delightful mostly because she was so careful about the value of every single item there. One of her biggest assets was her unending curiosity about historical items. What were they? Where did they come from? She was very agile on the computer so much of our history is safely on record. So my work as an archivist continued for several years. Now the Archivist is Anna Maria Prieto.

Clearly I have spent these years in profitable service.

House No. 20 – 1979

Orchid Lane – Long Beach, California

I purchased a nice little old two-bedroom mobile home. It was cozy. Mama could play her organ to her heart's content. She had her own bedroom again. I was happy about that. I was still working at Starr King School. But now I had an administrative position. It was helping to direct some special programs of the school. I liked it very much. The teachers seemed to like me in this work. So did Mildred. I am 55 years old. Mama is 83. She remains a sweet and docile woman. But it is harder for me to know what to do for her. Today I would know, but then I just couldn't seem to get any real help. Before I left for school in the morning I would place her corn flakes and fruit out on the table for her. Then I would fix a sandwich for her lunch. Oh how I desired to be right there with her. I could tell that she was more bewildered than ever. I was very sad to see this.

I didn't know that I would live here for almost nineteen years. So much happened during all of this time. I would continue to entertain my small family as I had done for the last several years. I had room enough for Mama to have her organ right there in the living room. There were times when she would just play so beautifully. All of those years as the Church organist made her touch so gentle and excellent. There would be special times when Dan and his family would come down to see us. It turned out that Meredith would watch her grandmother play, and then she would ask if she could play. Of course, this was a real pleasure to Mama and all of us.

During one of their visits, when Meredith had progressed a long way in her organ skills, I asked her if she would like to play on the same organ Mama used when she was the Parish organist. She, and all of us, was enthusiastic about this. So I phoned the Pastor and explained who I was, who Mama was, and asked him if it would be all right with him if Mama's granddaughter played some music on the Church organ.

We all went down to St. Athanasius on Market Street. Meredith did play some of her favorite pieces. I did notice at one point that the sacristy door opened. When I turned to look I could see the Pastor looking up at us, hoping that we were not ruining his precious organ. I was so very proud of Meredith.

There was so much going on with my life for the time I lived on Orchid Lane. It turned out to be the time when I would serve in several capacities in Public School.

The District needed someone with some 'moxie' to help in the School Improvement Office. I was asked if I would be interested. I was. One of the pluses was that Mr. Ed Pearlstein was the director. I liked him a lot, and vice versa. So I had to leave Starr King School after six years and settle in to my office cubicle at another school, John Burroughs School. My job turned out to be very similar to the one I had in the Community for 12 years, that of Supervisor.

Mr. Perlstein and I worked very well together because he discovered I could do all the jobs required while he took care of his work as principal of the school. I brought several good ideas to the task that the Principals and teachers appreciated.

Every day for two years I was either visiting an elementary school or meeting with someone in my office. Mr. Perlstein would have a conference with me on a regular basis so that we were working together, but changes were coming again. I did enjoy my two years in that job. Then I was approached about another promotion.

This time the Superintendent of schools called me and asked if I would consider a job as Vice-Principal. I was thrilled. I had spent those several years just relaxing by being a regular classroom teacher. Now, after two years in the School Improvement Office I was being promoted to Vice-Principal at US Grant Elementary School in North Long Beach.

This was the school I attended in third and fourth grade, when we lived on Lime Avenue. I had strange sensations every day when I would go to my office and begin the day. I never dreamed that I would ever return to my old school. I was in this position for two years. My boss was Bill Williams, a very good Principal and fine gentleman. He would give me tasks to do such as overseeing the teaching style of a teacher or deciding on discipline for a student. I seemed to do well because he must have recommended me for a promotion after two years.

I surprised when Mrs. Brewster, the Superintendent, called me down to her office? She said she was deciding that I would be a good Principal. I was hanging on her words to hear what school she was thinking of. Imagine my surprise when she said she was sending me to Starr King School. I was flabbergasted. That was where I had spent six happy years with Mildred as Principal. Now I had to get ready to return. By now I believe I am 59 years of age. I was really thinking that this would be my last assignment before retirement. Besides, it was a fine promotion financially.

I would serve at Starr King for three years before retiring. I was so pleased to finish my professional life doing what I loved – working with children.

I see that I have given a description of my professional life pretty fully. But, now I want to let you in on some of the very good times we had during this time. Mama was living with me in the coach for several years. I was so glad that I could include her in some of the wonderful times we had with Kath and Mildred. There were adventures traveling all over the Southwest. I also took Mama for trips to Portland, Castle Rock, and even to Calgary. It was fun packing up and going on a big "toot" as Mama used to love to say. I loved visiting relatives as much as Mama did.

Once we even went up to Portland with Carol Marie and her daughter Kathy. We started out in their nice big car, but it turned out that their car gave out up near Ventura. Carol had to phone her hubby Buddy to come and rescue us. He came to our rescue and picked us up and took us all back to Long Beach.

For awhile we were disappointed. But we were undaunted. We decided that we could continue our trip, but we would have to use my smaller car. I had not taken my car in for any oil or other preparation for a long trip so I was anxious. They said everything would be all right. Of course Mama was ready for the 'toot'. So we packed up and piled in, and started off.

It all went well. I was always nervous that my car would break down, but it only leaked what I thought was oil when we would stop somewhere. We had a very enjoyable visit with Aunt Hilda and Danny and family. We drove all around looking at the places of interest.

All went well except that every once in awhile when we would stop on the way home there would be a puddle of fluid under the front of the car. Now I wish I would have taken it in for servicing. We just kept right on driving down 101.

Finally we got home to Long Beach. I delivered Carol and Kathy to their home in Gardena. The very next morning I went out to my car to go somewhere. There was that big puddle again. I quickly got in and drove to the garage. After the mechanic checked it he said the motor would have been ruined if I had driven any further. My little car had been leaking transmission fluid for the entire trip. I didn't tell him that I had just finished a trip to Oregon, Washington and back. I was so thankful that we made it back without breaking down.

There were even trips to Europe. I have forgotten the dates of these wonderful times, but I was always so very grateful for the opportunities to see wonders of the world.

It was during one of our forays into a new place that Mama was injured. She fell and injured her hip so badly that she could not walk. I had to place her in a convalescent home, called Catered Manor, until she could walk again. I was still teaching, and working as Principal of a school, so I wasn't home during the day at all. Every day after school I would go to see Mama, take her out for a toot, or just visit. She seemed to be doing all right there. But it broke my heart every time I would have to leave her. I just felt so bad, and still do. Mama deserved only the best, and here I was visiting only late in the day. I can't write too much about this because I start to cry.

Everything was going along pretty well until one day I got a call from Catered Manor asking if Mama was home with me. I was horrified that she was not there. So I quickly rushed down there. I began searching the neighborhood. So did everyone else. After about a half-hour we got a phone call from a businesswoman two blocks down Atlantic Avenue.

It turned out that a very caring woman happened to be working in the front of the office building there. She said she noticed this white-haired lady sitting out on the bus bench. So she went out to see the woman, and noticed the woman was wearing a wristband. The band identified her as Martha Murphy who lived at Catered Manor. She quickly rushed inside and called the Manor. They, of course, were ecstatic that Martha was found. I and my friends and family recovered from heart attacks. I still think that there was a lack of care for her. After that I was twice as observant.

The best part was that I decided to retire from my schoolwork. What a relief it was for me because I was growing quite exhausted from the forty-six years of service I had given to God. And I wasn't finished yet.

So plans were made, parties and good wishes, and how I would manage to survive on my retirement salary. I was so grateful that I had worked in Public School for a modest salary. I was now able to care for Mama. She was still in the retirement home, but I was somewhat confident that she was getting good care.

There were so many things going on at this time that I just can't include them all. So I will try to tell you about Mama's last days. She seemed to be doing well at Catered Manor. But I was really wondering how she really was. So I would go down to visit her every day, and check up on her. We would visit awhile. She still recognized me, and would smile so sweetly when I would appear.

It was during one of these times that Lee Justin and I decided to take a three-day jaunt by car up to the foothills of the Sierras. I was feeling at ease about Mama because I always left her in the hands of Carol Marie. One of the things Lee and I would do was make a short visit to the local cemetery. It was so interesting just reading the names and dates. We spent the whole first day doing that until we found ourselves way up north in Placerville.

We stopped at a motel for the night. Before we were even unpacked I decided to call Carol to see how the day went. You can imagine my surprise when Buddy answered. I asked how Mama was. He said in a quavering voice that Carol wanted me to come right home. I kept asking why. Did something happen? Buddy told me that Mama was in the hospital and near death. I couldn't believe it because when we left Mama the day before she was looking so well, cheeks rosy, smiling. I still wonder what happened to bring on her death. I did all the driving because I was so nervous about what happened. Our trip took us about 8 hours of driving from Placerville up near Sacramento down to Long Beach. We arrived in Long Beach about 5 a.m. Oh, what prayers I was saying.

As we hurried into the hospital I was hoping I was in time to that see her alive, and kiss her goodbye. It was not meant to be. The nurse told me that she had passed away at 3 a.m. I burst into tears at my loss. I loved my mother more than anyone else in this world. I admired her brave way of living her life with so many problems to face.

Because Carol had been there all day and she was Mama's granddaughter, they thought she was the one in charge. Carol became exhausted and she knew I was on my way. So she went home at midnight. So from the time I arrived at the hospital there was activity. I was required to sign a myriad of papers. All the while I was in a daze of shock at what had happened.

I called my friends Kath Lucitt and Frannie Labonge,

They called a whole lot of IHMs. I believe I called our Community President. I asked Kath to come with me to visit the Rectory. It happened that the Pastor didn't know us at all. I was not a regular. Something happened that threw me for loop. I thought that Pastors were like Shepherds. The housekeeper told him that I needed to talk to him about it. He refused to come to the door.

It was true that we were not regulars. That meant no envelope. Later when our family told him that my Mother was the Church organist for 35 years since 1932 when the parish was founded, he wasn't too impressed. Nothing seemed to move him. I never talked to him in person. But I did find out that there was a parish organist who would play any songs I wished. The funeral Mass was well attended by IHMs, family, relatives from the North, and local friends. Because we were IHMs it was natural for someone to do some of the readings. I coordinated with the priest to insert our readings during the mass and funeral. I couldn't do any readings. I just couldn't. Kath Lucitt did the honors in every way. Mama's funeral was packed with IHMs. Mama is buried in Calvary Cemetery in East Los Angeles in a plot right next to her beloved Bernie. She wanted it that way. For years she would comment that she would be next to her beloved Bernie.

For the next few years I lived quietly in my mobile home. There were some problems with the coach though including termites and other pests. But the biggest problem became a raise in rent. I was beginning to find it a bit too much to pay from my meager income. So guess who came to my rescue? Carol Marie and Buddy of course. They came over and examined everything and decided it was just too much to try to fix up the coach so it would be livable again for me and my little cat, Fluffy.

They worked out the arrangements to sell the mobile home. I was one happy lady because I didn't know diddly about all the papers. You would think I would have some knowledge about it because Mildred and I had owned a neat little cabin for a few years. It turned out that Mildred didn't want to have anything to do with legal things. So I took on the job knowing absolutely nothing.

From here on Carol was chief 'cook and bottle washer' She was just magnificent with her help. I am so lucky that even though I had lost my dear sister, Beverly, I had her dear daughter right there to help me through some very difficult times.

I decided to retire in 1986. I had finished 45 years of service in education. I had spent the last 16 years in public schools. I was especially grateful for this because I finally had a true source of income. I qualified for Medicare, and had accrued enough savings in public school for a modest retirement.

So there I was. I didn't have to get up early to go to work. I spent my time working in my garden, petting my little Fluffy, and thinking about the future. I was only 62, and in fairly good health. I didn't want to get another job. Instead, I wanted to do something that would interest me as a volunteer in the Community.

Now I must describe another volunteer task I took on. This particular job was immensely gratifying. It became so important to me that I just could not stop until I was completely finished. It happened like this.

It was late 1980. I had retired from teaching in public school after sixteen years. I had not yet started volunteering with Stephanie in the Corita Gallery. Here I was with time on my hands. I began to think about what had happened to our Community during the past 20 years. Who would have thought that our own Cardinal would treat us in such a cavalier manner, by the Vatican? After much prayer and thought, and some outrage, I wondered how those in the future would even know about our travail. In my eyes the only way would be for someone to interview each member who consented to be interviewed to tell her story. After asking for good advice from my friend Liza Flynn who advised me on the interview outline, on the expected outcome, and the type of the recorder, the notes I would gather, and the photos I would place in a cherished album. I became more excited because if I truly finished this project it would be a wonderful gift to give to the Community for its historical collection.

I began contacting all IHMs who wore the habit before we made our changes, and who are still members of the Community. In my view it took an enormous amount of courage to examine life in the old days, and look at life in the new Community, and decide to continue membership. So I sent letters to over 140 IHMs telling them about my decision to gather as much information as possible in personal face-to-face interviews. I received affirmative replies from almost everyone. Even though I had volunteered to work in the Corita office two mornings a week, and later two mornings a week were devoted to my work as the archivist I had three mornings a week to get on the road and visit one IHM at a time. This visit contained a list of questions about the old and new Communities that I discussed with each IHM. I taped each interview, took notes, and finished up by taking a photograph of each interviewee.

Before I started the project I developed a series of questions to ask each IHM. I hoped that this method would capture wonderful stories about each person. The questions covered a life from childhood to a life as an IHM Sister and on.

I contacted Liza Flynn again who was in charge of the Education Department in the College. She had been my mentor all of those 12 years I was Supervisor of our schools. I explained what I wanted to do. She read everything, and asked me questions about my hopes for the end product. I said that I hoped it would become a valuable collection to add to our Community history. She didn't pause for a moment before saying, "This sounds like a wonderful idea. Your questions are great. I wouldn't change a word." At that moment Sister Aloyse spoke up and said, "I want to be first." And she was.

Soon after this I sent a letter to each IHM who had chosen to go modern. It was a momentous decision. I asked her permission to interview her using the questions I had sent to her. Almost all who qualified gave assent to be a part of this project. The interview was always held in the home of the member. I spent one or two days a week traveling around to each one. At the end of the interview I took a photograph of the IHM. These treasures are placed in albums along with a short vignette I wrote about my visit.

Now the collection consists of audio tapes of the interviews, photographs in albums, and a short description included in the album written by me. I simply describe my visit, which took place in the home of each person. It took me many years to complete the collection of all possible IHMs who wore the habit, and elected to remain with the new Community. The final count was 135. This completed collection is now a cherished addition to our Community Archives.

This has become a precious collection of 135 interviews. After several years, there was concern that the audio tapes would deteriorate. The decision was made to copy the tapes to CD. Equipment was purchased, and I started the task of copying the audio cassettes to the CDs. The process took several years.

After I retired from Community Archivist, Anna Maria Prieto, IHM, our new Community Archivist, has kindly transferred the information on the remaining tapes to CDs. She is very carefully caring for the Oral History Collection. I can't thank her enough, and all of those who graciously allowed me to interview them personally. I was amazed to find that when I completed all the interviews it had taken me over 20 years to complete the project.

House No. 21 – 1998

Barclay Street - Long Beach, California

There is a lot going on. If someone moves anywhere it becomes a major event. For me it was becoming an event for an elderly woman. This would be my 21st move that I would call permanent. As one can see this is one more traumatic time for me. So I will say "Goodbye" to my mobile home.

For several years I enjoyed it with my mother and my cat. But now that Mama has gone to Heaven I can move on.

It turned out that my stay in the mobile home was becoming impossible. I have mentioned a couple of things already. Who would want to live overrun by termites? And I mean overrun. Buddy and Carol helped me as much as they could, but the bugs kept moving in all over the place. Then, to top off everything our landlord decided that he could get more money by raising the rent. It was such a substantial amount that I was in danger of sinking.

Carol and Buddy had a nice little home in North Long Beach quite near to the mobile home I was in. They kindly asked me to live with them. When I finally moved in with Carol and Buddy I found a perfect apartment.

Everything was arranged so that Fluffy and I would be happy. They had a dog named MisterMr. We decided to keep our pets apart by building a Dutch door between the dining room and family room.

As time went on we realized that they stayed apart very well. There was one time that was traumatic for MisterMr because the Dutch door accidentally opened one day. I wasn't there, but Carol saw the whole thing. It seems that Fluffy came out of her spot in the front of the house. Carol said that MisterMr stood mesmerized because he hadn't seen her before. He just opened his eyes to stare at her, but there wasn't any dog-cat fight.

Of course life rolled along. Buddy would drive down to Boeing to pick up Carol after work. Carol could tell that if I was in the car we would be going out to dinner. Hurrah. Otherwise when Carol got home from work we would be enjoying dinner at home with a quiet evening. It is here that I have a very stupendous tale to relate. Very few persons would believe that I survived but it really happened to me.

It was a mild Wednesday morning in October 2006. I went through my usual routine of preparing to drive from Barclay Street up to the main IHM office in Los Feliz to volunteer in the Archive office. I had been doing this for years. So I got in my nice little Hyundai and made a U- turn out to the 710 freeway. I was making every effort to merge into the correct lane. The next thing I remember is noticing a sign by the Freeway that said "Hollywood turnoff". The airbags had deployed, I was covered in some kind of powder and it was difficult to steer the car. I was looking for the "5" Freeway that would take me to the IHM Office. How did I get all the way over to

Hollywood?

It turned out that I was not aware of my surroundings starting back at the beginning of "710" and it lasted until I reached Hollywood Boulevard. I couldn't believe it. That meant that I drove about 20 miles with my eyes open but not remembering seeing anything at all. How did I manage to keep driving, staying in the proper lane? There would have been lots of traffic as well as converging through several freeway changes. I parked and got out of the car to see what happened.

At first I couldn't tell what happened because I was standing in the street looking at my car. It was bent and scratched on the driver's side and across the front. But when I got on the sidewalk on the other side I almost had a heart attack. There was my beautiful little white Hyundai totally smashed in the front with large scrapes to the back. It looked just like an accordion. The front right tire was completely gone. I had been driving for 15 or 20 miles on the rim of the wheel. No policeman ever stopped me.

Then I began to shake. I went into a beauty salon to ask for help. I somehow called Carol to ask if she knew what happened. Of course she had no idea and asked if I could call the Auto Club. When the tow truck came, I just jumped into the front with the driver and directed him to my home in Long Beach. I couldn't remember my address but I could tell him how to get me home. I am in a daze the whole way. I checked myself for any injuries. There were none that I could tell. I wondered about other people. My car was really destroyed on one entire side. Someone must have been hurt.

When we arrived at Barclay both Carol and Buddy were out on the sidewalk waiting for me. I paid the driver after he deposited my car at the curbside. I could not explain to them what had happened. Carol called the police to see if there had been any accidents on the Hollywood Freeway because that is where I had taken the Hollywood Blvd. off ramp. The police said that there were no accidents reported anytime during that day on the Hollywood Freeway. Carol said she took one look at me and could tell that I was in some kind of distress. I could not tell them how the accidents happened or where it happened.

She told me later that I was acting very confused as well as not having any memory of any accident. She took me at once down to St. Mary's Hospital. The doctors examined me for about five or six days. They explained that I had a seizure similar to epilepsy, but I did not pass out. In fact, they said that they couldn't tell me exactly what caused it. But for some reason I was able to continue to drive until the shaking of the car "woke" me up. They said to come back to the neurologist if it happened again. It did happen three times again within two months.

The next morning after the accident, the Highway Patrol came to our house and asked if D. Murphy lived there. My smashed car was still sitting on the curb outside of the house so they knew that they had the right address. When Buddy answered the door, the officers had their hands on their guns. Buddy called Carol to the door to talk to the officers and she told them that I was in the hospital and that I had had an accident the day before but that I was not able to tell them what had happened. The police told them that I had hit two cars on the 710 Freeway and that I had just kept driving along like nothing had happened. As fate would have it, the two police officers at the door had been three cars behind me and had witnessed the accidents as they happened. They said that two cars were hit by a little white car driven by an elderly lady who just kept right on going. They had my license number from witnesses.

Carol gave them all of the information regarding the hospital, and the names of the doctors in charge. Later that day they called Carol to tell her that they were suspending my license and that hit and run charges may be forthcoming. They told her that no one was hurt in the accident. Carol also called my insurance company to report the accident. They instructed her not to talk to any insurance company but mine and to give them legal access to my medical records. My case would depend on whether or not I had suffered this seizure due to any pre-existing condition. I of course had never had a seizure before so therefore in the end I was not held responsible for the accident. My insurance company settled with both victims of the accident. My car of course was totaled.

Later after I was home from the hospital, I received a phone call from a policeman informing me that no one was hurt in either of my two accidents. He said he wouldn't arrest me for "hit and run" because the doctors told him that I had had a seizure. But he said he was taking my license away. That was ok because the whole event had scared me to death. Luckily my insurance covered everything. It was a miracle that I had only hit two cars and that no one was injured or killed. It still amazes me today to think that I drove all that way, on only three tires not even aware that I had side-swiped one car, totaled a second car as well as mine. Other than a huge bruise from my seat belt I was not injured nor were either of the other two drivers.

Since then my life proceeds along as usual except when I have another seizure. I never have a clue about when one will happen. I am completely blank, and I don't remember one moment of it. So far I have experienced eight seizures. I do take medication every day for this condition. Carol and Buddy took good care of me until I moved to the next house.

Carol took me to see the neurologist again. After examination he just threw up his hands and said, "All I can say is that you need to live in a place where there are more people so you can be watched more carefully."

It turned out that I lived with Carol and Buddy for ten years. We had many good times including cruises to Alaska, twice, the Panama Canal, Europe, including London, and many trips by car all over the West. It seemed as if there was no end to Carol's planning. So my life was always set up for packing. I enjoyed it all. On most of these trips my dear friend Mildred came too. Buddy and Carol are as dear as can be, but things changed for us all.

It happened after my hair-raising journey on the

freeways in a state of unconsciousness. The doctors couldn't tell me why I had this affliction. So I just returned home to Barclay Street. Carol and Buddy were probably holding their collective breath hoping that this is the end of the story. I was holding my breath too, but as fate would have it I had another seizure.

As soon as the Doctor said that I had to move and live with more people I was one of the luckiest elderly women on the planet because I was still a lifelong member of the Immaculate Heart Community.

I was aware that in the 70s the Community had purchased an apartment building for the sole purpose of inviting Community members who were ready, but had meager retirement means. In fact when I was still teaching during those years I would send a stipend for the purchase of the apartment house. So my story will come to a close in House number 21. Once again I had to move. Eventually it turned out that I would apply for an apartment in Kenmore House. So the rest of the story will be about my adventures there.

House No. 22 - 2007
Kenmore Ave. Los Angeles,
California

I just cannot believe that I am writing about this house. When I first started this book I really had no idea how far I would be able to go. So here I am in Kenmore. It may turn out to be my last house. I had been admiring it from afar for many years, so when the doctor who examined me when I lived at Barclay Street heard me say that I had another seizure, he quietly advised me to make arrangements to live with more people. I should not be left alone.

My heart fell. I had lived with Carol and Buddy for ten years. It would be quite wrenching to move again. After all, their home was the 21st house of my life. But Kenmore was not new to me. Luckily, I belonged to the IHMs who had the foresight to really provide a place for their retired and elderly members. This arrangement had been made about thirty years ago when so many of us were still out there working. I sent donations in for the mortgage. So here I was in a three-story apartment house I helped to buy.

I can't believe my good fortune. This is a lovely place. About twenty IHMs live here. We each have our own apartment with one bedroom, bath, living room, and kitchen and lots of cupboard space. I live on the first floor. One of the best features of this place is that we enjoy the presence of a lovely chapel that is available to us at all times. Another wonderful feature is that we all know one another. We are not surrounded by total strangers. No matter where I go I meet someone I know.

We also have a wonderful nursing staff that is stationed in the staff office right next to my apartment. When I need to go shopping for personal things I just ask Mrs. White. She is a great planner and a very generous helper to all of us. I feel very secure when she is here. She trains all the CNAs to do their tasks because she is our head nurse. 'Kindness' is her middle name.

The rules allow pets so I have met a little white dog named Melita. She belongs to Corinne de Hoyos who takes very good care of her. There are several Kitties like Travis who reigns supreme on the patio. He belongs to Pat Haid. Then there are a few more whose names elude me right now. A special treat is when Carol and Buddy bring their little dog up for a visit. His name is Curley. By the end of the visit he is actually sitting on my lap.

As I have mentioned before, that during all of the years since my retirement I have been busy volunteering in the Immaculate Heart Community. This usually meant that I would drive up there one or two days a week to help in some way. I enjoyed it so much that I spent the next 18 or 20 years lending a hand. I worked with so many wonderful IHM women. Some were Margaret Rose Welch, Marie Egan, Helen Kelley, Stephanie Baxter, Anna Maria Prieto. There are a hundred esteemed teachers I should add to the list.

This is a fine place to talk about my good friends. There were many Community activities for me to attend. I would touch bases with Paula Kraus, Rosalie Schneider, and Evelyn Delaney and many other

IHMs. Kathleen Lucitt was an IHM for many years. I spoke about her in earlier chapters; she and I became friends in the 60s when I was Elementary Supervisor.

As time passed we realized that we liked so many things together. I can't count the number of adventures we have enjoyed all over the place, driving, flying, and cruising. I must admit that she was the "idea woman" for many of our adventures. She learned to fly a small airplane, a glider, rowing down a wild river sometimes. She even obtained a glider pilot's license so we could go soaring if we had the nerve. We all seemed to get the nerve. Even Carol and her daughter Kathy went soaring with us.

Another good friend who was not an IHM was Mildred Hawley. Mildred was my dearest friend for many years. My whole family took both Kath and Mildred to their hearts so they were with us on many of our good times.

At this point in my story I can't believe that I am way, way past childhood. But by now I am beginning to realize that my old age has caught up with me.

Those of you who may be reading this little book must be familiar about places for the elderly and the infirm. Those of you in my near and extensive family certainly have had experience by now in caring for a loved one in a special way. You know how important the little things are. Now that I am 90 years of age I am not as active in anything anymore. I do manage to continue volunteering in the IHM Archives. I have spent a lot of time writing these memoirs, and I assist in a small way with the final presentation of the IHM oral history project. This all keeps me very busy.

I nap a lot and participate in Community activities here at Kenmore. This has turned out to be a loving and enjoyable place. We have celebrations for all birthdays and holidays. There is Rosalie Schneider, a friend from Cathedral Chapel days, another friend is Pat Haid. I can go on to JoAnn Vasquez, Phyllis Straling, Jeannette Melendrez, Eilene Berg, Catherine Smith, and many more. This place is rich with educated women who have a cart full of experiences. I am grateful that my life has neared its end giving me such blessings everywhere I turn.

Well, here I am near the end of my tale. I hope the reader has enjoyed learning about the Murphys. I know the first half of this story is about my early family and relatives, with nuggets of family information. While the last half is about the Murphy daughter, Doris's transition to Sister Peter and then back to Doris Murphy again.

I am most grateful to God for leading me so carefully and gently toward filling my lifelong goal. May God bless all of you who have had a place in my life.

Made in the USA
Lexington, KY
19 July 2016